Revolution
in Real Time

The Harvard Business Review Book Series

Revolution in Real Time

Managing Information Technology in the 1990s

With a Preface by
William G. McGowan
Chairman, Office of
the Chief Executive,
MCI Communications Corporation

A Harvard Business Review Book

Library of Congress Cataloging-in-Publication Data

Revolution in real time : managing information technology in the 1990s
/ with a preface by William G. McGowan.
    p. cm. — (A Harvard business review book)
  Includes bibliographical references and index.
  ISBN 0-87584-242-9 (acid-free paper) :
  1. Management—Data processing. 2. Information technology—
Management. I. Harvard business review. II. Series: Harvard
business review book series.
  HD30.2.R48 1990
  658.4′038—dc20   90-46351
                                                              CIP

The *Harvard Business Review* articles in this collection are available individually. Discounts apply to quantity purchases. For information and ordering contact Operations Department, Harvard Business School Publishing Division, Boston, MA 02163. Telephone: (617) 495-6192. Fax: (617) 495-6985.

95 94 93 92 91   5 4 3 2 1

Contents

v

example of the changing role of information
technology: competition is shifting from system
creation to effective modification of existing systems.

Part IV   Managing IT Applications

Preface

William G. McGowan

Not long ago, saying that a trillion dollars travels the world every day through electronic channels caused a moment of contemplation—as the size of the figure and its implications settled in.

It was a very serviceable fact for the times, a tidy illustration of the sweeping impact of technological change. Now it's just another statement; not unimportant, but no more surprising than the fact that there is a global economy. That October 19, 1987 was a bad day on Wall Street. That Nolan Ryan can still throw a baseball.

Today, little in information technology surpasses the imagination, and anything that can be imagined is probably being developed. And we will no doubt have it sooner than we thought.

However, even for someone like myself, who has enjoyed the information technology revolution from a front row seat, there still remains the capacity for amazement at the scale and depth of the changes that the information revolution is creating. Is there any business, or any part of a business, where technology isn't reworking how things happen? Any function where technology isn't being applied to make it faster or to give it more value? Find one and you've probably found a vacuum waiting to be filled.

The collection of articles that comprise *Revolution in Real Time* takes a broad and penetrating look at how information technology is fundamentally altering how organizations are structured and how they function. These articles also detail the novel demands that these changes place on the people who run organizations and work in them. They combine six years of study and opinion—current history in many industries, but a virtual epoch in the light-speed progress of information technology—into a fascinating oversight of how thinking, technology, and strategy have taken shape.

Ranking high on the order of technological impact is the role of information in changing the shape, location, and even the nature of organizations. The past foundations of a successful company are breaking down and reforming into new shapes appropriate to changing markets, new customer demands, and the new tools that hold the altered shapes together.

A solid hierarchy, deeply ingrained institutional mores, neatly drawn compartments of authority and lines of command, and an iron control of its own assets are no longer hallmarks of a formidable institution.

The emerging organizational supports, as Peter Drucker says in "The Coming of the New Organization," aren't foundations at all—at least not in the sense of a rigid infrastructure. They are more likely to be power information-based filaments that hold an organization's vital parts together in a configuration that is designed to bring special areas of knowledge together where, when, and how they're needed. The bucket brigade—where research hands off to manufacturing, which hands off to marketing, which hands off to sales—is fading fast. The new organization depends on teams, where all the key functions appropriate to a project are involved from the outset.

All of that, of course, raises a host of challenges. How, in such an organization, do you allocate rewards and career opportunities? How do you create a unified vision? And how do you feed and nurture the supply of top management talent? These are just three questions in a long and growing list.

While the answers are not yet clear, the critical need to find and act on them is.

Just as the division walls of the hierarchical organization are breaking down, so are the walls between companies—even competitors. Change is coming so fast and the competitive demands are so great that no one company can do it all, all the time. More are finding the value-adding benefits of combination.

Companies undergoing organizational change are doing so on the shifting sands of markets that are also evolving. For many companies, in fact, the questions must be asked: What is the market? And where is it? As we move toward the twenty-first century, the answer is increasingly found on the screen of a computer.

One of the early impacts of the revolution was that companies began to tie themselves to their markets through electronic links to their customers. With many variations, customers could enter the supplier's inventory and take out goods. Supplier and market, the thinking went, would become closely bound. And in many specialized industries, it works. But a funny thing happened on the way to the Decade of the Customer. Customers began to ask, "If I can order directly from one company, why can't I tap into a whole electronic marketplace?"

Now they can. Customers are strolling—or scrolling—through electronic markets that they expect their suppliers to furnish. Retailing and financial services are fast becoming electronic shopping centers. Technology's impact on reaching customers long ago helped fragment once monolithic markets to splinter-size niches. The splinters are growing smaller—down to a market of one.

The armada of information technologies driving new structures and other changes is formidable.

Today, that curious sound of a connecting fax machine is as familiar as the dial tone that precedes it. Electronic mail and voice mail have tied companies closer together even as they disperse geographically. Global networks can move data at speeds of 1.8 kilobits per second, 50,000 pages of manuscript with each tick of the clock.

The marriage of computers and telecommunications gives us computers that communicate like telephones and telephone switches that work like computers. Indeed, the global network of fiber and satellite that comprises today's worldwide communications systems is one large computer. Once an inert collection of hardware, these systems are thinking, flexible, and infinitely improvable communications tools.

What technological surprises will jump out of the next century's information jack-in-the-box is anybody's guess. But there are some safe bets.

Data transmission speeds now in development will move the entire contents of the Library of Congress in just four minutes. We will have desktop computers that rival the power of today's supercomputers. Neural networks will mimic human thought patterns, giving machines the ability, for example, to "mine" data, making independent decisions as they burrow through layers of vast data bases. Voice recognition technology already has machinery that is learning to recognize complex speech patterns: "Please write a letter right now to Mrs. Wright."

Such technologies are powerful. And they're important. But even more important, particularly to gaining and keeping competitive advantage in world markets, is how well we use them. The same technology that bestows competitive advantage can also snatch it back. As the strategic use of information becomes the norm, the competitive advantage it yields may last only as long as the competitors' next bold leap.

The margin of competitive advantage is measured by how you make that global collection of cables and switches perform: what they can do to give the customer the transmission flexibility and power that help generate "superior knowledge" and, in turn, competitive advantage.

Reading through the following explorations of new organizations, new competitive measures, new demands on chief executives, new applications, and new managerial requisites makes clear that we have, in fact, been in the midst of a revolution.

The revolution is far from over. We are firmly locked into a cycle of technology driving strategy driving technology. Each opportunity that new technologies create demands in turn more technology. There is no end in sight—in how widely and deeply technology is driving the transformation of how we do business and the performance potential for companies that truly understand the nature of the revolution and the power it can provide.

PART

I

How IT Reshapes
Organizations

1
The Coming of the New Organization

Peter F. Drucker

The typical large business 20 years hence will have fewer than half the levels of management of its counterpart today, and no more than a third the managers. In its structure, and in its management problems and concerns, it will bear little resemblance to the typical manufacturing company, circa 1950, which our textbooks still consider the norm. Instead it is far more likely to resemble organizations that neither the practicing manager nor the management scholar pays much attention to today: the hospital, the university, the symphony orchestra. For like them, the typical business will be knowledge-based, an organization composed largely of specialists who direct and discipline their own performance through organized feedback from colleagues, customers, and headquarters. For this reason, it will be what I call an information-based organization.

Businesses, especially large ones, have little choice but to become information-based. Demographics, for one, demands the shift. The center of gravity in employment is moving fast from manual and clerical workers to knowledge workers who resist the command-and-control model that business took from the military 100 years ago. Economics also dictates change, especially the need for large businesses to innovate and to be entrepreneurs. But above all, information technology demands the shift.

Advanced data-processing technology isn't necessary to create an information-based organization, of course. As we shall see, the British built just such an organization in India when "information technology" meant the quill pen, and barefoot runners were the "telecommunications" systems. But as advanced technology becomes more and more prevalent, we have to engage in analysis and diagnosis—that is, in "information"—even more intensively or risk being swamped by the data we generate.

So far most computer users still use the new technology only to do faster what they have always done before, crunch conventional numbers. But as soon as a company takes the first tentative steps from data to information, its decision processes, management structure, and even the way its work gets done begin to be transformed. In fact, this is already happening, quite fast, in a number of companies throughout the world.

The Transformation of Work

We can readily see the first step in this transformation process when we consider the impact of computer technology on capital-investment decisions. We have known for a long time that there is no one right way to analyze a proposed capital investment. To understand it we need at least six analyses: the expected rate of return; the payout period and the investment's expected productive life; the discounted present value of all returns through the productive lifetime of the investment; the risk in not making the investment or deferring it; the cost and risk in case of failure; and finally, the opportunity cost. Every accounting student is taught these concepts. But before the advent of data-processing capacity, the actual analyses would have taken man-years of clerical toil to complete. Now anyone with a spreadsheet should be able to do them in a few hours.

The availability of this information transforms the capital-investment analysis from opinion into diagnosis, that is, into the rational weighing of alternative assumptions. Then the information transforms the capital-investment decision from an opportunistic, financial decision governed by the numbers into a business decision based on the probability of alternative strategic assumptions. So the decision both presupposes a business strategy and challenges that strategy and its assumptions. What was once a budget exercise becomes an analysis of policy.

The second area that is affected when a company focuses its data-processing capacity on producing information is its organization structure. Almost immediately, it becomes clear that both the number of management levels and the number of managers can be sharply cut. The reason is straightforward: it turns out that whole layers of management neither make decisions nor lead. Instead, their main, if not their only, function is to serve as "relays"—human boosters for the faint, unfocused signals that pass for communication in the traditional pre-information organization.

One of America's largest defense contractors made this discovery when it asked what information its top corporate and operating managers needed to do their jobs. Where did it come from? What form was it in? How did it flow? The search for answers soon revealed that whole layers of management—perhaps as many as 6 out of a total of 14—existed only because these questions had not been asked before. The company had had data galore. But it had always used its copious data for control rather than for information.

Information is data endowed with relevance and purpose. Converting data into information thus requires knowledge. And knowledge, by definition, is specialized. (In fact, truly knowledgeable people tend toward overspecialization, whatever their field, precisely because there is always so much more to know.)

The information-based organization requires far more specialists overall than the command-and-control companies we are accustomed to. Moreover, the specialists are found in operations, not at corporate headquarters. Indeed, the operating organization tends to become an organization of specialists of all kinds.

Information-based organizations need central operating work such as legal counsel, public relations, and labor relations as much as ever. But the need for service staffs—that is, for people without operating responsibilities who only advise, counsel, or coordinate—shrinks drastically. In its *central* management, the information-based organization needs few, if any, specialists.

Because of its flatter structure, the large, information-based organization will more closely resemble the businesses of a century ago than today's big companies. Back then, however, all the knowledge, such as it was, lay with the very top people. The rest were helpers or hands, who mostly did the same work and did as they were told. In the information-based organization, the knowledge will be primarily at the bottom, in the minds of the specialists who do different work and direct themselves. So today's typical organization in which knowledge tends to be concentrated in service staffs, perched rather insecurely between top management and the operating people, will likely be labeled a phase, an attempt to infuse knowledge from the top rather than obtain information from below.

Finally, a good deal of work will be done differently in the information-based organization. Traditional departments will serve as guardians of standards, as centers for training and the assignment of specialists; they won't be where the work gets done. That will happen largely in task-focused teams.

This change is already under way in what used to be the most clearly defined of all departments—research. In pharmaceuticals, in telecommunications, in papermaking, the traditional *sequence* of research, development, manufacturing, and marketing is being replaced by *synchrony*: specialists from all these functions work together as a team, from the inception of research to a product's establishment in the market.

How task forces will develop to tackle other business opportunities and problems remains to be seen. I suspect, however, that the need for a task force, its assignment, its composition, and its leadership will have to be decided on case by case. So the organization that will be developed will go beyond the matrix and may indeed be quite different from it. One thing is clear, though: it will require greater self-discipline and even greater emphasis on individual responsibility for relationships and for communications.

From Hierarchy to Symphony

To say that information technology is transforming business enterprises is simple. What this transformation will require of companies and top managements is much harder to decipher. That is why I find it helpful to look for clues in other kinds of information-based organizations, such as the hospital, the symphony orchestra, and the British administration in India.

A fair-sized hospital of about 400 beds will have a staff of several hundred physicians and 1,200 to 1,500 paramedics divided among some 60 medical and paramedical specialities. Each specialty has its own knowledge, its own training, its own language. In each specialty, especially the paramedical ones like the clinical lab and physical therapy, there is a head person who is a working specialist rather than a full-time manager. The head of each specialty reports directly to the top, and there is little middle management. A good deal of the work is done in ad hoc teams as required by an individual patient's diagnosis and condition.

A large symphony orchestra is even more instructive, since for some works there may be a few hundred musicians on stage playing together. According to organization theory then, there should be several group vice president conductors and perhaps a half-dozen division VP conductors. But that's not how it works. There is only the conductor-CEO—and every one of the musicians plays directly to that person without an intermediary. And each is a high-grade specialist, indeed an artist.

But the best example of a large and successful information-based organization, and one without any middle management at all, is the British civil administration in India.[1]

The British ran the Indian subcontinent for 200 years, from the middle of the eighteenth century through World War II, without making any fundamental changes in organization structure or administrative policy. The Indian civil service never had more than 1,000 members to administer the vast and densely populated subcontinent—a tiny fraction (at most 1%) of the legions of Confucian mandarins and palace eunuchs employed next door to administer a not-much-more populous China. Most of the Britishers were quite young; a 30-year-old was a survivor, especially in the early years. Most lived alone in isolated outposts with the nearest countryman a day or two of travel away, and for the first hundred years there was no telegraph or railroad.

The organization structure was totally flat. Each district officer reported directly to the "Coo," the provincial political secretary. And since there were nine provinces, each political secretary had at least 100 people reporting directly to him, many times what the doctrine of the span of control would allow. Nevertheless, the system worked remarkably well, in large part because it was designed to ensure that each of its members had the information he needed to do his job.

Each month the district officer spent a whole day writing a full report to the political secretary in the provincial capital. He discussed each of his principal tasks—there were only four, each clearly delineated. He put down in detail what he had expected would happen with respect to each of them, what actually did happen, and why, if there was a discrepancy, the two differed. Then he wrote down what he expected would happen in the ensuing month with respect to each key task and what he was going to do about it, asked questions about policy, and commented on long-term opportunities, threats, and needs. In turn, the political secretary "minuted" every one of those reports—that is, he wrote back a full comment.

On the basis of these examples, what can we say about the requirements of the information-based organization? And what are its management problems likely to be? Let's look first at the requirements. Several hundred musicians and their CEO, the conductor, can play together because they all have the same score. It tells both flutist and timpanist what to play and when. And it tells the conductor what to expect from each and when. Similarly, all the specialists in the hospital share a common mission: the care and cure of the sick. The diagnosis is their "score"; it dictates specific action for the X-ray lab, the dietitian, the physical therapist, and the rest of the medical team.

Information-based organizations, in other words, require clear, simple, common objectives that translate into particular actions. At the same time, however, as these examples indicate, information-based organizations also need concentration on one objective or, at most, on a few.

Because the "players" in an information-based organization are specialists, they cannot be told how to do their work. There are probably few orchestra conductors who could coax even one note out of a French horn, let alone show the horn player how to do it. But the conductor can focus the horn player's skill and knowledge on the musicians' joint performance. And this focus is what the leaders of an information-based business must be able to achieve.

Yet a business has no "score" to play by except the score it writes as it plays. And whereas neither a first-rate performance of a symphony nor a miserable one will change what the composer wrote, the performance of a business continually creates new and different scores against which its performance is assessed. So an information-based business must be structured around goals that clearly state management's performance expectations for the enterprise and for each part and specialist and around organized feedback that compares results with these performance expectations so that every member can exercise self-control.

The other requirement of an information-based organization is that everyone take information responsibility. The bassoonist in the orchestra does so every time she plays a note. Doctors and paramedics work with an elaborate system of reports and an information center, the nurse's station on the patient's floor. The district officer in India acted on this responsibility every time he filed a report.

The key to such a system is that everyone asks: Who in this

organization depends on me for what information? And on whom, in turn, do I depend? Each person's list will always include superiors and subordinates. But the most important names on it will be those of colleagues, people with whom one's primary relationship is coordination. The relationship of the internist, the surgeon, and the anesthesiologist is one example. But the relationship of a biochemist, a pharmacologist, the medical director in charge of clinical testing, and a marketing specialist in a pharmaceutical company is no different. It, too, requires each party to take the fullest information responsibility.

Information responsibility to others is increasingly understood, especially in middle-sized companies. But information responsibility to oneself is still largely neglected. That is, everyone in an organization should constantly be thinking through what information he or she needs to do the job and to make a contribution.

This may well be the most radical break with the way even the most highly computerized businesses are still being run today. There, people either assume the more data, the more information—which was a perfectly valid assumption yesterday when data were scarce, but leads to data overload and information blackout now that they are plentiful. Or they believe that information specialists know what data executives and professionals need in order to have information. But information specialists are tool makers. They can tell us what tool to use to hammer upholstery nails into a chair. We need to decide whether we should be upholstering a chair at all.

Executives and professional specialists need to think through what information is for them, what data they need: first, to know what they are doing; then, to be able to decide what they should be doing; and finally, to appraise how well they are doing. Until this happens MIS departments are likely to remain cost centers rather than become the result centers they could be.

The New Management Challenges

Most large businesses have little in common with the examples we have been looking at. Yet to remain competitive—maybe even to survive—they will have to convert themselves into information-based organizations, and fairly quickly. They will have to change old habits and acquire new ones. And the more successful a company has been, the more difficult and painful this process is apt to be. It will threaten the jobs, status, and opportunities of a good many people in the organization, especially the long-serving, middle-aged people in middle management who tend to be the least mobile and to feel most secure in their work, their positions, their relationships, and their behavior.

The information-based organization will also pose its own special management problems. I see as particularly critical:

1. Developing rewards, recognition, and career opportunities for specialists.
2. Creating unified vision in an organization of specialists.
3. Devising the management structure for an organization of task forces.
4. Ensuring the supply, preparation, and testing of top management people.

Bassoonists presumably neither want nor expect to be anything but bassoonists. Their career opportunities consist of moving from second bassoon to first bassoon and perhaps of moving from a second-rank orchestra to a better, more prestigious one. Similarly, many medical technologists neither expect nor want to be anything but medical technologists. Their career opportunities consist of a fairly good chance of moving up to senior technician, and a very slim chance of becoming lab director. For those who make it to lab director, about 1 out of every 25 or 30 technicians, there is also the opportunity to move to a bigger, richer hospital. The district officer in India had practically no chance for professional growth except possibly to be relocated, after a three-year stint, to a bigger district.

Opportunities for specialists in an information-based business organization should be more plentiful than they are in an orchestra or hospital, let alone in the Indian civil service. But as in these organizations, they will primarily be opportunities for advancement within the specialty, and for limited advancement at that. Advancement into "management" will be the exception, for the simple reason that there will be far fewer middle-management positions to move into. This contrasts sharply with the traditional organization where, except in the research lab, the main line of advancement in rank is out of the specialty and into general management.

More than 30 years ago General Electric tackled this problem by creating "parallel opportunities" for "individual professional contributors." Many companies have followed this example. But professional specialists themselves have largely rejected it as a solution. To them—and to their management colleagues—the only meaningful opportunities are promotions into management. And the prevailing compensation structure in practically all businesses reinforces this attitude because it is heavily biased toward managerial positions and titles.

There are no easy answers to this problem. Some help may come from looking at large law and consulting firms, where even the most senior partners tend to be specialists, and associates who will not make partner are outplaced fairly early on. But whatever scheme is eventually developed will work only if the values and compensation structure of business are drastically changed.

The second challenge that management faces is giving its organization of specialists a common vision, a view of the whole.

In the Indian civil service, the district officer was expected to see the "whole" of his district. But to enable him to concentrate on it, the government services that arose one after the other in the nineteenth century (forestry, irrigation, the archaeological survey, public health and sanitation, roads) were organized outside the administrative structure, and had virtually no contact with the district officer. This meant that the district officer became increasingly isolated from the activities that often had the greatest impact on—and the greatest importance for—his district. In the end, only the provincial government or the central government in Delhi had a view of the "whole," and it was an increasingly abstract one at that.

A business simply cannot function this way. It needs a view of the whole and a focus on the whole to be shared among a great many of its professional specialists, certainly among the senior ones. And yet it will have to accept, indeed will have to foster, the pride and professionalism of its specialists—if only because, in the absence of opportunities to move into middle management, their motivation must come from that pride and professionalism.

One way to foster professionalism, of course, is through assignments to task forces. And the information-based business will use more and more smaller self-governing units, assigning them tasks tidy enough for "a good man to get his arms around," as the old phrase has it. But to what extent should information-based businesses rotate performing specialists out of their specialties and into new ones? And to what extent will top management have to accept as its top priority making and maintaining a common vision across professional specialties?

Heavy reliance on task-force teams assuages one problem. But it aggravates another: the management structure of the information-based organization. Who will the business's managers be? Will they be task-force leaders? Or will there be a two-headed monster—a specialist structure, comparable, perhaps, to the way attending physicians function in a hospital, and an administrative structure of task-force leaders?

The decisions we face on the role and function of the task-force leaders are risky and controversial. Is theirs a permanent assignment, analogous to the job of the supervisory nurse in the hospital? Or is it a function of the task that changes as the task does? Is it an assignment or a position? Does it carry any rank at all? And if it does, will the task-force leaders become in time what the product managers have been at Procter & Gamble: the basic units of management and the company's field officers? Might the task-force leaders eventually replace department heads and vice presidents?

Signs of every one of these developments exist, but there is neither a clear trend nor much understanding as to what each entails. Yet each would give rise to a different organizational structure from any we are familiar with.

Finally, the toughest problem will probably be to ensure the supply, preparation, and testing of top management people. This is, of course, an old and central dilemma as well as a major reason for the general acceptance of decentralization in large businesses in the last 40 years. But the existing business organization has a great many middle-management positions that are supposed to prepare and test a person. As a result, there are usually a good many people to choose from when filling a senior management slot. With the number of middle-management positions sharply cut, where will the information-based organization's top executives come from? What will be their preparation? How will they have been tested?

Decentralization into autonomous units will surely be even more critical than it is now. Perhaps we will even copy the German *Gruppe* in which the decentralized units are set up as separate companies with their own top managements. The Germans use this model precisely because of their tradition of promoting people in their specialties, especially in research and engineering; if they did not have available commands in near-independent subsidiaries to put people in, they would have little opportunity to train and test their most promising professionals. These subsidiaries are thus somewhat like the farm teams of a major-league baseball club.

We may also find that more and more top management jobs in big companies are filled by hiring people away from smaller companies. This is the way that major orchestras get their conductors— a young conductor earns his or her spurs in a small orchestra or opera house, only to be hired away by a larger one. And the heads of a good many large hospitals have had similar careers.

Can business follow the example of the orchestra and hospital where top management has become a separate career? Conductors and hospital administrators come out of courses in conducting or schools of hospital administration, respectively. We see something of this sort in France, where large companies are often run by men who have spent their entire previous careers in government service. But in most countries this would be unacceptable to the organization (only France has the *mystique* of the *grandes écoles*). And even in France, businesses, especially large ones, are becoming too demanding to be run by people without firsthand experience and a proven success record.

Thus the entire top management process—preparation, testing, succession—will become even more problematic than it already is. There will be a growing need for experienced businesspeople to go back to school. And business schools will surely need to work out what successful professional specialists must know to prepare themselves for high-level positions as *business* executives and *business* leaders.

The Third Evolution

Since modern business enterprise first arose, after the Civil War in the United States and the Franco-Prussian War in Europe, there have been two major evolutions in the concept and structure of organizations. The first took place in the ten years between 1895 and 1905. It distinguished management from ownership and established management as work and task in its own right. This happened first in Germany, when Georg Siemens, the founder and head of Germany's premier bank, Deutsche Bank, saved the electrical apparatus company his cousin Werner had founded after Werner's sons and heirs had mismanaged it into near collapse. By threatening to cut off the bank's loans, he forced his cousins to turn the company's management over to professionals. A little later, J.P. Morgan, Andrew Carnegie, and John D. Rockefeller, Sr. followed suit in their massive restructurings of U.S. railroads and industries.

The second evolutionary change took place 20 years later. The development of what we still see as the modern corporation began with Pierre S. du Pont's restructuring of his family company in the early twenties and continued with Alfred P. Sloan's redesign of General Motors a few years later. This introduced the command-and-control organization of today, with its emphasis on decentralization, central service staffs, personnel management, the whole apparatus of budgets and controls, and the important distinction between policy and operations. This stage culminated in the massive reorganization of General Electric in the early 1950s, an action that perfected the model most big businesses around the world (including Japanese organizations) still follow.[2]

Now we are entering a third period of change: the shift from the command-and-control organization, the organization of departments and divisions, to the information-based organization, the organization of knowledge specialists. We can perceive, though perhaps only dimly, what this organization will look like. We can identify some of its main characteristics and requirements. We can point to central problems of values, structure, and behavior. But the job of actually building the information-based organization is still ahead of us—it is the managerial challenge of the future.

Notes

1. The standard account is Philip Wooddruff, *The Men Who Ruled India,* especially the first volume, *The Founders of Modern India* (New York: St. Martin's, 1954). How the system worked day by day is charmingly told in *Sowing* (New York: Harcourt Brace Jovanovich, 1962), volume one of the autobiography of Leonard Woolf (Virginia Woolf's husband).

2. Alfred D. Chandler, Jr., has masterfully chronicled the process in his two books *Strategy and Structure* (Cambridge: MIT Press, 1962) and *The Visible Hand* (Cambridge: Harvard University

Press, 1977)—surely the best studies of the administrative history of any major institution. The process itself and its results were presented and analyzed in two of my books: *The Concept of the Corporation* (New York: John Day, 1946) and *The Practice of Management* (New York: Harper Brothers, 1954).

2
Beyond Vertical Integration—The Rise of the Value-Adding Partnership

Russell Johnston and Paul R. Lawrence

For decades large, vertically integrated companies have reaped the benefits of their size, growing stronger with every competitor they eliminated or engulfed. But the elephants aren't grazing so freely anymore. Another beast has been nibbling at the herbage, and its presence is beginning to be felt.

That beast is the "value-adding partnership"—a set of independent companies that works closely together to manage the flow of goods and services along the entire value-added chain. (See Exhibit I.) It is an organizational form much like the putting-out system of the early Industrial Revolution, whereby manufacturing was done in cottages and coordinated by a merchant-manufacturer who supplied the raw materials and sold the final product. But the value-adding partnership, or VAP, is not an anachronism. It is a product of its time, and its time may well have come.

Most historians agree that the development of cheap, centralized power and efficient but costly production machinery tipped the competitive advantage toward large companies that could achieve economies of scale. Today, low-cost computing and communication seem to be tipping the competitive advantage back toward partnerships of smaller companies, each of which performs one part of the value-added chain and coordinates its activities with the rest of the chain. (See Exhibit II.)

VAPs are not, however, necessarily technology driven. They may emerge as the result of computerized links between companies or they may exist before the technical links have been made.

Exhibit I.   What's a Value-Added Chain?

The term *value-added chain* comes from the field of microeconomics, where it is used to describe the various steps a good or service goes through from raw material to final consumption. Economics has traditionally conceived of transactions between steps in the chain as being arm's-length relationships or hierarchies of common ownership. Value-adding partnerships are an alternative to those two types of relationships. Usually, the partnerships first develop between organizations that perform adjacent steps in the chain.

A value-added chain for packaged foods might look like this:

farmer ——▶ broker ——▶ basic ——▶ packaged ——▶ distributor ——▶ retailer ——▶ consumer
                      processor   goods
                                    producer

Exhibit II.   New Technological Tools Help Create VAPs

Tools	Implications
Minicomputers and PCs; user friendly languages; inexpensive general-purpose software packages	Drastically improves the economics of small scale, providing wider access to information power to include the *smallest* organizations and the *lowest* organizational levels.
Data standards; bar codes	Enable rapid, inexpensive, accurate capture and use of information in electronic form, lowering transaction costs *between* organizations.
Information networking capability	Permits instantaneous sharing of information *between* organizations with shared interests—thus increasing speed and economy of coordinated response to market changes.
Computer-aided design	Improves speed and economy of response to customer needs by improving coordination *between* organizations in design functions.
Computer-aided manufacturing	Permits use of just-in-time practices *between* organizations.

In all cases, they depend largely on the attitudes and practices of the participating managers. Computers simply make it easier to communicate, share information, and respond quickly to shifts in demand. They facilitate VAPs but alone don't create them.

To better understand what a value-adding partnership is and how it works, let's look at some that are doing especially well.[1]

McKesson Corporation

McKesson Corporation, the $6.67 billion distributor of drugs, health care products, and other consumer goods, is among the most successful. The business press has often cited McKesson for its innovative use of information technology to improve customer service and cut order-entry costs. But McKesson's story is much richer than most people know. Once a conventional wholesale distributor squeezed by vertically integrated chain stores, McKesson has transformed itself into the hub of a large value-adding partnership that can more than hold its own against the chains.

McKesson's evolution to a VAP was triggered by fierce competition from large drugstore chains, which were eating into the business of the independent stores McKesson serviced. McKesson realized that if the independents died, it would soon follow suit. To protect their business, McKesson's managers began to look for ways to help customers.

Their search focused on a rudimentary order-entry system at one of McKesson's warehouses. In the early stages, the system included data-collection devices, powered by car batteries, that were wheeled around customers' stores in shopping carts. The system dramatically cut the costs of processing orders by expediting the steps of checking inventory, calling in an order, manually recording the order, and eventually packing and shipping it. McKesson soon discovered that the system could also specify how to pack orders so that they coincided with the arrangement of customers' shelves. Doing so made restocking more efficient.

These successful uses of information technology spurred the search for others. McKesson managers soon realized they could use the computer to manipulate data to help customers set prices and design store layouts to maximize the profits of each particular store. They also began using it to perform accounting services, such as producing balance sheets and income statements. And they discovered that the system could be used to warn consumers of potentially harmful drug combinations by tracking prescription histories.

McKesson thus offered the independent drugstores many advantages of computerized systems that no one store could afford by itself. The drugstores were able to offer their customers better prices, a more targeted product mix, and better service, all of which helped them stand up against the chains. Still, the drugstores maintained their autonomy, so they could be responsive to the needs of the local area and form lasting ties with the community. This actually gave them an advantage over the chain stores, whose managers had to answer to headquarters and could be transferred from one location to another.

McKesson, of course, benefited from the independents' good health. The user fees covered the cost of service development plus provided a return on the investment. Since the system was introduced in 1976, sales to pharmacies have soared from $900 million to over $5 billion. And the more efficient ordering systems allowed the company to reduce its warehouses from 130 to 54, eliminate 500 clerical jobs devoted to taking telephone orders, strengthen its customer base from 20,000 customers averaging $4,000 a month in orders to 15,000 customers averaging $12,000 to $15,000 a month, and reduce the average number of shipments per customer from two per day to two per week while lowering its own and customers' inventory costs.

The close and productive link with customers wasn't good enough, however, to satisfy McKesson's imagination. The company recognized that the up-to-date information on sales had immense value to product managers of consumer goods manufacturers and proceeded to sell it to its own suppliers. Suppliers used it to make more timely shipments to McKesson in much the same way as McKesson had done with the drugstores. Computer-to-computer ordering from suppliers permitted McKesson to cut its staff of buyers from 140 to 12. Meanwhile, suppliers could schedule production more efficiently and streamline their inventories.

Another McKesson innovation was to use the computer system to help process insurance claim applications for prescription reimbursement. This strengthened the ties among insurance companies, consumers, and drugstores by speeding payments and smoothing administrative hassles. McKesson's total network thus includes manufacturer, distributor, retailer, consumer, and third-party insurance supplier.

What makes McKesson so powerful—and what makes it a VAP—is the understanding that each player in the value-added chain has a stake in the others' success. McKesson managers see the entire

VAP—not just one part of it—as one competitive unit. It was this awareness that allowed McKesson's managers to look for opportunities beyond their own corporate boundaries. They looked for ways the resources at one part of the value-added chain could be used in another. And their efforts to be competitive went beyond cost cutting. Many companies focus on trimming costs to increase profits, and they consider opportunities only within the unit defined by ownership. McKesson also looks for ways to add value by creating new services.

This ability to see beyond the corporate boundaries has another important advantage. It permits recognition of serious threats that lie elsewhere along the value-added chain. Because McKesson knows its own fate depends on that of its suppliers and customers, the company monitors competitive dynamics throughout the chain and tries to fix weaknesses wherever they occur. When all the partners are strong, the entire value-added chain can stand up to the toughest of competitors, integrated or not.

The McKesson partnership is so successful that others in the pharmacy distribution business have emulated it or withdrawn entirely. But most have missed the point. It is easy to make the mistake of thinking that McKesson's network is nothing more than a computer system with terminals in someone else's building. The wires and processors are not what make McKesson successful. True, the McKesson VAP grew out of the company's computer system, but information technology did not create the VAP. Rather, it was the managers who understood the relationships along the entire value-added chain and the need for each link in the chain to be as strong as possible. Information technology is not even a necessary ingredient in a VAP, as the next example demonstrates.

The Italian Textile Industry

The textile industry of central Italy comprises many successful VAPs, which have evolved very differently from McKesson.[2] Over the past 20 years, 15,000 to 20,000 smaller companies have replaced all but one of the large, vertically integrated textile mills of the Prato area. By 1982, these companies were employing 70,000 people and exporting about $1.5 billion worth of products. The industry's disintegration may have begun partly to avoid labor legislation, but the new structure has allowed the industry to thrive for more basic reasons.

The Italian story really begins in the early 1970s, when Massimo Menichetti took over a large, integrated textile mill from his father.[3] At that time the company's future—indeed that of the whole Italian textile industry—looked bleak. Labor costs were soaring throughout Italy, and foreign competition was intensifying. Furthermore, a trend toward greater product variety meant that companies had to be able to create new designs quickly and efficiently, shifting production from one product to another without wasting time or materials. Innovation and flexibility had become critical to survival. Increasingly squeezed between rising production costs and falling market prices, Menichetti's mill had been losing money for several years.

Menichetti believed that the company had become too big and bureaucratic to adapt to the new competitive demands, so he proceeded to break the company into eight independent organizations. He arranged to sell between 30% and 50% of the stock in those companies to key employees, who would make the purchases with company profits—thus enabling them to become part owners without putting up any of their own money. The ownership transfer was to be gradual, over the course of three years. By the end of that period, the new enterprises would have to make half their sales to outside companies—to avoid a slip into complacency. To demonstrate his resolve to play only an advisory role and keep out of operations, Menichetti also started a marketing company in New York. He stipulated that it could represent no more than 30% of the production volume of the Menichetti group.

Within three years, the dismantling of the Menichetti mill was complete and business was being conducted very differently. Since then, other integrated mills have patterned themselves after the Menichetti VAP. Small companies with cooperative relationships are now spread through the entire Prato area of central Italy.

Formerly, in each large mill, one group of managers oversaw the entire process, from assessing the market to designing fabric to supervising every detail of production. Now, small groups—sometimes a family—take total responsibility for their part in the process. Each shop has certain special skills. One may be particularly good at producing high-quality knits for dresses; another may be expert at mixing colors. Work is contracted out to whichever shop can meet the market's needs at the time. Each, therefore, has great incentive to stay in touch with fashion trends and environmental changes and to be ready to react quickly. Otherwise, it would lose business to other producers and might even go out of business.

At the center of each set of small companies is an independent master broker, or *impannatore*. In the Menichetti VAP, Massimo Menichetti himself plays this role. The *impannatores* manage the relationships among the various shops. They are facilitators and problem solvers who carry information from one place along the value-added chain to wherever it will be most useful. They get involved in all aspects of the textile business: raw materials purchases, fabric design, production contracts, transportation, and sales. They look at the weaver's samples for next year and if they think they will sell, take them to customers all over the world. If the market objects to the weaver's price, the *impannatores* may help the weaver find ways to trim costs. They also negotiate with raw materials suppliers and transportation providers.

Being close to the customer, the *impannatores* were the first to realize that market changes required increased innovation and flexibility. They took the lesson to heart and, more importantly, carried the word back to the small manufacturers. To avoid losing business because of an inability to react fast enough, the production shops have adopted the latest textile machinery, including numerically controlled looms. Whole chains, not just individual players, adapted quickly to the market information, and all have benefited.

Realizing that their partners must also be financially sound, efficient, and marketwise if they themselves are to be competitive, the players in the Italian textile VAPs are eager to share information and cooperate. In recent years, they have developed computer systems that rush information from partner to partner. The technology enhances coordination and boosts the speed and quality of responses to the market. The computer systems enhance the VAPs, but again, do not create them.

Of course, sharing information is very different from sharing rewards. In a VAP, as in any other industrial or organizational structure, innovation and adaptation must be rewarded if they are to be encouraged. In the Prato area, the *impannatores* can ensure that the rewards are shared appropriately by influencing prices and channeling work only to cooperative members. They can, for instance, withhold work from a shop that is trying to drive out otherwise successful competitors through predatory pricing.

The Prato mammoths gave way quietly and gracefully to the

extraordinarily successful VAPs. Systematic, close coordination is now the rule, not the exception. In fact, the ties exist not only vertically, with suppliers and customers, but also horizontally, with what would usually be considered direct competitors. A weaver that guesses wrong one season might well receive overflow orders from a competitor that guessed right. They both understand that next year their roles may be reversed. And they know that if they help each other through tough times, they can avoid building over-capacity that could eventually hurt them all. Computer networks have been extended to interconnect the Italian VAPs, so when one VAP cannot deliver, another can be called on right away.

After only five years, all Menichetti's productive units had over 90% utilization of their machines. Both labor and machine productivity had increased. New machines had been added, increasing capacity by 25%. Product variety was increased in each of the eight units from an average of 600 to 6,000 different yarns. Average in-process and finished-goods inventory dropped from four months to 15 days. What works for Menichetti works for the Italian textile industry as a whole. From 1970 to 1982, Prato production of textiles more than doubled, while that in the rest of Europe declined steeply.

Other Successful VAPs

Other VAPs are alive and well and show that Prato and McKesson are not flukes. The construction industry is a third example. It has operated like a value-adding partnership since the time of the Roman Empire. General contractors subcontract almost all the work on a construction job, soliciting bids from a selected set of subcontractors they trust and making contracts with "partners" who offer reasonable prices—not always the lowest bid.

Japanese trading companies are venerable VAPs that are even more extensive than those in the construction industry. They arrange for the buying and selling of goods at every step of the value-added chain, from mines to household consumers, across several continents. They never get involved in operations. Although some Japanese companies are now choosing to develop their own brand images and find their own way to foreign markets, trading companies remain central to Japan's economic success.

Japanese auto companies also operate as VAPs. Toyota, for example, directly produces only 20% or so of the value of its cars, while GM and Ford produce 70% and 50%, respectively. Chrysler's comeback was due in part to the creation of a VAP with its suppliers, distributors, and union. It produces only around 30% of the value of the cars it sells. Many industry observers attribute Ford's recent gains on GM to Ford's aggressive moves to form partnerships with suppliers.

In the past 30 years, book publishing has evolved toward a VAP. The leading competitors have taken turns divesting various operations that were formerly vertically integrated. The printing function was one of the first to be farmed out, followed by graphics and artwork. Now the usual core function of publishing is brokerage and marketing.

The movie industry has been moving in a somewhat parallel way. Full-blown movie studios that hold exclusive long-term contracts with actors and directors, have a staff of full-time composers and scriptwriters, and own and operate fully equipped production lots are a thing of the past. Now the studios act like brokers who negotiate a set of contracts for a single film production. Old-fashioned studios have been unable to compete.

The Demise of Vertical Intergration

At least in theory, whenever a nonintegrated company deals with another company that performs the next phase of the value-added chain, both stand to benefit from the other's success. But usually, such companies hold each other at arm's length and struggle to keep any economic gains to themselves. In fact, organizations often try to weaken a supplier or customer to ensure their own control of profits. This is understandable, given that the widely followed competitive model suggests that companies will lose bargaining power—and therefore the ability to control profits—as suppliers or customers gain strength.

The relationship between companies connected only by free-market business transactions and guided by such a model of competitiveness is often guarded, if not antagonistic, and rooted in fear that the other will become a competitor or engage in some other opportunistic behavior. Naturally, such companies tend to share as little information as possible, and consequently managers often lack knowledge of the activities elsewhere along the value-added chain. If a company perceives a trading partner as an adversary, it may ship shoddy materials, squeeze margins, delay payments, pirate employees, steal ideas, start price wars, or corner a critical resource—all practices that reveal a lack of concern for the supplier's or customer's well-being.

The conventional solution for ending such destructive games and for controlling resources is vertical integration. When organizations along the value chain are under one management, it is presumed that they can coordinate their activities and work toward a common purpose. And, of course, they can often realize economies of scale.

But vertical integration has its weaknesses. In the process of exploiting their distinctive competences, many large, integrated companies emphasize one competitive dimension. In an integrated company, such focus can actually be a liability, because the strong culture that supports that focus makes it hard to perform tasks that require distinctly different orientations and values. A business that emphasizes low cost, for instance, may run its factories well, but its R&D, design, or marketing functions may have trouble innovating. In a chemical company dominated by commodity production, the culture may inhibit specialty operations. The packaging division of a large paper manufacturer that emphasizes mass production may have trouble responding to the market as an independent competitor.

Perhaps the best example of this problem is in manufacturing. Many manufacturing companies that have invested heavily in flexible manufacturing systems in recent years have had trouble making the new technology achieve its potential. The culture and practices that support long production runs of standardized parts don't fit the new emphasis on wide product variety.

The problem of focus applies to horizontally integrated companies as well. A manufacturer of automobile parts is unlikely to be equally successful at making other products. Although the similarities may be many, whatever differences exist are likely to keep one or the other lines from doing as well as it could if it were the company's sole product. And in many companies, large size itself creates a certain complexity that inhibits communication, innovation, and flexibility.

In a VAP, each small operating company focuses on doing just one step of the value-added chain. Therefore, each unit can tailor all aspects of the organization to this single task. Personnel, plant and equipment, compensation schemes, career tracks, accounting systems, and management styles—all vary depending on the work to be done. The drugstores in the McKesson VAP can attend to their customers' needs and let someone else concentrate on getting the products on the shelf at the right time. In the Prato area, the small companies that produce fabric strive for low cost, coupled with flexibility; those who design the fabric emphasize innovation and creativity.

This sense of focus translates into low overhead, lean staff, and few middle managers. Decisions are made and executed quickly, so response time is short. Creative ideas are less likely to be suppressed, and more employees are exposed to the demands of the market. The fact that each company in a VAP is free to be different from the others creates a diversity that can be the seedbed of innovation. And marketing orientation becomes not an edict nor a difficult task. It follows naturally from the free flow of information throughout the value-added chain to so many of the people who actually do the work.

At the same time, value-adding partnerships have some of the advantages of vertically integrated companies. Managers in a VAP take an interest in the success of other companies in the value-added chain. Their partnership orientation means they work toward the common goal of making the whole VAP competitive. They have command of facts about the market and empathy for the other organizations they deal with. Because information is shared throughout the chain, they know a lot about the competition. And they coordinate their activities with those of their trading partners.

VAPs can also secure the benefits of economies of scale by sharing such things as purchasing services, warehouses, research and development centers, and of course information. McKesson's partners share access to the computer system. Partners in the Menichetti VAP are so congenial that they are housed under one roof; lines on the floor mark where one ends and the other begins. And that VAP has a cooperative transport system.

The power of the VAP is undeniable. To a great extent, VAPs have the best of both worlds: the coordination and scale associated with large companies and the flexibility, creativity, and low overhead usually found in small companies. VAPs share knowledge and insight but aren't burdened with guidelines from a distant headquarters. They don't have long forms to fill out and weekly reports to render. They can act promptly, without having to consult a thick manual of standard operating procedures. In an increasing number of industries, they are proving to be fiercely competitive against both large companies and small independents.

Indeed, the spate of failed mergers and subsequent divestitures and spin-offs, what some people call downsizing, demonstrates that conglomerates and vertically integrated corporations are not always the most competitive organizational forms. The largest organizations in the United States seem to be losing their footing. Employment at the approximately 800 companies ranked in the *Forbes* "500" on sales, profits, assets, or market value declined from more than 23 million in 1979 to 20.6 million in 1986. Average employment at the companies declined from nearly 29,000 to just over 26,000 during the same period. These numbers fell despite a significant rise in total U.S. employment, not to mention the acquisition programs many of these large companies pursued.

Small size alone is not the answer. Many small companies that have open-market relationships with other businesses survive only at the whim of a larger competitor, customer, or supplier that could readily drive it out of business or acquire it if margins become attractive enough. Always constrained by fierce competitiveness and trading partners that know no loyalty, they have little freedom to make financial and operating decisions that are best in the long run.

Ground Rules of Vaps

The delicate issue of control raises questions about the viability of a VAP over time. Let's not forget how creative businesspeople can be. They can invent dozens of ways to take advantage of each other. What prevents them from playing destructive games with their VAP partners, that are, after all, potential competitors? What prevents hostile takeovers? In short, what is to stop a VAP from devolving into anarchy or back to a vertically integrated giant?

For a VAP to exist, its partners must adopt and adhere to a set of ground rules that generates trustworthy transactions. The sense of partnership must become an enforceable reality, despite the many uncertainties and opportunities for playing games. Advice on the best way to do this comes not only from the examples of successful VAPs but also from economists and political scientists who have experimented with the "prisoner's dilemma." The prisoner's dilemma is a game in which two "prisoners" are separated.

Each has the option of either squealing on the other, thereby getting more lenient treatment for himself, or remaining silent, thereby saving both himself and his partner in crime. Of course, if one prisoner remains silent but the partner squeals, the silent person will suffer.

When the games are repeated over and over again, the strategy proving most beneficial is "tit for tat." That is, those players who cooperate on the first round and thereafter do whatever the other player did on the previous move are more successful. Those who don't catch on get eliminated. Robert Axelrod has summarized the extensive studies of the prisoner's dilemma in his 1984 book, *The Evolution of Cooperation*. His advice is particularly relevant to businesspeople in a VAP: (1) don't be the first to play games, (2) reciprocate with both cooperation and lack of it, (3) don't be too greedy, and (4) don't be too clever and try to outsmart your partner.

Studies of existing VAPs are far from conclusive, but early indications are that VAPs follow Axelrod's advice intuitively. They are thus very different from the theoretically perfect markets of economic theory, in which bidders balance supply and demand around price and caveat emptor is the guiding principle. Each company in a VAP cultivates relationships with only a few (from two to six) suppliers of critical items and customers. Having too many partners means few repeat transactions and no time for close relationships to develop. At the same time, partners avoid becoming overdependent on one relationship. A company can keep potential partners "on reserve" through occasional transactions so its welfare won't be harmed if a regular player fails to cooperate.

If partners are to help one another, VAPs must have ways of sharing information. If a partner's costs are creeping out of line, others must know so they can explore ways of helping with cost controls. Technological developments are making it easier for companies to exchange information (see the accompanying list of computer tools and their implications). But also important, successful VAPs must be able to punish partners for acts of opportunism and gaming.

In the Prato textile area, late delivery sometimes calls for withholding of new orders until the problem is rectified. And the construction industry has invented many ways to cope with changes in job specifications and raw materials costs as well as strikes and bad weather. The ultimate sanction, of course, is to terminate the partnership. In the Prato area, this could happen if, for instance, an *impannatore* failed to pass orders back to the weaver who had supplied the fabric design that was being sold.

It seems clear that, for at least some value-added chains, a value-adding partnership is a viable and advantageous means of achieving the benefits of vertical integration. By observing the characteristics of and the processes followed by successful partnerships, executives can determine whether VAPs might pay off for their organizations. Business relationships premised on the need to achieve bargaining power may be more aggressively competitive than is in their best interest. Remember that the examples cited earlier—U.S. automobiles, Italian textiles, and drug distribution—all evolved from competitive, sometimes acrimonious, relationships.

The economic logic of the VAP is compelling. And at least for now, VAPs are part of the business landscape. Others should mind their feeding grounds and watering holes, for even giants have their vulnerabilities.

Notes

1. For other discussions of the new organizational forms see Raymond Miles and Charles Snow, "Network Organizations: New Concepts for New Forms," *California Management Review*, Spring 1987, p. 62; Robert G. Eccles, "The Quasifirm in the Contruction Industry," *Journal of Economic Behavior and Organization*, December 1981, p. 335; Calvin Pava, "Managing the New Information Technology: Design or Default?" in *HRM Trends and Challenges*, eds. Richard E. Walton and Paul R. Lawrence (Boston: Harvard Business School Press, 1985); and Andrea Larson, "Networks as Organizatons," unpublished manuscript, 1987.

2. This description draws heavily on Michael J. Piore and Charles F. Sabel, *The Second Industrial Divide* (New York: Basci Books, 1984) and on Gianni Lorenzoni, *Una Politica Innovative* (Milan: Etas Libri, 1979).

3. The facts about Massimo Menichetti are excerpted from the Harvard Business School case, "Massimo Menichetti (B)," 686-135, revised October 1986, prepared by Ramchandran Jaikumar.

3
Information Technology and Tomorrow's Manager

Lynda M. Applegate, James I. Cash, Jr., and D. Quinn Mills

The year is 1958. It's a time of prosperity, productivity, and industrial growth for U.S. corporations, which dominate the world economy. Organizations are growing bigger and more complex by the day. Transatlantic cable service, which has just been initiated, and advances in transportation are allowing companies to expand into international markets. To handle the growth, companies are decentralizing decision making. To keep track of these burgeoning operations, they are hiring middle managers in droves. In fact, for the first time ever, white-collar workers outnumber blue-collar workers. Large companies are installing their first computers to automate routine clerical and production tasks, and "participatory management" is the buzzword.

It's also the year Harold J. Leavitt and Thomas L. Whisler predicted what corporate life would be like 30 years later. Their article "Management in the 1980s" (*Harvard Business Review*, November–December 1958) and its predictions ran counter to the trends that were then underway. Leavitt and Whisler said, for instance, that by the late 1980s, the combination of management science and information technology would cause middle-management ranks to shrink, top management to take on more of the creative functions, and large organizations to centralize again. Through the 1960s, 1970s, and early 1980s, Leavitt and Whisler's predictions met strong criticism. But as the 1980s draw to a close, they don't seem so farfetched. Instead, they seem downright visionary.

They predicted that in the 1980s . . .

. . . the role and scope of middle managers would change. Many of the existing middle management jobs would become more structured and would move downward in status and compensation. The number of middle managers would decrease, creating a flatter organization. Those middle-management positions that remained would be more technical and specialized. New mid-level positions with titles like "analyst" would be created.

. . . top management would take on more of the innovating, planning, and creating. The rate of obsolescence and change would quicken, and top management would have to continually focus on the horizon.

. . . large organizations would recentralize. New information technologies would give top managers more information and would extend top management's control over the decisions of subordinates. Top executives chose to decentralize only because they were unable to keep up with the changing size and complexity of their organizations. Given the chance, however, they would use information technology to take more control and recentralize.

Downsizing and "flattening" have been common in recent years. One estimate has it that organizations have shed more than one million managers and staff professionals since 1979. As companies have reduced the number of middle managers, senior managers have increased their span of control and assumed additional responsibilities. Consider these two examples.

Within weeks after a comprehensive restructuring thinned management by 40%, the president of a large oil company requested an improved management control system for his newly appointed senior management team. In response, a sophisticated, online executive information system was developed. It did the work of scores of analysts and mid-level managers whose responsibilities had been to produce charts and graphs, communicate this information, and coordinate operations with others in the company. The president also mandated the use of electronic mail to streamline communication throughout the business.

A large manufacturing company recently undertook a massive restructuring to cut the cost and time required to bring a new product to market. The effort included layoffs, divestitures, and early retirements, which thinned middle management by 30%. The company adopted a sophisticated telecommunications network, which linked all parts of the multinational company, and a centralized corporate data base, which integrated all aspects of the highly decentralized business. Senior managers used the data base and networks to summarize and display data from inside and outside the company and to signal to employees the kinds of things they should focus on.

Information technology, which had once been a tool for organizational expansion, has become a tool for downsizing and restructuring. Both these companies used technology to improve centralized control and to create new information channels. But this improved centralized control did not come at the expense of decentralized decision making. In fact, the need to be responsive led to even more decentralized decision making. The companies reduced the number of middle managers, and the computer systems assumed many of the communication, coordination, and control functions that middle managers previously performed. The line managers who remained were liberated from some routine tasks and had more responsibility.

These effects are similar to what Leavitt and Whisler predicted. Taking their clues from the management science and technology research of the 1950s, Leavitt and Whisler contemplated how technology would influence the shape and nature of the organization. They understood that technology would enable senior management to monitor and control large organizations more effectively and that fewer middle managers would be needed to analyze and relay information. They did not anticipate, however, that microcomputers would enable simultaneous improvement in decentralized decision making.

In the past, managers had to choose between a centralized and a decentralized structure. Today there is a third option: technology-driven control systems that support the flexibility and responsiveness of a decentralized organization as well as the integration and control of a centralized organization.

What Next?

Now that this wave of information technology has worked its way into practice, it's time to think about where we're headed next. When we turn to research to see what technical breakthroughs are on the horizon, as Leavitt and Whisler did, we find that the horizon itself has changed. It's now much closer. Since the 1950s, development time has been cut in half. What once took 30 years to get from pure research to commercial application now takes only 10 to 15.

Moreover, when earlier generations of technology were commercialized, managers tended to adopt the technology first and then try to figure out what to do with the new information and how to cope with the organizational implications. But for many companies, that approach is now grossly inadequate. The new technology is more powerful, more diverse, and increasingly entwined with the organization's critical business processes. Continuing to merely react to new technology and the organizational change it triggers could throw a business into a tailspin.

At the same time, the business environment is changing ever faster, and organizations must be more responsive to it. Yet certain facts of life restrain them from doing so. Companies want to be more flexible, yet job descriptions, compensation schemes, and control mechanisms are rigid. They want to use their resources effectively, yet it's not always clear who can contribute most to a project, especially among people in different functional areas. They want to be productive, but every time an employee goes to another company, a little bit of corporate history and experience walks out the door.

With the help of technology, managers will be able to overcome these problems and make their organizations far more responsive than they are today. We can look forward, in fact, to an era in which managers will do the shaping. Large organization or small, centralized or not—business leaders will have options they've never had before. The technology will be there to turn the vision into reality and to change it as circumstances evolve. With that in mind, making a next round of predictions and waiting to see if they come true seems too passive. It makes more sense to begin thinking about the kind of organization we want and taking the steps necessary to prepare for it.

We already see glimpses of the future in some progressive companies that have used technology creatively, but even they do not give us a complete picture of the kind of organization that will be possible—maybe even prevalent—in the twenty-first century. Some companies will choose to adopt a new organizational form that we call the "cluster organization."[1] By doing so, they will be able to run their large companies like small ones and achieve the benefits of both.

In the cluster organization, groups of people will work together to solve business problems or define a process and will then disband when the job is done. Team members may be geographically dispersed and unacquainted with each other, but information and communication systems will enable those with complementary skills to work together. The systems will help the teams carry out their activities and track the results of their decisions. Reporting relationships, control mechanisms, compensation schemes—all will be different in the cluster organization.

Technology will offer new options even to companies that don't wish to make all of the changes the cluster organization implies. The first step in understanding these options is to look, as Leavitt and Whisler did, at the technologies that will make them possible.

Tomorrow's Machines

Much of the technology that will give managers the freedom to shape their organizations is already being commercialized—expert systems, group and cooperative work systems, and executive information systems. Expert and knowledge-based systems (a subset of artificial intelligence technology) are rapidly appearing in commercial settings. Every large company we've polled expects to have at least one production system using this technology by late 1989. Group and cooperative work systems have sprung up in a number of companies, primarily for use by multidisciplinary teams. Executive information systems, which track both internal and external information, enable senior managers to monitor and control large, geographically dispersed and complex organizations.

By the turn of the century, these and other technologies will be widely available. Companies will be able to pick and choose applications that fit their requirements. Computers will be faster, smaller, more reliable, and easier to use. They'll store vast amounts of information, and they'll be flexible enough to allow companies to change their information and communication systems as the environment changes.

In the twenty-first century, desktop computers will be as powerful as today's supercomputers, and supercomputers will run at speeds over a thousand times faster than today's. Computer chips now with one million processing elements will have more than one billion, and parallel processing (the ability to share a task among a number of processing units) will boost power tremendously.

It will be possible to communicate voluminous amounts of information in a variety of forms over long distances within seconds.

Standard telephone lines and advanced cellular radio technology will provide access to high-speed networks that will whisk data, text, graphics, voice, and video information from one part of the world to another instantly. Improved reliability and security will accompany the significantly higher network speeds and the improved performance.

Plugging all shapes and sizes of computers into tomorrow's network will be as easy as plugging in a telephone today. Telephones, in fact, will be replaced by computer phones that can convert speech into machine-readable text and can simultaneously transmit video images, voice, and data. Storing messages, transferring documents, paying bills, and shopping at home will all be possible through the same connection.

Computers the size of a small book will have the information processing power and storage capabilities of today's desktop workstations, yet will fit in a briefcase. They'll enable us to create and revise documents, review and answer mail, and even hold video conference meetings from anyplace that has a phone jack. Cellular terminals will allow even more freedom, since they won't require a wired telephone connection. And we will no longer be a slave to the keyboard; voice recognition technology will allow us to dictate messages and create and revise text as easily as using a dictaphone.

As computers become faster at processing and communicating information, we'll need better ways of storing and managing it. Optical storage media, similar to the compact-disk technology that is used today to store music, will hold much more information than is possible today and will retrieve information much more quickly.

And no longer will it be necessary to store data in static data bases that must be reprogrammed every time the business changes. Flexible, dynamic information networks called associative networks will do away with these rigid systems. Associative networks will allow us to store and manipulate information in a manner similar to the way we think. They will store data, voice, video, text, and graphics—but beyond that, they will store the relationships between information elements. As needs change and the network is reconfigured, the relationships among the data remain intact. Primitive associative information systems, used primarily to process large-text data bases (e.g., hypertext), are currently on the market. We can expect significant enhancements to these associative information systems in the next several years.

Tomorrow's computers will truly be more intelligent. Today's computers are designed to process information sequentially, one command at a time. This capability works well if the problem or task is structured and can be broken down into a series of steps. It doesn't work well for complex, unstructured tasks involving insight, creativity, and judgment. "Neural network" computers will change that.

Rather than processing commands one at a time, a neural network computer uses associative reasoning to store information as patterns of connections among millions of tiny processors, all of which are linked together. These computers attempt to mimic the actions of the human brain. When faced with a new pattern, the computer follows rules of logic to ask questions that help it figure out what to do with the anomaly.

Prototypes of neural network computers already exist. One group of researchers developed a neural network computer that contained the logic to understand English phonetics. The researchers gave the computer typed transcripts, containing 1,024 words, from a child in first grade, and it proceeded to read out loud. A human instructor "told" the computer each time it made a mistake, and within ten tries, the computer was reading the text in an understandable way. Within 50 tries, the computer was reading at 95% accuracy. No software programming was ever done.[2] The computer learned to read in much the same way that humans do.

We can also expect that by the twenty-first century there will be many companies that routinely use expert systems and other artificial intelligence applications. Knowledge bases, in which expertise is stored along with information, will become as commonplace as data bases are today. Technology will increasingly help people perform tasks requiring judgment and expert knowledge. Already, fighter aircraft technology is moving toward having the plane respond to what the pilot is thinking rather than his physical movements.

This type of technology will no longer simply make things more efficient; instead, the computer will become a tool for creativity, discovery, and education. Interactive technology based on optical storage is currently used in flight simulators to help pilots learn to make decisions. Some companies are experimenting with similar systems, described as digital video interactive, to help planners, analysts, researchers, functional specialists, and managers learn to make decisions without the risk and time associated with traditional experiential learning. These should help managers learn to be effective much more quickly.

Technologies will be well developed to meet the needs of senior

executives. Sophisticated analytical, graphical, and computer interface capabilities will be able to aggregate, integrate, and present
data in flexible and easy-to-use formats. Computers and special
software will support executive planning, decision making, communication, and control activities. Some executives already use
these applications to manage their businesses.

While in the past computers primarily supported individual
work, the computer systems of the future will also be geared toward
groups. Research on computer support for cooperative work has
gained momentum over the past five years, and many companies
are developing promising new technologies. Several companies are
installing automated meeting rooms, and a number of vendors are
working on software to support group activities. Researchers are
now testing electronic brainstorming, group consensus, and nego-
tiation software, and general meeting support systems. To help
geographically dispersed group members work together, some companies are developing electronic communication software and applications that make communication and the exchange of
documents and ideas faster and easier. These applications will
allow skills to be better allocated.

The Structure, the Process, and the People

These and other advanced technologies will give managers a
whole new set of options for structuring and operating their businesses. In the twenty-first century, like today, some companies will
be small, some will be large; some will be decentralized, others
will not. But technology will enable new organizational structures
and management processes to spring up around the familiar ones,
and the business world will be a very different place as a result.
Here we describe the organizational structures, management processes, and human resource management strategies associated with
the cluster organization and how the technology will make them
possible in years to come.

ORGANIZATIONAL STRUCTURE

Companies will have the benefits of small scale and large scale
simultaneously.

Even large organizations will be able to adopt more flexible and dynamic structures.

The distinctions between centralized and decentralized control will blur.

The focus will be on projects and processes rather than on tasks and standard procedures.

The hierarchy and the matrix are the most common formal organizational designs for large companies today. They structure communication, responsibility, and accountability to help reduce complexity and provide stability. But, as implemented today, they also tend to stifle innovation. With the environment changing as quickly as it does, the challenge has been to make large companies, with their economies of scale and other size advantages, as responsive as small ones.

Small companies, of course, have fewer layers of management and less bureaucracy, so the organization is less rigid. They adapt more easily to change and allow for creativity. Leadership and control are generally easier in small businesses because top management can communicate directly with workers and can readily trace the contribution individuals make. Information is also easier to track. Much of the knowledge is in people's heads, and everyone knows whom to go to for expertise on a particular subject. People often have a chance to get involved with a broad range of responsibilities and therefore have a better understanding of the business as a whole.

These small organizations, especially those that are information-intensive and have a large percentage of professional employees, tend to be structured differently. We have termed the most fluid and flexible forms "cluster." Other authors talk of a network organization or an adhocracy.[3] In the network organization, rigid hierarchies are replaced by formal and informal communication networks that connect all parts of the company. In the adhocracy, a set of project-oriented work groups replaces the hierarchy. Both of these forms are well known for their flexibility and adaptiveness. The Manned Space Flight Center of NASA, an example of an adhocracy, changed its organization structure 17 times in the first eight years of its existence.[4]

In what will be an even faster changing world than the one we now know, businesses of all sizes will need the ability to adapt to the dynamics of the external environment. Automated information and communication networks will support the sharing of information throughout a large, widely dispersed, complex company. The systems will form the organization's infrastructure and change the role of formal reporting procedures. Even in large corporations, each individual will be able to communicate with any other—just as if he or she worked in a small company.

The technologies that will allow these more fluid organizational forms are already coming into use in the form of electronic mail, voice mail, fax, data networks, and computer and video conferencing. Speed and performance improvements will collapse the time and distance that now separate people who could benefit from working together. The large organizations of the future will seem as tightly connected as small ones.

Computers will also help identify who in the company has the expertise needed to work on a particular problem. Data bases of employees' skills and backgrounds will ensure that the mix of talent can be tailor-made for every task that arises. The systems will keep track of who knows what, and how to prepare an individual for the next project.

Managers in large companies will also have technological help in keeping track of where information resides and how to analyze it. Associative information networks and neural network computers will preserve the relationships among data elements and will store and manage information in a manner similar to the way we think. They will provide concise snapshots of the vast activities and resources of a large corporation. This will prevent managers from being overwhelmed by the scale and complexity.

Executives and senior managers will be less insulated from operations because executive information systems will help them get the information they need to monitor, coordinate, and control their businesses. Rather than waiting for the analysts and middle managers to prepare reports at the end of a prolonged reporting period, executives will have immediate access to information. Software will help do the analysis and present it in a usable format. With such immediate feedback, managers will be able to adjust their strategy and tactics as circumstances evolve rather than at fixed time intervals. And if a change in tactics or strategy is warranted, advanced communication technology will send the message to employees promptly.

Top management's ability to know what is going on throughout the organization won't automatically lead to centralization. With feedback on operations readily available at the top, the rigid policies and procedures that now aim to keep line managers on track can be relaxed. The systems will also liberate business managers by giving them the information and analytic support they need to make decisions and control their operations. Individuals and project teams will be able to operate fairly autonomously while senior management monitors the overall effects of their actions by the hour or day.

Most of the day-to-day activity will be project oriented. Because circumstances will change even faster than they do now, no two situations will be exactly alike or call for the same set of experts or procedures. The employees' skills and the approach will vary with the task at hand, so teams of people will form around particular projects and subsequently dissolve. Most responsibilities, then, will be handed over to project managers. Associative information networks will help those managers deploy resources, and software specially designed to support group work will aid communication, decision making, and consensus reaching. People who work together only infrequently will have the tools they need to be at least as effective as the permanent management team in a small company.

MANAGEMENT PROCESSES

Decision making will be better understood.

Control will be separate from reporting relationships.

Computers will support creativity at all organizational levels.

Information and communication systems will retain corporate history, experience, and expertise.

Decision making is not well understood in most organizations. Managers often make choices based on thought processes they themselves cannot explain. They gather the information they think is relevant and reach what seems like the best conclusion. In the future, sophisticated expert systems and knowledge bases will help to capture those decision-making processes. Companies can then analyze and improve them.

As the decision processes become more explicit and well defined and as companies learn what information is required, the level of the person making the decision becomes less important. It will still be important to monitor the outcome and to make sure the circumstances surrounding the decision haven't completely changed.

Management control is now exerted through the formal organizational chart. A manager at a given level in the organization is responsible for everything that happens below that level. That same person channels information up through the organization to the person he or she reports to.

But when technology allows top management to monitor data at the lowest organizational level without the help of intermediaries and when employees at all levels and in all functions can communicate directly, formal control systems do not have to be embedded in organizational reporting relationships. The ability to separate control from reporting relationships means that both systems can be handled most effectively. For instance, top management can exercise control directly by monitoring results at all levels, while a different set of relationships exists for reporting purposes. These reporting relationships would focus on employee motivation, creativity, and socialization.

By doing a lot of the analytical work, expert systems and artificial intelligence tools will free up workers at all levels to be more creative. Up to now, only top management jobs have been structured to allow as much time as possible for creative thinking. As technology helps managers with coordination, control, decision making, and communication, they too will have the time and encouragement to make discoveries and use the new resources innovatively.

The transience of even specialized workers won't be nearly the problem in the twenty-first century that it is today. Information systems will maintain the corporate history, experience, and expertise that long-time employees now hold. The information systems themselves—not the people—can become the stable structure of the organization. People will be free to come and go, but the value of their experience will be incorporated in the systems that will help them and their successors run the business.

In this environment, companies will need fewer managers. Those managers that do assume executive positions, however, will lack the experiential learning acquired through years as a middle manager. Their career paths will not take them through positions of increasing responsibility where they oversee the work of others. Executive information systems will enable them to "get up to speed" quickly on all parts of the business. Sophisticated business analysis and simulation models will help them analyze business situations and recognize the consequences, thereby decreasing and managing risk.

HUMAN RESOURCES

Workers will be better trained, more autonomous, and more transient.

The work environment will be exciting and engaging.

Management will be for some people a part-time activity that is shared and rotated.

Job descriptions tied to narrowly defined tasks will become obsolete.

Compensation will be tied more directly to contribution.

In the 1950s and 1960s, computers took on many operational and routine tasks. In the 1970s and 1980s, they assumed some middle-management decision-making, coordinating, and controlling tasks. As the technology affects even more aspects of the business, work itself will change and require a different set of skills. People will need to be technically sophisticated and better educated in order to cope with the demands on them. Employees must be capable of leading—rather than being led by—the technology, capable of using technology as a lever against the increased complexity and pace of change in their business environments.

As top management seizes on its ability to monitor without restricting freedom, employees will have more control over their own work. There will be fewer rigid policies from a less visible headquarters. Also, as the nature of the work changes from implementing a particular company's standard operating procedures to participating in a series of projects that call on one's expertise, workers will be less tied to any one organization, and building loyalty to a company will be harder than it is today. In some companies, loyalty may be less critical than having access to the skills a given employee has to offer. As companies pull together the resources they need on a project-by-project basis and as information and communication networks extend beyond the organization, company boundaries will be harder to define. Organizations may draw on expertise that lies in a supplier or an independent consultant if appropriate.

Because workers will be highly skilled and the organization will offer fewer opportunities for advancement, employees will expect the work environment to be rewarding. If they are not stimulated or if their independence is threatened, they will go elsewhere.

In these ways, companies of the future will closely resemble professional service firms today. The most successful firms attract and retain employees by providing an environment that is intellectually engaging. The work is challenging, the projects diverse, and the relationships with clients fairly independent. Some professionals work with more than one firm—like doctors who admit patients to several hospitals.

Management will be a part-time job as group members share responsibility and rotate leadership. Except at the top of the organization, there will be few jobs that consist solely of overseeing the work of others—and then primarily for measurement and control purposes. Each work group may have a different leader. In addition, the leadership of a single group may rotate among members, depending on what the business problem requires. Employees will take on a management role for short periods, and as a result, will have a better understanding of the entire business.

Detailed, task-oriented job descriptions will be less important because the job will be changing all the time. In a sense, everyone will be doing the same job—lending their special skills and expertise to one project after another. In another sense, every job will be unique—people with different kinds of expertise will work on different sets of projects. Information systems will be able to account for the work each person does and the skills and experience he or she possesses.

The ability to track each individual's skill and participation in the company outside the traditional organizational forms creates a whole new freedom: the ability to pay each person for his or her actual contribution to the organization without upsetting an entire pay scale or hierarchical structure. Currently, if the company wants to create an incentive for a particular person, it is often constrained by the compensation system itself. To raise one person's salary requires boosting everyone else above that point in the hierarchy.

Flexible, dynamic compensation packages will allow companies to treat individuals as unique contributors and to reward them based on their particular skills. In some companies, an employee's compensation may follow the pattern of a normal distribution curve, matching the employee's desired work pattern and contribution to the company. Salaries would increase and peak between ages 40 and 50, and then decline.

Be Creative But Be Careful

The new technologies hold great promise that our large, rigid hierarchies will become more adaptive, responsive, and better suited to the fast-paced world of the twenty-first century. But these technologies do not come without risk. Processing information faster may seem like a good idea, but it is possible to process information too fast. As speed increases, efficiency of a process improves only to a point. That point is reached when it is no longer possible to monitor and control the results of the process. Beyond that point, the process of collecting information, making decisions, monitoring feedback, and evaluating performance breaks down. The experience of some companies during the stock market crash of October 19, 1987 shows what can happen when information is processed faster than we can monitor and control it.

There are also risks associated with integrating data from diverse sources. For one thing, we run the risk of data overload, in which case people unable to understand or use the information and the tools that convert data into information may fail. Also, the creation of integrated data bases may lead to unintended liabilities. For example, when an elevator manufacturer created a centralized service and repair center, it also created a legal liability. A large, centralized data base containing the maintenance and repair records of all of their elevators in North America provided an attractive target for subpoena by any suitor.

Computerization of critical business processes may also create security risks. Sabotage, fraud, record falsification, and theft become more threatening than ever. And with more information stored electronically, privacy issues become more acute.

Leavitt and Whisler were wise to believe that information technology would influence the structure of organizations, their management processes, and the nature of managerial work. Our 30-year history of information technology use in organizations suggests that in the future managers must be much more actively involved in directing technology and managing its influence on organizations.

Technology will not be an easy solution to serious problems and it won't guarantee competitiveness. As always, it will require thoughtful planning and responsible management. But as never before, it will tax the creative powers of the business leaders who must decide when to use it—and to what end.

Notes

1. See D. Quinn Mills, *Rebirth of the Corporation* (New York: John Wiley, forthcoming).
2. Terrence Sejnowski and Charles Rosenberg, "Parallel Networks That Learn to Pronounce English Text," *Complex Systems,* vol. 1, 1987, p. 145.
3. See Robert G. Eccles and Dwight B. Crane, "Managing Through Networks in Investment Banking," *California Management Review,* Fall 1987, p. 176; and Henry Mintzberg, "The Adhocracy," in *The Strategy Process,* eds. James Brian Quinn, Henry Mintzberg, and Robert M. James (Englewood Cliffs, N.J.: Prentice-Hall, 1988), p. 607.
4. As reported in Henry Mintzberg, *Structuring in Fives: Designing Effective Organizations* (Englewood Cliffs, N.J.: Prentice-Hall, 1983).

4
The Logic of Electronic Markets

Thomas W. Malone, JoAnne Yates, and Robert I. Benjamin

Innovative companies like American Hospital Supply, United Airlines, and McKesson have been widely applauded for their clever use of information technology. By using computers to help customers order supplies or make airline reservations, such companies have boosted their profits and net worth and permanently altered the competitive dynamics of their industries.

But companies that try to imitate these mavericks by "locking in" customers may be left behind by an evolution away from single-source electronic sales channels toward "electronic markets" that include many suppliers' offerings. United's airline reservations system has in fact already become an electronic market, listing flights from other airlines. AHS's system (now operated by Baxter Healthcare after the merger of AHS and Baxter Travenol) seems to be following suit. Hospitals can now use Baxter's computer network to order products from several of Baxter's competitors.

We believe that the dynamics that have caused these single-source sales channels to evolve are generic and that many of the single-source sales channels that have proliferated in recent years will ultimately follow the same path toward electronic markets. This evolution of computer-aided buying and selling will disrupt conventional marketing and distribution patterns.

As the competitive landscape changes, some companies will emerge as winners—like those that make electronic markets or those that use them wisely. Others will lose out—like those that are unwittingly eliminated from the distribution chain and those that try to lock in customers through obsolete arrangements.

Ultimately, the electronic links between suppliers and customers will have an even more important effect on our economy. By reducing the costs of negotiating and consummating deals and by helping buyers find the best supplier, electronic markets will make it more attractive to buy certain goods and services than to make them. Therefore, vertical integration will be less appealing to many companies. Networks of companies that perform different steps in the value-added chain, also known as value-adding partnerships, may well become a major industry structure.[1]

Talkin' about an Evolution

Beginning in the 1970s, a number of suppliers created single-source electronic sales channels. Electronic terminals on customers' premises would link the customers and the sponsoring vendor— but only for that vendor's products. Some of those early channels failed, but others have grown and changed.

The electronic sales channels that work do so because they give customers something of real value. For one thing, having on-site terminals is often simply more convenient than contacting a sales representative. Also electronic sales channels eliminate much of the paper handling and clerical work associated with making a purchase: processing the order, billing the customer, tracking the delivery, and accounting for the sale require many people and take a long time. Electronic sales channels streamline much of that. Some systems let customers reduce their materials inventories by arranging just-in-time deliveries of components. All of this translates either directly or indirectly into savings for the customer.

The advantages to the seller can be even more substantial. Customers who become accustomed to the convenience of electronic terminals on their premises give the vendor a captive audience. Competitors must bend over backward to lure customers away.

Inland Steel has a single-source sales channel that lets customers access the company's mainframe computer to place orders and track steel shipments. And Digital Equipment Corporation has one: an on-line catalog and ordering service, called Digital's Electronic Store, through which customers can order a number of computer products the company makes.

But even customers who appreciate the convenience and savings of single-source sales channels don't like being locked into one supplier. They would rather be able to compare a number of competing products to be sure of getting the product features they want, at the best price.

That's where electronic markets come in. Electronic markets offer cross-company electronic connections, just as single-source sales channels do, and therefore give customers the same convenience. But they include offerings from competing suppliers. Not only do customers have electronic connections to their suppliers but they can also choose which supplier they want to use. From the customers' perspective, then, electronic markets are more desirable than single-source sales channels.

If the technology exists to create electronic markets and customers want them, it is just a matter of time until services arise to meet that need. Companies that have created single-source sales channels are often the first to respond to that demand by adding competitors' products to their data base, thereby creating an electronic market. They risk losing their customer franchise, but if they try to keep their customers captive too long, they risk losing those customers entirely. Consider what happened in the airline industry.

In 1976, United Airlines created a single-source sales channel called Apollo that allowed travel agents to book flights on United. The system provided a competitive advantage for a while, but then American Airlines did United one better. It created Sabre, a system of its own—but one that soon included flights from other airlines. Travel agents of course liked the range of choices. To prevent agents from choosing Sabre over Apollo, United quickly responded by adding other airlines' flights to its own system.

But the inclusion of other air carriers didn't complete the evolution of Sabre and Apollo. Even while offering competitors' flights, the airlines tried to retain some advantage: knowing that agents tend to book flights near the top of the list, they listed their own flights first. The airline companies had moved from single-source sales channels to electronic markets for competitive reasons, but the markets they created were biased. The defunct Civil Aeronautics Board intervened. To protect consumers and the smaller airlines, it required Sabre and Apollo to eliminate the bias in the listing order.

Making an unbiased electronic market is a potentially profitable business in its own right. Last year, United sold a half interest in the Apollo system for $500 million. For some organizations, like Inventory Locator Service, Inc., market making is their main activity. Not long ago, when an airplane needed a replacement part, a repair person would have to call parts dealers and brokers to see if they could provide the item. The search was slow and somewhat random because it relied heavily on personal relationships. The caller, who was usually pressed for time, often didn't compare prices but made a purchase as soon as a broker or dealer found the part.

In 1979, Inventory Locator Service started its data base with information from the Air Transport Association, the trade organization of major U.S. air carriers. The company (subsequently acquired by Ryder System and operating as an independent division) now lists all the suppliers that have a certain item in stock along with their telephone numbers and a few other pieces of information. Subscribers can simply dial into the data base using terminals or personal computers to get information on the parts they need. Planes that used to be grounded for days are now flying within hours.

Recently, electronic connections between companies and retail customers have proliferated. In 1988, J.C. Penney launched Telaction, an electronic home-shopping system designed to simulate shopping at a mall. Customers "shop" via a cable television channel and can get more detailed information about the products by using their push-button phone. Sears, Roebuck and IBM have jointly created Prodigy, a home-shopping and entertainment system that users can access through personal computers. And many cities now have computer-based multiple listing services for residential real estate that help buyers find the houses they want to see in person.

The Comp-U-Card system lets buyers call an operator at a toll-free number to order any of a wide variety of consumer goods listed in the system's data base. With this service, marketed by Citibank and a number of other banks, buyers can either get information about the alternatives in a product category—like color televisions—or get price information about a particular brand name product—say, a 19-inch Sony color television. In either case, if the buyer decides to purchase an item, the system automatically selects the lowest price supplier for that item, and the product is directly shipped and charged to the buyer.

Comp-U-Store, an extension of Comp-U-Card, provides a similar service for personal computer users. Users dial up the system either directly through their personal computers or through an information service like Dow Jones News/Retrieval or CompuServe

Information Service. Customers then enter the characteristics of products they are interested in, and the system lists all the products that meet those requirements. If the buyer decides to buy one of them, the system selects the lowest price supplier and transmits the order directly to the supplier's shipping center.

Although not all of these electronic buyer-supplier connections are realizing the same degree of success, they are evidence of a real and irreversible trend toward electronic markets. Ultimately, many, if not most, business transactions will be conducted electronically.

Getting off the Bench

All market participants should consider how computer-aided buying and selling is likely to affect them. Early developers of single-source or biased sales channels should plan for the transition to unbiased electronic markets. That way, they can continue to derive revenues from the market-making activity. Other companies should think about creating or using an electronic market.

One way sellers can decide if electronic markets are likely to be useful in their industries is to consider whether customers can make purchase decisions based on information in a computerized data base. If so, then a full electronic market is feasible. Since commodities are by definition simple to describe, they clearly lend themselves to electronic markets, as do products that are standardized.

When products are unique to each buyer, there may be little value in being able to compare alternative products electronically. But even if a product is somewhat complex, an electronic market that lets customers narrow their search according to a few important product features might succeed. And in some cases, customers may find value in a single-source sales channel just to reduce paperwork.

Manufacturers are well positioned to create an electronic market. They can leverage the fact that they are both buyer and seller. Digital Equipment Corporation, for example, has a data base of software products—developed internally and by other companies— that runs on Digital's computers. The system, called SOFTbase, helps Digital employees find externally developed software. It also helps Digital sales representatives find the best programs available to meet customers' needs.

Companies that stand to benefit from electronic markets but lack such services can build their own data bases of information about alternative products. Ryder System created an electronic market for its employees called MedFacts. This service lists fees, educational backgrounds, and specialities of more than 1,400 physicians in the Miami area.

Companies that are powerful in their markets can require suppliers to provide the information they need in a form that fits their data bases. General Motors demands that its primary suppliers conform to the computer hardware and communications standards the Automotive Industry Action Group established. Buyer groups in the grocery, chemical, insurance, and aluminum industries are developing similar standards.

Because electronic markets are essentially a brokering service, they offer an opportunity as well as a threat to existing brokers. When Inventory Locator Service was introduced, brokers and dealers subscribed to the service, and the airlines continued to turn to them. But now that many airlines subscribe, the brokers and dealers are in a precarious situation.

Retailers are also vulnerable to distributors who circumvent them electronically. SelectQuote Insurance Services of San Francisco and Insurance Information, Inc. of Methuen, Massachusetts, bypass retail insurance agents by offering consumers access to a data base of information about life insurance from a wide range of providers. Brokers can survive by following Inventory Locator Service's example and creating their own electronic market. Retailers could use an electronic market as one more outlet, like mail order or a new store.

When no single player is powerful enough to create an electronic market on its own, an industry association may be able to help— if only by setting standards and promoting the idea. In the U.S. insurance industry, for instance, a group of independent agents, concerned about their loss of market share to direct sales forces from State Farm and Allstate, developed industrywide standards for electronic data interchange. This effort eventually led to the development of an independent network, IVANS (Insurance Value Added Network Services), based in White Plains, New York. It links insurance agents, insurance carriers, and many other information sources for agents.

Other examples include a cooperative association of cotton farmers in Oklahoma and Texas who established TELCOT, an electronic market for cotton. No one farmer could have created TELCOT, but now more than 12,000 farmers use it to sell their product. And a trade association, the Motor and Equipment Manufacturers Association, operates MEMA/Transnet, an electronic order system for automotive parts that serves more than 100 manufacturers and 4,000 customers.

Such collaborations also make sense when competitors, customers, or third parties are likely to form electronic interconnections. Smaller players can pool their efforts and succeed even against big players with established electronic systems.

Banks and other financial institutions already participate in many markets by transferring funds or extending credit. This involvement can be the basis for an electronic market, as it was for Citibank when it gave its credit card holders access to the Comp-U-Card system. Similarly, Chemical Bank created an electronic market to give customers stock price and home retailing information.

Vendors of hardware, networks, and software also have opportunities to create markets. Orion Network Enterprises, which sells the technology to build networks, created an electronic market for auto parts by linking about 600 junkyards across the country. And in France, the national telephone company subsidized the installation of simple computer terminals for many of its telephone subscribers so they could access directories electronically. The phone company also encourages independent companies to use its Minitel system to set up on-line services to which customers subscribe. The number of these services has exploded. Some U.S. telephone companies are exploring an "electronic yellow pages," which would let customers place orders as well as locate suppliers.

Out with Firms, in with Markets

As electronic markets spur companies to reposition themselves and to rethink the way they conduct business, they will create more fundamental changes in the economy. The emergence of electronic markets will reduce the benefits of vertical integration for many organizations. Separate companies—not vertically integrated companies—will perform different steps along the value-added chain, and the exchanges between those independent players will be more efficient.

Vertically integrated companies have a certain economic logic. It used to be true—and of course in many cases still is—that the costs associated with locating vendors, comparing their products or services, negotiating with them, and handling the paperwork were a big factor in the make-or-buy decision. A company that made machined fittings for many different customers could, through economies of scale, produce them cheaply. But for some customers, the so-called transaction costs offset the potential savings in production costs. For those would-be customers, it made more sense to make the items.

For reasons already explained, electronic markets reduce transaction costs. Where it once made sense to make a product or perform a service in-house, it suddenly makes sense to buy it. This leads to more market activity overall.

As market activity increases, electronic networks will help companies and consumers find the most efficient providers of goods and services. Comp-U-Card is a case in point. Even if consumers were to visit several stores to compare prices, they still would have no way of knowing if the item were available at a lower price in another city or state. Comp-U-Card ensures that they get the item at the best price. Inventory Locator Service makes markets efficient in a slightly different way: by helping companies find the specific item they need as soon as possible.

With such sound underlying economics, electronic markets are not a fad. They are in fact inevitable. And their continued proliferation and evolution will be felt throughout our economy. They will touch even those businesses that choose not to participate in them. Clearly, managers need to watch this trend, for it is full of threats to the unwary and full of opportunities for those who are prepared.

Note

1. For discussion of value-adding partnerships, see Russell Johnston and Paul R. Lawrence, "Beyond Vertical Integration—the Rise of the Value-Adding Partnership." The article is Chapter 2 of Part I in this collection.

PART
II
How IT Influences Strategy

1
How Information Gives You Competitive Advantage

Michael E. Porter and Victor E. Millar

The information revolution is sweeping through our economy. No company can escape its effects. Dramatic reductions in the cost of obtaining, processing, and transmitting information are changing the way we do business.

Most general managers know that the revolution is under way, and few dispute its importance. As more and more of their time and investment capital are absorbed in information technology and its effects, executives have a growing awareness that the technology can no longer be the exclusive territory of EDP or IS departments. As they see their rivals use information for competitive advantage, these executives recognize the need to become directly involved in the management of the new technology. In the face of rapid change, however, they don't know how.

This article aims to help general managers respond to the challenges of the information revolution. How will advances in information technology affect competition and the sources of competitive advantage? What strategies should a company pursue to exploit the technology? What are the implications of actions that competitors may already have taken? Of the many opportunities for investment in information technology, which are the most urgent?

To answer these questions, managers must first understand that information technology is more than just computers. Today, infor-

Authors' note: We wish to thank Monitor Company and Arthur Andersen for their assistance in preparing this article. F. Warren McFarlan also provided valuable comments.

mation technology must be conceived of broadly to encompass the information that businesses create and use as well as a wide spectrum of increasingly convergent and linked technologies that processes the information. In addition to computers, then, data recognition equipment, communications technologies, factory automation, and other hardware and services are involved.

The information revolution is affecting competition in three vital ways.

It changes industry structure and, in so doing, alters the rules of competition.

It creates competitive advantage by giving companies new ways to outperform their rivals.

It spawns whole new businesses, often from within a company's existing operations.

We discuss the reasons why information technology has acquired strategic significance and how it is affecting all businesses. We then describe how the new technology changes the nature of competition and how astute companies have exploited this. Finally, we outline a procedure managers can use to assess the role of information technology in their business and to help define investment priorities to turn the technology to their competitive advantage.

Strategic Significance

Information technology is changing the way companies operate. It is affecting the entire process by which companies create their products. Furthermore, it is reshaping the product itself: the entire package of physical goods, services, and information companies provide to create value for their buyers.

An important concept that highlights the role of information technology in competition is the "value chain."[1] This concept divides a company's activities into the technologically and economically distinct activities it performs to do business. We call these "value activities." The value a company creates is measured by the amount that buyers are willing to pay for a product or service. A business is profitable if the value it creates exceeds the cost of performing the value activities. To gain competitive advantage over its rivals, a company must either perform these activities at a lower cost or perform them in a way that leads to differentiation and a premium price (more value).[2]

A company's value activities fall into nine generic categories (see Exhibit I). Primary activities are those involved in the physical creation of the product, its marketing and delivery to buyers, and its support and servicing after sale. Support activities provide the inputs and infrastructure that allow the primary activities to take place. Every activity employs purchased inputs, human resources, and a combination of technologies. Firm infrastructure, including such functions as general management, legal work, and accounting, supports the entire chain. Within each of these generic categories, a company will perform a number of discrete activities, depending on the particular business. Service, for example, frequently includes activities such as installation, repair, adjustment, upgrading, and parts inventory management.

A company's value chain is a system of interdependent activities, which are connected by linkages. Linkages exist when the way in which one activity is performed affects the cost or effectiveness of other activities. Linkages often create trade-offs in performing different activities that should be optimized. This optimization may require trade-offs. For example, a more costly product design and more expensive raw materials can reduce after-sale service costs. A company must resolve such trade-offs, in accordance with its strategy, to achieve competitive advantage.

Linkages also require activities to be coordinated. On-time delivery requires that operations, outbound logistics, and service activities (installation, for example) should function smoothly together. Good coordination allows on-time delivery without the need for costly inventory. Careful management of linkages is often a powerful source of competitive advantage because of the difficulty rivals have in perceiving them and in resolving trade-offs across organizational lines.

The value chain for a company in a particular industry is embedded in a larger stream of activities that we term the "value system" (see Exhibit II). The value system includes the value chains of suppliers, who provide inputs (such as raw materials, components, and purchased services) to the company's value chain. The company's product often passes through its channels' value chains on its way to the ultimate buyer. Finally, the product becomes a purchased input to the value chains of its buyers, who use it to perform one or more buyer activities.

Exhibit 1. The Value Chain

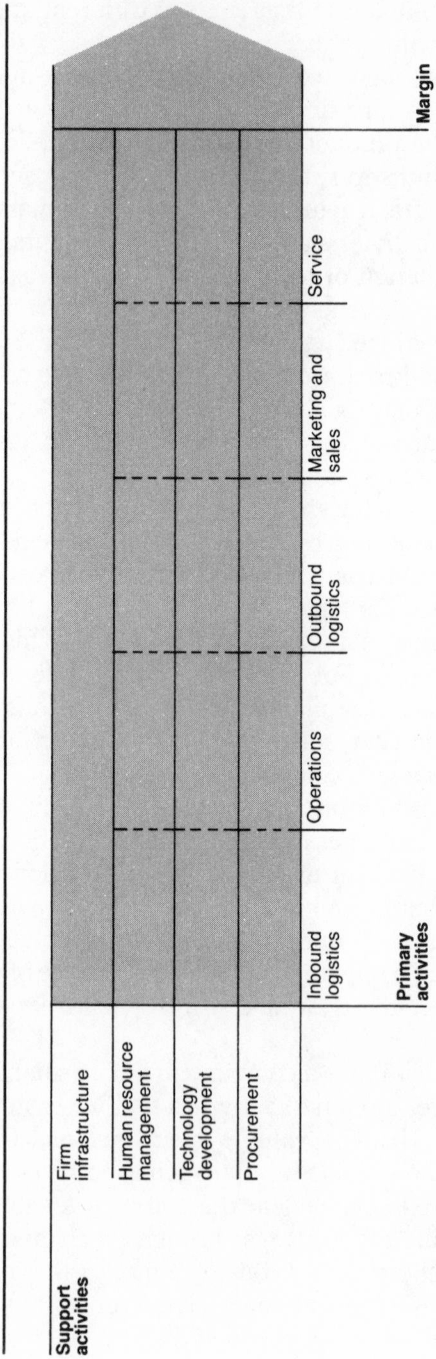

Exhibit II.   The Value System

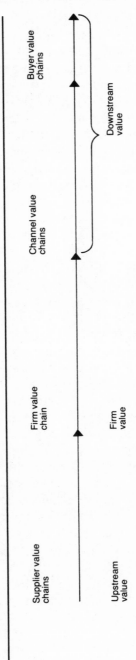

Linkages not only connect value activities inside a company but also create interdependencies between its value chain and those of its suppliers and channels. A company can create competitive advantage by optimizing or coordinating these links to the outside. For example, a candy manufacturer may save processing steps by persuading its suppliers to deliver chocolate in liquid form rather than in molded bars. Just-in-time deliveries by the supplier may have the same effect. But the opportunities for savings through coordinating with suppliers and channels go far beyond logistics and order processing. The company, suppliers, and channels can all benefit through better recognition and exploitation of such linkages.

Competitive advantage in either cost or differentiation is a function of a company's value chain. A company's cost position reflects the collective cost of performing all its value activities relative to rivals. Each value activity has cost drivers that determine the potential sources of a cost advantage. Similarly, a company's ability to differentiate itself reflects the contribution of each value activity toward fulfillment of buyer needs. Many of a company's activities—not just its physical product or service—contribute to differentiation. Buyer needs, in turn, depend not only on the impact of the company's product on the buyer but also on the company's other activities (for example, logistics or after-sale services).

In the search for competitive advantage, companies often differ in competitive scope—or the breadth of their activities. Competitive scope has four key dimensions: segment scope, vertical scope (degree of vertical integration), geographic scope, and industry scope (or the range of related industries in which the company competes).

Competitive scope is a powerful tool for creating competitive advantage. Broad scope can allow the company to exploit interrelationships between the value chains serving different industry segments, geographic areas, or related industries. For example, two business units may share one sales force to sell their products, or the units may coordinate the procurement of common components. Competing nationally or globally with a coordinated strategy can yield a competitive advantage over local or domestic rivals. By employing a broad vertical scope, a company can exploit the potential benefits of performing more activities internally rather than use outside suppliers.

By selecting a narrow scope, on the other hand, a company may be able to tailor the value chain to a particular target segment to achieve lower cost or differentiation. The competitive advantage of a narrow scope comes from customizing the value chain to best serve particular product varieties, buyers, or geographic regions. If the target segment has unusual needs, broad-scope competitors will not serve it well.

TRANSFORMING THE VALUE CHAIN

Information technology is permeating the value chain at every point, transforming the way value activities are performed and the nature of the linkages among them. It also is affecting competitive scope and reshaping the way products meet buyer needs. These basic effects explain why information technology has acquired strategic significance and is different from the many other technologies businesses use.

Every value activity has both a physical and an information-processing component. The physical component includes all the physical tasks required to perform the activity. The information-processing component encompasses the steps required to capture, manipulate, and channel the data necessary to perform the activity.

Every value activity creates and uses information of some kind. A logistics activity, for example, uses information like scheduling promises, transportation rates, and production plans to ensure timely and cost-effective delivery. A service activity uses information about service requests to schedule calls and order parts, and generates information on product failures that a company can use to revise product designs and manufacturing methods.

An activity's physical and information-processing components may be simple or quite complex. Different activities require a different mix of the two components. For instance, metal stamping uses more physical processing than information processing; processing of insurance claims requires just the opposite balance.

For most of industrial history, technological progress principally affected the physical component of what businesses do. During the Industrial Revolution, companies achieved competitive advantage by substituting machines for human labor. Information processing at that time was mostly the result of human effort.

Now the pace of technological change is reversed. Information technology is advancing faster than technologies for physical processing. The costs of information storage, manipulation, and transmittal are falling rapidly and the boundaries of what is feasible in information processing are at the same time expanding. During the Industrial Revolution, the railroad cut the travel time from Boston, Massachusetts, to Concord, New Hampshire, from five days to four hours, a factor of 30.[3] But the advances in information technology are even greater. The cost of computer power relative to the cost of manual information processing is at least 8,000 times less expensive than the cost 30 years ago. Between 1958 and 1980 the time for one electronic operation fell by a factor of 80 million. Department of Defense studies show that the error rate in recording data through bar coding is 1 in 3,000,000, compared to 1 error in 300 manual data entries.[4]

This technological transformation is expanding the limits of what companies can do faster than managers can explore the opportunities. The information revolution affects all nine categories of value activity, from allowing computer-aided design in technology development to incorporating automation in warehouses (see Exhibit III). The new technology substitutes machines for human effort in information processing. Paper ledgers and rules of thumb have given way to computers.

Initially, companies used information technology mainly for accounting and record-keeping functions. In these applications, the computers automated repetitive clerical functions such as order processing. Today information technology is spreading throughout the value chain and is performing optimization and control functions as well as more judgmental executive functions. General Electric, for instance, uses a data base that includes the accumulated experience and (often intuitive) knowledge of its appliance service engineers to provide support to customers by phone.

Information technology is generating more data as a company performs its activities and is permitting it to collect or capture information that was not available before. Such technology also makes room for a more comprehensive analysis and use of the expanded data. The number of variables that a company can analyze or control has grown dramatically. Hunt-Wesson, for example, developed a computer model to aid it in studying distribution-center expansion and relocation issues. The model enabled the company to evaluate many more different variables, scenarios, and alternative strategies than had been possible before. Similarly, information technology helped Sulzer Brothers' engineers improve the design of diesel engines in ways that manual calculations could not.

Exhibit III.   *Information Technology Permeates the Value Chain*

Support activities	Firm infrastructure	Planning models				
	Human resource management	Automated personnel scheduling				
	Technology development	Computer-aided design	Electronic market research			
	Procurement	On-line procurement of parts				
		Automated warehouse	Flexible manufacturing	Automated order processing	Telemarketing Remote terminals for salespersons	Remote servicing of equipment Computer scheduling and routing of repair trucks
		Inbound logistics	Operations	Outbound logistics	Marketing and sales	Service
		Primary activities				

Margin

Information technology is also transforming the physical processing component of activities. Computer-controlled machine tools are faster, more accurate, and more flexible in manufacturing than the older, manually operated machines. Schlumberger has developed an electronic device permitting engineers to measure the angle of a drill bit, the temperature of a rock, and other variables while drilling oil wells. The result: drilling time is reduced and some well-logging steps are eliminated. On the West Coast, some fishermen now use weather satellite data on ocean temperatures to identify promising fishing grounds. This practice greatly reduces the fishermen's steaming time and fuel costs.

Information technology not only affects how individual activities are performed but, through new information flows, it is also greatly enhancing a company's ability to exploit linkages between activities, both within and outside the company. The technology is creating new linkages between activities, and companies can now coordinate their actions more closely with those of their buyers and suppliers. For example, McKesson, the nation's largest drug distributor, provides its drugstore customers with terminals. The company makes it so easy for clients to order, receive, and prepare invoices that the customers, in return, are willing to place larger orders. At the same time, McKesson has streamlined its order processing.

Finally, the new technology has a powerful effect on competitive scope. Information systems allow companies to coordinate value activities in far-flung geographic locations. (For example, Boeing engineers work on designs on-line with foreign suppliers.) Information technology is also creating many new interrelationships among businesses, expanding the scope of industries in which a company must compete to achieve competitive advantage.

So pervasive is the impact of information technology that it confronts executives with a tough problem: too much information. This problem creates new uses of information technology to store and analyze the flood of information available to executives.

TRANSFORMING THE PRODUCT

Most products have always had both a physical and an information component. The latter, broadly defined, is everything that the buyer needs to know to obtain the product and use it to achieve the desired result. That is, a product includes information about its characteristics and how it should be used and supported. For example, convenient, accessible information on maintenance and service procedures is an important buyer criterion in consumer appliances.

Historically, a product's physical component has been more important than its information component. The new technology, however, makes it feasible to supply far more information along with the physical product. For example, General Electric's appliance service data base supports a consumer hotline that helps differentiate GE's service support from its rivals'. Similarly, some railroad and trucking companies offer up-to-the-minute information on the whereabouts of shippers' freight, which improves coordination between shippers and the railroad. The new technology is also making it increasingly possible to offer products with no physical component at all. Compustat's customers have access to corporate financial data filed with the Securities and Exchange Commission, and many companies have sprung up to perform energy use analyses of buildings.

Many products also process information in their normal functioning. A dishwasher, for example, requires a control system that directs the various components of the unit through the washing cycle and displays the process to the user. The new information technology is enhancing product performance and is making it easier to boost a product's information content. Electronic control of the automobile, for example, is becoming more visible in dashboard displays, talking dashboards, diagnostic messages, and the like.

There is an unmistakable trend toward expanding the information content in products. This component, combined with changes in companies' value chains, underscores the increasingly strategic role of information technology. There are no longer mature industries; rather, there are mature ways of doing business.

DIRECTION AND PACE OF CHANGE

Although a trend toward information intensity in companies and products is evident, the role and importance of the technology differs in each industry. Banking and insurance, for example, have always been information intensive. Such industries were naturally

Exhibit IV. Information Intensity Matrix

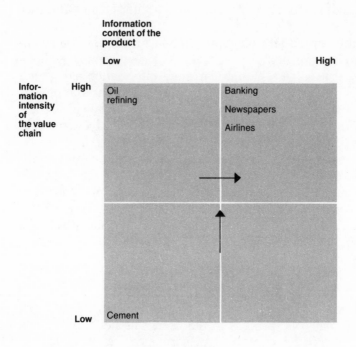

among the first and most enthusiastic users of data processing. On the other hand, physical processing will continue to dominate in industries that produce, say, cement, despite increased information processing in such businesses.

Exhibit IV, which relates information intensity in the value chain to information content in the product, illuminates the differences in the role and intensity of information among various industries. The banking and newspaper industries have a high information-technology content in both product and process. The oil-refining industry has a high use of information in the refining process but a relatively low information content in the product dimension.

Because of the falling cost and growing capacity of the new technology, many industries seem to be moving toward a higher information content in both product and process. It should be emphasized that technology will continue to improve rapidly. The cost of hardware will continue to drop, and managers will continue to distribute the technology among even the lower levels of the company. The cost of developing software, now a key constraint, will fall as more packages become available that are easily tailored to customers' circumstances. The applications of information technology that companies are using today are only a beginning.

Information technology is not only transforming products and processes but also the nature of competition itself. Despite the growing use of information technology, industries will always differ in their position in Exhibit IV and their pace of change.

Changing the Nature of Competition

After surveying a wide range of industries, we find that information technology is changing the rules of competition in three ways. First, advances in information technology are changing the industry structure. Second, information technology is an increasingly important lever that companies can use to create competitive advantage. A company's search for competitive advantage through information technology often also spreads to affect industry structure as competitors imitate the leader's strategic innovations. Finally, the information revolution is spawning completely new businesses. These three effects are critical for understanding the impact of information technology on a particular industry and for formulating effective strategic responses.

CHANGING INDUSTRY STRUCTURE

The structure of an industry is embodied in five competitive forces that collectively determine industry profitability: the power of buyers, the power of suppliers, the threat of new entrants, the threat of substitute products, and the rivalry among existing competitors (see Exhibit V). The collective strength of the five forces varies from industry to industry, as does average profitability. The strength of each of the five forces can also change, either improving or eroding the attractiveness of an industry.[5]

Information technology can alter each of the five competitive forces and, hence, industry attractiveness as well. The technology

Exhibit V.   Determinants of Industry Attractiveness

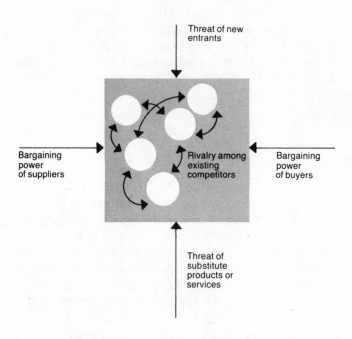

is unfreezing the structure of many industries, creating the need and opportunity for change. For example.

Information technology increases the power of buyers in industries assembling purchased components. Automated bills for materials and vendor quotation files make it easier for buyers to evaluate sources of materials and make-or-buy decisions.

Information technologies requiring large investments in complex software have raised the barriers to entry. For example, banks competing in cash management services for corporate clients now need advanced software to give customers on-line account information. These banks may also need to invest in improved computer hardware and other facilities.

Flexible computer-aided design and manufacturing systems have influenced the threat of substitution in many industries by making it quicker, easier, and cheaper to incorporate enhanced features into products.

The automation of order processing and customer billing has increased rivalry in many distribution industries. The new technology raises fixed costs at the same time as it displaces people. As a result, distributors must often fight harder for incremental volume.

Industries such as airlines, financial services, distribution, and information suppliers (see the upper right-hand corner of Exhibit IV) have felt these effects so far.[6]

Information technology has had a particularly strong impact on bargaining relationships between suppliers and buyers since it affects the linkages between companies and their suppliers, channels, and buyers. Information systems that cross company lines are becoming common. In some cases, the boundaries of industries themselves have changed.[7]

Systems that connect buyers and suppliers are spreading. Xerox gives manufacturing data to suppliers electronically to help them deliver materials. To speed up order entry, Westinghouse Electric Supply Company and American Hospital Supply have furnished their customers with terminals. Among other things, many systems raise the costs of switching to a new partner because of the disruption and retraining required. These systems tend to tie companies more closely to their buyers and suppliers.

Information technology is altering the relationship among scale, automation, and flexibility with potentially profound consequences. Large-scale production is no longer essential to achieve automation. As a result, entry barriers in a number of industries are falling.

At the same time, automation no longer necessarily leads to inflexibility. For example, General Electric rebuilt its Erie locomotive facility as a large-scale yet flexible factory using computers to store all design and manufacturing data. Ten types of motor frames can be accommodated without manual adjustments to the machines. After installation of a "smart" manufacturing system, BMW can build customized cars (each with its own tailored gearbox, transmission system, interior, and other features) on the normal assembly line. Automation and flexibility are achieved simultaneously, a pairing that changes the pattern of rivalry among competitors.

The increasing flexibility in performing many value activities combined with the falling costs of designing products has triggered an avalanche of opportunities to customize and to serve small market niches. Computer-aided design capability not only reduces the cost of designing new products but also dramatically reduces the cost of modifying or adding features to existing products. The cost of tailoring products to market segments is falling, again affecting the pattern of industry rivalry.

While managers can use information technology to improve their industry structure, the technology also has the potential to destroy that structure. For example, information systems now permit the airline industry to alter fares frequently and to charge many different fares between any two points. At the same time, however, the technology makes the flight and fare schedules more readily available and allows travel agents and individuals to shop around quickly for the lowest fare. The result is a lower fare structure than might otherwise exist. Information technology has made a number of professional service industries less attractive by reducing personal interaction and making service more of a commodity. Managers must look carefully at the structural implications of the new technology to realize its advantages or to be prepared for its consequences.

CREATING COMPETITIVE ADVANTAGE

In any company, information technology has a powerful effect on competitive advantage in either cost or differentiation. The technology affects value activities themselves or allows companies to gain competitive advantage by exploiting changes in competitive scope.

LOWERING COST.   As we have seen, information technology can alter a company's costs in any part of the value chain. The technology's historical impact on cost was confined to activities in which repetitive information processing played a large part. These limits no longer exist, however. Even activities like assembly that mainly involve physical processing now have a large information-processing component.

Canon, for example, built a low-cost copier assembly process around an automated parts-selection and materials-handling system. Assembly workers have bins containing all the parts needed for the particular copier. Canon's success with this system derives from the software that controls parts inventory and selection. In insurance brokerage, a number of insurance companies usually participate in underwriting a contract. The costs of documenting each company's participation are high. Now a computer model can optimize (and often reduce) the number of insurers per contract, lowering the broker's total cost. In garment production, equipment such as automated pattern drawers, fabric cutters, and systems for delivering cloth to the final sewing station have reduced the labor time for manufacturing by up to 50%.

In addition to playing a direct role in cost, information technology often alters the cost drivers of activities in ways that can improve (or erode) a company's relative cost position. For example, Louisiana Oil & Tire has taken all ten of its salespeople off the road and made them into telemarketers. As a result, sales expenses have fallen by 10% and sales volume has doubled. However, the move has made the national scale of operations the key determinant of the cost of selling, rather than regional scale.

ENHANCING DIFFERENTIATION.   The impact of information technology on differentiation strategies is equally dramatic. As noted earlier, the role of a company and its product in the buyer's value chain is the key determinant of differentiation. The new information technology makes it possible to customize products. Using automation, for instance, Sulzer Brothers has increased from five to eight the number of cylinder bore sizes of new low-speed marine diesel engines. Shipowners now choose an engine that is more precisely suited to their needs and thereby recoup significant fuel savings. Similarly, Digital Equipment's artificial intelligence system, XCON, uses decision rules to develop custom computer configurations. This dramatically reduces the time required to fill orders and increases accuracy—which enhances Digital's image as a quality provider.

By bundling more information with the physical product package sold to the buyer, the new technology affects a company's ability to differentiate itself. For example, a magazine distributor offers retailers processing credits for unsold items more efficiently than its competitors. Similarly, the embedding of information systems in the physical product itself is an increasingly powerful way to distinguish it from competing goods.

CHANGING COMPETITIVE SCOPE. Information technology can alter the relationship between competitive scope and competitive advantage. The technology increases a company's ability to coordinate its activities regionally, nationally, and globally. It can unlock the power of broader geographic scope to create competitive advantage. Consider the newspaper industry. Dow Jones, publisher of *The Wall Street Journal*, pioneered the page transmission technology that links its 17 U.S. printing plants to produce a truly national newspaper. Such advances in communication plants have also made it possible to move toward a global strategy. Dow Jones has started *The Asian Wall Street Journal* and *The Wall Street Journal-European Edition* and shares much of the editorial content while printing the papers in plants all over the world.

The information revolution is creating interrelationships among industries that were previously separate. The merging of computer and telecommunications technologies is an important example. This convergence has profound effects on the structure of both industries. For example, AT&T is using its position in telecommunications as a staging point for entry into the computer industry. IBM, which recently acquired Rolm, the telecommunications equipment manufacturer, is now joining the competition from the other direction. Information technology is also at the core of growing interrelationships in financial services, where the banking, insurance, and brokerage industries are merging, and in office equipment, where once distinct functions such as typing, photocopying, and data and voice communications can now be combined.

Broad-line companies are increasingly able to segment their offerings in ways that were previously feasible only for focused companies. In the trucking industry, Intermodal Transportation Services, Inc. of Cincinnati has completely changed its system for quoting prices. In the past, each local office set prices using manual procedures. Intermodal now uses microcomputers to link its offices to a center that calculates all prices. The new system gives the company the capacity to introduce a new pricing policy to offer discounts to national accounts, which place their orders from all over the country. Intermodal is tailoring its value chain to large national customers in a way that was previously impossible.

As information technology becomes more widespread, the opportunities to take advantage of a new competitive scope will only increase. The benefits of scope (and the achievement of linkages), however, can accrue only when the information technology spread throughout the organization can communicate. Completely decentralized organizational design and application of information technology will thwart these possibilities, because the information technology introduced in various parts of a company will not be compatible.

SPAWNING NEW BUSINESSES

The information revolution is giving birth to completely new industries in three distinct ways. First, it makes new businesses technologically feasible. For example, modern imaging and telecommunications technology blend to support new facsimile services such as Federal Express's Zapmail. Similarly, advances in microelectronics made personal computing possible. Services such as Merrill Lynch's Cash Management Account required new information technology to combine several financial products into one.

Second, information technology can also spawn new businesses by creating derived demand for new products. One example is Western Union's EasyLink service, a sophisticated, high-speed, data-communications network that allows personal computers, word processors, and other electronic devices to send messages to each other and to telex machines throughout the world. This service was not needed before the spread of information technology caused a demand for it.

Third, information technology creates new businesses within old ones. A company with information processing embedded in its value chain may have excess capacity or skills that can be sold outside. Sears took advantage of its skills in processing credit card accounts and of its massive scale to provide similar services to others. It sells credit-authorization and transaction-processing services to Phillips Petroleum and retail remittance-processing services to Mellon Bank. Similarly, a manufacturer of automotive parts, A.O. Smith, developed data-communications expertise to meet the needs of its traditional businesses. When a bank consortium went looking for a contractor to run a network of automated teller machines, A.O. Smith got the job. Eastman Kodak recently began offering long-distance telephone and data-transmission services through its internal telecommunications system. Where the information technology used in a company's value chain is sensitive to scale, a company may improve its overall competitive advantage by increasing the scale of information processing and lowering costs. By selling extra capacity outside, it is at the same time generating new revenue.

Companies also are increasingly able to create and sell to others information that is a by-product of their operations. National Benefit Life reportedly merged with American Can in part to gain access to data on the nine million customers of American Can's direct-mail retailing subsidiary. The use of bar-code scanners in supermarket retailing has turned grocery stores into market research labs. Retailers can run an ad in the morning newspaper and find out its effect by early afternoon. They can also sell this data to market research companies and to food processors.

Competing in the Age of Information

Senior executives can follow five steps to take advantage of opportunities that the information revolution has created.

1. ASSESS INFORMATION INTENSITY.   A company's first task is to evaluate the existing and potential information intensity of the products and processes of its business units. To help managers accomplish this, we have developed some measures of the potential importance of information technology.

It is very likely that information technology will play a strategic role in an industry that is characterized by one or more of the following features.

Potentially high information intensity in the value chain—a large number of suppliers or customers with whom the company deals directly, a product requiring a large quantity of information in selling, a product line with many distinct product varieties, a product composed of many parts, a large number of steps in a company's manufacturing process, a long cycle time from the initial order to the delivered product.

Potentially high information intensity in the product—a product that mainly provides information, a product whose operation involves substantial information processing, a product whose use requires the buyer to process a lot of information, a product requiring especially high costs for buyer training, a product that has many alternative uses or is sold to a buyer with high information intensity in his or her own business.

These may help identify priority business units for investment in information technology. When selecting priority areas, remember the breadth of information technology—it involves more than simple computing.

2. DETERMINE THE ROLE OF INFORMATION TECHNOLOGY IN INDUSTRY STRUCTURE. Managers should predict the likely impact of information technology on their industry's structure. They must examine how information technology might affect each of the five competitive forces. Not only is each force likely to change but industry boundaries may change as well. Chances are that a new definition of the industry may be necessary.

Many companies are partly in control of the nature and pace of change in the industry structure. Companies have permanently altered the bases of competition in their favor in many industries through aggressive investments in information technology and have forced other companies to follow. Citibank, with its automated teller machines and transaction processing; American Airlines, with its computerized reservations system; and *USA Today*, with its newspaper page transmission to decentralized printing plants, are pioneers that have used information technology to alter industry structure. A company should understand how structural change is forcing it to respond and look for ways to lead change in the industry.

3. IDENTIFY AND RANK THE WAYS IN WHICH INFORMATION TECHNOLOGY MIGHT CREATE COMPETITIVE ADVANTAGE. The starting assumption must be that the technology is likely to affect every activity in the value chain. Equally important is the possibility that new linkages among activities are being made possible. By taking a careful look, managers can identify the value activities that are likely to be most affected in terms of cost and differentiation. Obviously, activities that represent a large proportion of cost or that are critical to differentiation bear closest scrutiny, particularly if they have a significant information-processing component. Activities with important links to other activities inside and outside the company are also critical. Executives must examine such activities for ways in which information technology can create sustainable competitive advantage.

In addition to taking a hard look at its value chain, a company should consider how information technology might allow a change in competitive scope. Can information technology help the company serve new segments? Will the flexibility of information technology allow broad-line competitors to invade areas that were once the province of niche competitors? Will information technology provide the leverage to expand the business globally? Can managers harness information technology to exploit interrelationships with other industries? Or, can the technology help a company create competitive advantage by narrowing its scope?

A fresh look at the company's product may also be in order.

Can the company bundle more information with the product?

Can the company embed information technology in it?

4. INVESTIGATE HOW INFORMATION TECHNOLOGY MIGHT SPAWN NEW BUSINESSES.   Managers should consider opportunities to create new businesses from existing ones. Information technology is an increasingly important avenue for corporate diversification. Lockheed, for example, entered the data base business by perceiving an opportunity to use its spare computer capacity.

Identifying opportunities to spawn new businesses requires answering questions such as.

What information generated (or potentially generated) in the business could the company sell?

What information-processing capacity exists internally to start a new business?

Does information technology make it feasible to produce new items related to the company's product?

5. DEVELOP A PLAN FOR TAKING ADVANTAGE OF INFORMATION TECHNOLOGY.   The first four steps should lead to an action plan to capitalize on the information revolution. This action plan should rank the strategic investments necessary in hardware and software, and in new product development activities that reflect the increasing information content in products. Organizational changes that reflect the role that the technology plays in linking activities inside and outside the company are likely to be necessary.

The management of information technology can no longer be the sole province of the EDP department. Increasingly, companies must employ information technology with a sophisticated understanding of the requirements for competitive advantage. Organizations need to distribute the responsibility for systems development more widely in the organization. At the same time, general managers must be involved to ensure that cross-functional linkages, more possible to achieve with information technology, are exploited.

These changes do not mean that a central information-technology function should play an insignificant role. Rather than control information technology, however, an IS manager should coordinate the architecture and standards of the many applications throughout the organization, as well as provide assistance and coaching in systems development. Unless the numerous applications of information technology inside a company are compatible with each other, many benefits may be lost.

Information technology can help in the strategy implementation process. Reporting systems can track progress toward milestones and success factors. By using information systems, companies can measure their activities more precisely and help motivate managers to implement strategies successfully.

The importance of the information revolution is not in dispute. The question is not whether information technology will have a significant impact on a company's competitive position; rather the question is when and how this impact will strike. Companies that anticipate the power of information technology will be in control of events. Companies that do not respond will be forced to accept changes that others initiate and will find themselves at a competitive disadvantage.

Notes

1. For more on the value chain concept, see Michael E. Porter, *Competitive Advantage* (New York: Free Press, 1985).

2. For a discussion of the two basic types of competitive advantage, see Michael E. Porter, *Competitive Strategy* (New York: Free Press, 1980), Chapter 2.

3. Alfred D. Chandler, Jr., *The Visible Hand* (Cambridge: Belknap Press of Harvard University Press, 1977), p. 86.

4. James L. McKenney and F. Warren McFarlan, "The Information Archipelago—Maps and Bridges," *Harvard Business Review*, September-October 1982, p. 109.

5. See Michael E. Porter, "How Competitive Forces Shape Strategy," *Harvard Business Review*, March-April 1979, p. 137.

6. See F. Warren McFarlan, "Information Technology Changes the Way You Compete," *Harvard Business Review*, May-June 1984, p. 98. Article is Chapter 2 in Part II of this collection.

7. James I. Cash, Jr., and Benn R. Konsynski, "IS Redraws Competitive Boundaries," *Harvard Business Review*, March-April 1985, p. 134. Article is Chapter 3 in Part II of this collection.

8. See Gregory L. Parsons, "Information Technology: A New Competitive Weapon," *Sloan Management Review*, Fall 1983, p. 3.

9. Victor E. Millar, "Decision-Oriented Information," *Datamation*, January 1984, p. 159.

2
Information Technology Changes the Way You Compete

F. Warren McFarlan

To solve customer service problems, a major distributor installs an on-line network to its key customers so that they can directly enter orders into its computer. The computer's main purpose is to cut order-entry costs and to provide more flexibility to customers in the time and process of order submission. The system yields a larger competitive advantage, adding value for customers and a substantial rise in their sales. The resulting sharp increase in the company's market share forces a primary competitor into a corporate reorganization and a massive systems development effort to contain the damage, but these corrective actions have gained only partial success.

A regional airline testifies before the U.S. Congress that it has been badly hurt by the reservation system of a national carrier. It claims that the larger airline, through access to the reservation levels on every one of the smaller line's flights, can pinpoint all mutually competitive routes where the regional is performing well and take competitive pricing and service action. Since the regional airline lacks access to the bigger carrier's data, it allegedly is at decided competitive disadvantage.

A large aerospace company has required major suppliers to acquire CAD (computer-aided design) equipment to link directly to its CAD installation. It claims this has dramatically reduced total cost and time of design changes, parts acquisition, and inventory, making it more competitive.

These examples are not unusual. With great speed, the sharp reduction in the cost of information systems (IS) technology (i.e., computers, remote devices, and telecommunications[1]) has allowed computer systems to move from applications for back-office support to those offering significant competitive advantage. Particularly outstanding are systems that link customer and supplier. Though such links offer an opportunity for a competitive edge, they also bring a risk of strategic vulnerability. In the case of the aerospace manufacturer, operating procedures have shown much improvement, but this has been at the cost of vastly greater dependence, since it is now much harder for the manufacturer to change suppliers.

In many cases, the new technology has opened up a singular, one-time opportunity for a company to redeploy its assets and rethink its strategy. The technology has given the organization the potential for forging sharp new tools that can produce lasting gains in market share.

Of course, such opportunities vary widely from one company to another just as the intensity and the rules of competition vary widely from one industry to another. Similarly, a company's location, size, and basic product technology also shape potential IS technology applications. Computer advances have affected even the smallest companies. (Recently, for example, a $6 million manufacturer of electronic components profitably acquired CAD technology.) Further, in different situations, a company may appropriately attempt to be either a leader or an alert follower. The stakes can be so high, however, that this must be an explicit, well-planned decision.

Search for Opportunity

In assessing the ultimate impact of IS technology, companies must address the five questions that follow. If their answer to one or more of these questions is yes, information technology represents a strategic resource that requires attention at the highest level.

CAN IS TECHNOLOGY BUILD BARRIERS TO ENTRY?

In the example of the distributor, the company was able to open up a new electronic channel to its customers. Not only was the move highly successful but other companies could not replicate it. Customers did not want devices from different vendors on their premises.

A successful entry barrier offers not only a new service to appeal to customers but also features that keep the customers "hooked." The harder the service is to emulate, the higher the barrier for the competition. An example of such a defensible barrier is the development of a complex software package that adds value and is capable of evolution and refinement. A large financial services firm used this approach to launch a different and highly attractive financial product, depending on sophisticated software. Because of the complexity of the concept and its software, competitors lagged behind, giving the firm valuable time to establish market position. Further, the firm has been able to enhance its original product significantly, thus making itself a moving target.

The payoff from value-added features that increase both sales and market share is particularly noteworthy for industries in which there are great economies of scale and price is important to the customer. By moving first down the learning curve, a company can gain a cost advantage that enables it to put great pressure on its competitors.

Electronic tools for salespeople that increase the scope and speed of price quotes represent another kind of barrier. By permitting the sales force to prepare complex quotations on the customer's premises, portable microcomputers not only give better support but also make the sales force feel more confident (whether or not they have any reason to) and hence sell more aggressively. The sophisticated financial planning packages being used by sales forces of major insurance companies build similar barriers.

The flip side, of course, is the large capital investments these projects require and the uncertainty of their ultimate benefits. Further, in difficult economic times, investment in these electronic systems may create both serious cost rigidity and exit barriers against an orderly withdrawal from the industry. It is difficult, for example, for a large airline to scale its computing activity down sharply to deal with reduced operations or great cost pressures.

While a company may have difficulty in maintaining an individual advantage, it can parlay a series of innovations into a valuable image; it can be seen as a company that is at the leading edge. For example, Merrill Lynch has consistently improved the features of its Cash Management Account. This image can help maintain market position, especially in periods when a line of products is not successfully competitive.

CAN IS TECHNOLOGY BUILD IN SWITCHING COSTS?

Are there ways to encourage customers to rely increasingly on the supplier's electronic support, building it into their operations so that increased operational dependence and normal human inertia make switching to a competitor unattractive? In the ideal case, the electronic support system is simple to use. It also contains, however, a series of increasingly complex and useful procedures that insinuate themselves into the customer's routines. Finally, the customer will have to spend too much time and money to change suppliers. Electronic home banking is a good example of this. When a customer has learned to use such a system and has coded all monthly creditors for the system, he or she will be much more reluctant to change banks than before.

A heavy machine manufacturer provides another example of electronic services and features that add value to and support a company's basic product line while increasing the switching cost. The company has attached electronic devices to its machinery installed on customer premises. In case of mechanical failure, the device signals a computer program at corporate headquarters and the program analyzes the data, diagnoses the problem, and either suggests changes in the machine's control settings or pinpoints the cause of the failure and identifies the defective parts. In the same vein, another manufacturer has supplemented such a service with immediate dispatching of spare parts.

CAN THE TECHNOLOGY CHANGE THE BASIS OF COMPETITION?

One revealing way to characterize competitive strategies is by means of Michael E. Porter's analysis.[2] He discusses three types, each with different ground rules. One is cost based, when a company can produce at a much lower cost than its competition. Companies selling commodities and high-technology products can use such strategies. A second type is based on product differentiation, when a company offers a different mix of product features such as service and quality. The third type is specialization in only one niche of a market, distinguishing itself by unusual cost or product features. Its strategies may be called focused.

In some industries dominated by cost-based competition, IS technology has permitted development of product features that are so different that they cause the basis of competition to change radically. For example, in the mid-1970s, a major distributor of magazines to newsstands and stores was in an industry segment dominated by cost-based competition. For years it had used electronic technology to drive costs down by developing cheaper methods of sorting and distributing magazines. While using less staff and lower inventory, it had achieved the position of low-cost producer.

In 1977, however, the distributor decided to build on the fact that its customers were small, unsophisticated, and unaware of their profit structures. By using its records of weekly shipments and returns from a newsstand, the distributor could identify what was selling on the newsstand. It developed programs that calculated profit per square foot for every magazine and compared these data with information from newsstands in economically and ethnically similar neighborhoods that often carried very different mixes of merchandise. The distributor could thus tell each newsstand every month how it could improve the product mix. Instead of just distributing magazines, the company has used technology to add a valuable inventory management feature that has permitted it to raise prices substantially and has changed the basis of competition from cost to product differentiation.

Other companies have used IS technology to change the basis of competition from product differentiation to low cost. For example, the suppliers to the aerospace manufacturer described earlier used to compete on the basis of quality, speedy handling of rush orders, and ability to meet customized requests as well as cost. The CAD-to-CAD link and the move to numerically controlled machine tools have negated the value of many of these elements of differentiation and made overall cost more important.

Dramatic cost reduction can significantly alter the old ground rules of competition. In a low-cost competitive environment, companies should look for a strategic opportunity from IS technology either through sharp cost reduction (for example, staff reduction or ability to grow without hiring staff, improved material use, increased machine efficiency through better scheduling or more cost-effective maintenance, and lower inventories) or by adding value to their products that will permit a change to competing on the basis of product differentiation. In the airline industry in the 1960s, American Airlines pioneered a new kind of reservation service, which brought a large increase in market share and competition. Today in the industry, airlines are fighting to get their on-line reservation systems into travel agencies and, through positioning of flight recommendations on a CRT screen, to influence the travel agent's purchase recommendation. In another example, relentless competition is taking place in the diversified financial services industry as insurance companies, banks, and brokerage houses merge, and companies jockey for position.

A large insurance carrier recently identified systems development as its biggest bottleneck in the introduction of new insurance products. It is, therefore, heavily investing in software packages and outside staff to complement its large (500-person) development organization. A cost-cutting activity in the 1960s and 1970s, the IS organization has become vital to the implementation of a product differentiation strategy in the 1980s. This company, which is cutting staff and financial expenditures overall, is increasing IS expenditures and staff as a strategic investment.

Just ahead are the risks and opportunities that will come with the timing and packaging of videotex and cable services as a new way of retailing, particularly to the upscale market. In many cases in a short time these changes could dramatically alter old processes and structures. No example is more striking than the situation confronting libraries. They have a 1,000-year-plus tradition of storing books made of parchment and wood pulp. Soaring materials costs, the advent of cheap microfiche and microfilm, expansion of computer data bases, and electronic links between libraries will make the research facility of the year 2000 unrecognizable from the large library of today. Those libraries that persist in spending 65% of their budget to keep aged wood pulp warm (and cool) will be irrelevant to the needs of their readers.

Though in the early stages it is difficult to distinguish the intriguing but ephemeral from an important structural innovation, if managers misread the issues in either direction the consequences can be devastating.

CAN IS CHANGE THE BALANCE OF POWER IN SUPPLIER RELATIONSHIPS?

The development of interorganizational systems can be a powerful asset; for example, just-in-time delivery systems can drastically reduce inventory levels in the automotive and other industries, thus permitting big cost savings. Similarly, electronic CAD links from one organization to another permit faster response, smaller inventory, and better service to the final consumer. In one case, a large retailer has linked his materials-ordering system electronically to his suppliers' order-entry system. If he wants 100 sofas for a particular region, his computer automatically checks the order-entry system of his primary sofa suppliers, and the one with the lowest cost gets the order.

Equally important, the retailer's computer continually monitors the suppliers' finished-goods inventories, factory scheduling, and commitments against his schedule to make sure enough inventory will be available to meet unexpected demand by the retailer. If inventories are inadequate, the retailer alerts the supplier. If suppliers are unwilling to go along with this system they may find their overall share of business dropping until they are replaced by others.

Such interorganizational systems can redistribute power between buyer and supplier. In the case of the aerospace manufacturer, the CAD-CAD systems increased dependence on an individual supplier, became hard to replace, and left the company vulnerable to major price increases. The retailer, on the other hand, was in a much stronger position to dictate the terms of its relationship to its suppliers.

CAN IS TECHNOLOGY GENERATE NEW PRODUCTS?

As described earlier, IS can lead to products that are of higher quality, that can be delivered faster, or that are cheaper. Similarly, at little extra cost, existing products can be tailored to customers' needs. Some companies may be able to combine one or more of these advantages. They should ask themselves if they can join an electronic support service with a product to increase the value in the consumer's eyes. Sometimes this can be done at little additional cost, as in the case of the on-line diagnostic system for machine failure described earlier.

Sometimes the data a company already has can be bundled or packaged to generate revenue. For example, Data Resources, Inc., the large econometrics subsidiary of McGraw-Hill, introduced a new product called VISILINK that for the first time permitted owners of personal computers to use DRI's econometrics data base and to extract desired information. This service significantly broadened DRI's appeal and allowed it to reach many small companies and individuals who either were unaware of DRI or who previously could not afford DRI's service. Similarly, the software developed to support a product may have commercial value.

The Challenge

Achieving advantages requires broad IS management and user dialogue plus imagination. The process is complicated by the fact that many IS products are strategic though the potential benefits are very subjective and not easily verified. Often a strict ROI focus by senior management may turn attention toward narrow, well-defined targets as opposed to broader strategic opportunities that are harder to analyze.

Visualizing their systems in terms of a strategic grid,[3] senior and IS management in a number of organizations have concluded that their company or business unit is located in either the support or the factory quadrant (see Exhibit I). They have set up staffing, organization, and planning activities accordingly. As a result of both the sharp change in IS technology performance and the evolution of competitive conditions, this categorization may be wrong. For the new conditions, for example, the competitor of the distributor described above was complacent about its position in the support box. The company never realized what had happened until it was too late. Playing catch-up ball is difficult and expensive in this area.

A number of companies and industry groups are and will remain appropriately in the support and factory boxes. Technical changes,

Exhibit I. *Position of Information Systems in Various Types of Companies*

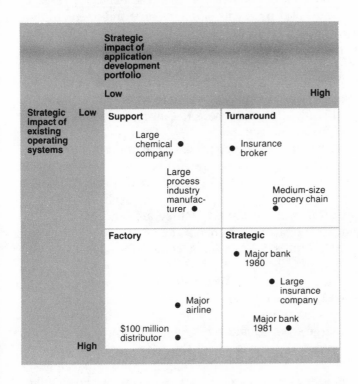

however, have been so sudden in the past several years that the role of a company's IS function needs reexamination to ensure its placement is still appropriate.

A New Point of View

Addressing the issues raised here requires management to change the way it operates.

The CEO must insist that the end products of IS planning clearly communicate the true competitive impact of the expenditures involved. Exhibit II shows how to accomplish this by identifying priorities for the allocation of financial and staff resources. In this connection, managers should realize that an embarrassingly large amount of development effort must be devoted to repair worn-out systems and to maintain them to meet changed business conditions.[4] Also, a vital but often unrecognized need exists for research and development to keep up with IS technology and to ensure that the company knows the full range of possibilities (for appropriate investments in the early phases).[5] Distinctly separate are the areas where a company spends money to obtain pure competitive advantage (very exciting) or to regain or maintain competitive parity (not so exciting because the company is trying to recover from its shortsightedness). Finally, projects where the investment is defined for measurable ROI are also separate.

The aim underlying the ranking process in Exhibit II is to allocate resources to areas with the most growth potential. Each company should have a summary of the IS plan of about three pages that vividly communicates to the CEO the data derived from Exhibit II, why IS expenditures are allocated as they are, and what explicit types of competitive business benefits the company might expect from its IS expenditures. Today, many companies fall short of this goal.

Till now, it has been the industry norm for organizations and individuals to share data widely about information systems technology and plans, on the ground that no lasting competitive advantage would emerge from IS and that collaboration would allow all to reduce administrative headaches. But today, managers should take appropriate steps to ensure the confidentiality of strategic IS plans and thinking. Great care should be taken in choosing the attendees at industry meetings and in determining what they can talk about and what information they can share with vendors and competitors.

Executives should not permit the use of simplistic rules to calculate desirable IS expense levels. Judging an IS budget as a percentage of something, such as sales, has always been an easy way to compare the performance of different companies. In today's more volatile competitive arena, such comparisons are very dangerous. I have observed some companies that are spending 6% of their total sales in this area and which are clearly underinvesting. I have seen others making an outlay of 1% of their sales volume that are overspending.

Interorganizational IS systems have hidden, second-order effects, that is, repercussions in other parts of the business. Managers should not ignore them. Interorganizational IS systems are not

Exhibit II.   Resource Allocation Priorities by Strategic Business Unit

Goal of IS expenditure	Growing, highly competitive industry	Relatively stable industry, known ground rules	Static or declining industry
Rehabilitate and maintain system	1	1	1
Experiment with new technology	2	3	3
Attain competitive advantage	2	2	3*
Maintain or regain competitive parity	2	3	4
Defined return on investment†	3	3	4

*Assuming the change is not so dramatic as to revolutionize the industry's overall performance.

†In an intensely cost-competitive environment, defined ROI is the same as gaining competitive advantage.

Note:
Numbers indicate relative attractiveness or importance of the investment, with 1 having the highest priority.

necessarily good in and of themselves just because they work and are technically sound. Both their development and operation pose opportunity for shifts in the balance of power between companies. Sourcing inflexibility, pricing, vulnerability, systems inefficiencies, and excess expense are examples of these secondary effects. Assessing their implication requires careful examination.

Managers must not be too efficiency-oriented in IS resource allocation. They must encourage creativity in R&D during this period of technological discontinuity. The support or factory role (see Exhibit I) is correct for IS in some organizations; however, such a decision should result from careful, creative analysis.

Notes

1. See my article with James L. McKenney, "The Information Archipelago—Maps and Bridges," *Harvard Business Review*, September-October 1982, p. 109.

2. Michael E. Porter, "How Competitive Forces Shape Strategy," *Harvard Business Review*, March-April 1979, p. 137.

3. See my article with James L. McKenney, and Philip Pyburn, "The Information Archipelago—Plotting a Course," *Harvard Business Review*, January-February 1983, p. 145.

4. See Martin D. J. Buss, "Penny-Wise Approach to Data Processing," *Harvard Business Review*, July-August 1981, p. 111.

5. See "The Information Archipelago—Plotting a Course."

3

IS Redraws Competitive Boundaries

James I. Cash, Jr., and Benn R. Konsynski

In a 1966 HBR article, Felix Kaufman implored general managers to think beyond their own organizational boundaries to the possibilities of extra-corporate systems.[1] His was a visionary argument about newly introduced computer time-sharing and networking capabilities. In the nearly 20 years since that article was written, developments in information systems technology (IS) have made feasible many new applications of strategic importance.[2]

Today the most dramatic and potentially powerful uses of information systems technology involve networks that transcend company boundaries. Some of these interorganizational systems (referred to hereafter as IOSs) also have important social and public policy implications. These systems, defined as automated information systems shared by two or more companies, will significantly contribute to enhanced productivity, flexibility, and competitiveness of many companies. However, current examples illustrate that some IOSs will radically change the balance of power in buyer-supplier relationships, provide entry and exit barriers in industry segments, and in most instances, shift the competitive position of intraindustry competitors. For example, a major automotive manufacturer has established computer-to-computer communication with its primary suppliers to implement just-in-time inventory systems.

As an extension, the automotive manufacturer could add instructions to scan the computers of its primary suppliers and place an order with the company's computer that contained the lowest bid or price for the desired product (assuming that other things such as product quality are equal). It is easy to see that such a system would encourage competition among the vendors and that this rivalry would enhance the manufacturer's bargaining power with them.

Unfortunately, despite the great stakes involved, companies are making the decision whether to participate in these systems without an appreciation of the broader strategic implications: in some cases such a decision is made at the production clerk level. In about half these instances, under the guise of faster information flow and greater data integrity, the new system suddenly shifts inventory holding costs and business risk to a supplier. Such an imbalance would clearly far outweigh any advantages that the more efficient information system brings to the supplier.

Some IOSs already have 10- to 15-year histories, which clearly illustrate the impact that such systems may have. The most dramatic and best-documented example is from the airline industry. It involves airline reservation systems, which are a class of IOS shared by intraindustry competitors and organizations that have a buyer-supplier relationship. In testimony before the Civil Aeronautics Board (CAB), Frontier Airlines alleged that United Airlines, developer-owner of APOLLO, a widely used reservation system, was enjoying unfair competitive advantage by monitoring loading factors of competitors and then using the system to either lower prices or broadcast special messages to travel agents. Since two major carriers, American and United, own reservation systems that provide the primary market access for almost two-thirds of the travelers who make reservations through travel agents, this issue generated a great deal of public interest in 1983.

Given the rapid diffusion of computer and communications technology into most organizations, the potential for similar IOS growth and impact in a broad range of industries is great. The CAB's airline reservation system inquiry has shown the necessity for participants to anticipate the effects of an IOS. Further, it illustrated a need for social, regulatory, and strategic business perspectives in this rapidly evolving area.

In the following discussion, we will describe the trends contributing to IOS development; show what an IOS is and how it works; describe frameworks for analyzing business, industry, and organizational impact; and, finally, suggest a way to think about the alternative forms of participation in these systems.

IOS Development

The growth of interorganizational systems is due to various technological, economic, and organizational changes.

The need for fast, reliable information exchange in response to rapidly changing markets, products, and services is mainly based on shifts in increasing international competition, shrinking geographic separation, and deregulation with more open competition. The shift in world economics is shown by the change in the world GNP. Shortly after World War II, the U.S. GNP was about half the world GNP. By 1983, the U.S. GNP was about a fourth of world GNP. This shift has greatly stepped up international competition, and vice versa.

The injection of new international competitors that have different cost structures (for example, the relative labor component of total costs), manufacturing and production processes, and so on has in many industries changed fundamental characteristics of products (cars, for example), reduced the time span of product life cycles, and added much new productive capacity (which generally limits prices and margins and/or increases costs).

Increased deregulation in industries that range from trucking to petroleum to airline and financial services has combined with the shifts already mentioned to foster redefinition of products, relationships between buyers and suppliers in a product-service delivery chain, and ancillary services to the end consumer. Some industry segments that are still heavily regulated, such as the insurance industry, are also affected by this trend.

As a response to the need for better and faster information exchange, interest has grown in developing standard definitions, protocols, and product encoding. Historically, government regulation was the primary impetus for establishing standards. But now organizations such as industry associations and industry groups are also introducing standards. Two examples are the universal product code (UPC) in the grocery industry and magnetic ink character (MICR) sets and magnetic strips on credit cards and cards for automatic teller machines in retail banking. By forcing consistency of message content and product form, such standards make it much easier for a wider range of organizations to establish and participate in interorganizational systems.

The combination of decreasing costs and increasing capability has resulted in a broader range of internal computer applications. As more and more data are stored in computers, the natural next step is to transmit these data in machine-readable form wherever they are needed. This prevents redundant encoding of data and makes information readily accessible. Both the money and the time saved easily justify such data and resource sharing. The combination of more internal company data on computers, standards for intercompany exchange of information, and clear economic justification makes participation in interorganizational systems very attractive.

As IS technology has become increasingly reliable, companies can use IOSs in business-sensitive areas, such as in dealing with customers. For example, with automatic teller machines (ATMs), the customer's perception of a bank's service is tested at each use of the machine. Too frequent problems may cause users to change banks. Favorable experience with internal computer and communications systems has led companies to explore external application of these technologies.

IS technology is used more and more to distinguish a product or company. An example of such use is a large construction company that first developed for its own internal use a program for more efficient project management. Next, the company gave "dumb" terminals (those that have no independent processing ability) to its clients so that they could make use of the program to track progress of the project, analyze changes in specifications, and forecast maintenance schedules and costs. In this second step, the company sought to distinguish itself from its competitors, who lacked such computer backup.

Finally, the company gave "intelligent" terminals to customers to use primarily for special maintenance management programs that originate with the construction company's computer. In competitive bidding, this service differentiates the construction company from its competitors. Further, after the project is completed, it links the customer in a manner that encourages a continuing relationship with the company.

IOS versus DDP

Although some larger companies have well-established IOSs, many executives barely understand the concept of such a system. The most frequent response to a general description of an inter-organizational system is, "What's different about it? Isn't it a special form of distributed data processing (DDP)?"

In the broadest terms, an *IOS* consists of a computer and communication infrastructure that permit the sharing of an application, such as programs for making reservations or for ordering supplies. The players in a system are either participants or facilitators.[3] An IOS *participant* is an organization that develops, operates, or uses an IOS to exchange information that supports a primary business process. Participants can be competitors, organizations in the buyer-supplier chain, or a combination of these. An IOS *facilitator* is an organization that aids in the development, operation, or use of such a network for exchange of information among participants. The supporting products or services are a part of the primary business of the facilitator.

It is possible to distinguish an IOS from distributed data processing in four important ways.

1. Whereas DDP is under the control of a single company, an IOS crosses company boundaries. Thus an employee in one company can directly allocate resources and initiate business processes in another company. This capability introduces very different challenges for a company's internal control, planning, and resource allocation systems. As a result, most companies need to revise these management control systems to permit the requisite coordination across organization boundaries.

2. With an IOS, in contrast to DDP, the question of government regulation arises as a result of the information exchange across the boundaries of separate organizations and hence across separate legal entities. Among the numerous potential issues are questions of legal liability. For example, in an IOS, when does the electronic message passing over communication lines actually become an order? When an IOS involves competitors, as illustrated by airline reservation systems, what constitutes unfair business practice? When an IOS involves participants engaged in interstate commerce, are current regulations sufficient to protect consumer interests?

3. The IOS facilitator is a player that doesn't exist in DDP. Although

intermediaries are not new in most industry segments, their role in interorganizational electronic communication is new. An example of an IOS facilitator is the CIRRUS nationwide network of automated teller machines. CIRRUS, which is not a bank, permits subscribing banks to give their customers 24-hour coast-to-coast access to their ATM system. The home banking system network offered by CompuServe is another example of an IOS facilitator.

4. An IOS frequently has a broader and more significant potential competitive impact than the traditional internal uses of IS technology. For example, a major bank has developed an application it calls the Treasury Decision Support System (TDSS). TDSS is a microcomputer-based system that the bank makes available to its largest customers for use by the company treasurer. The system communicates with the bank's host computer and will accept input from a range of other systems. TDSS permits a treasurer to track, report, analyze, and perform simple manipulation of data concerning the company's funds.

Data for TDSS can be transferred from several sources, including the company's computer or computers owned by competitive banks. It's conceivable that the company will ask other banks or repositories to transfer to TDSS, in machine-readable form, data on company funds under their control. Currently, the bank that developed TDSS is the only organization in addition to the (customer) company that can examine all the data in the microcomputer. This examination would yield a complete profile of the company's funds management and would, the bank hopes, provide an excellent basis for developing a new (and tailored) product offering for the customer.

Analyzing the Impact

The variety and use of existing IOSs are as broad and complex as the industries in which they have evolved. To facilitate planning, analyzing, and deciding whether to participate in (or develop) an IOS, companies need a comprehensive framework. The framework must show use of computer and communications technology from a strategic rather than a tactical perspective. Michael Porter's industry and competitive analysis (ICA) framework, originally directed to general managers and business planners with no reference to information systems technology, can be used in this manner. Porter argues that many strategic planning frameworks view competition too narrowly and pessimistically because they are primarily based on projections of market share and market growth.[4]

He asserts that the economic and competitive forces in an industry segment result from a broader range of factors than the established combatants in a particular industry. According to him, the state of competition in an industry depends on five forces: (1) bargaining power of suppliers, (2) bargaining power of buyers, (3) threat of new entrants into the industry segment, (4) threat of substitute products or services, and (5) positioning of traditional intraindustry rivals.

Exhibit I shows the potential effect of an IOS using the ICA framework of the five competitive forces. Note that in a given industry segment not all forces are equal. Suppliers dominate some industries (as OPEC does the petroleum industry), and others are preoccupied with the threat of new entrants and/or substitute products (as the banking industry is). This model describes possible strategic uses of IOSs and thus helps in planning. It should be noted that implementation of an IOS is not guaranteed to improve return on investment, productivity, or operational efficiency demonstrably. The impact of such systems may be more subtle.

IOS and Generic Strategy

Companies that have a strategic planning process formulate their competitive strategy in two steps. The first step involves using some kind of framework (such as the industry competitive analysis framework of Michael Porter) to describe their competitive environment. In the next step managers consider the resources available to derive and implement company strategy. Traditionally, most companies have not explicitly considered the potential uses of information systems resources as part of this process. In a previous article in this collection, F. Warren McFarlan shows how companies could use information systems technology to implement one of the three generic competitive strategies as defined by Porter (overall cost leadership, product differentiation, and special market focus) and cites companies in which the technology has changed the basis of competition.

As part of the two-step strategic planning process, managers

Exhibit I. Potential Uses of an IOS to Combat Competitive Forces

Competitive force	Implications	Uses of an IOS
New entrants	New capacity Need for substantial resources Reduced prices or inflated incumbents' costs	To provide: Entry barriers, greater economies of scale, switching costs, product differentiation, limited access to distribution channels To control market access
Buyers	Lower prices Higher quality More services More competition	To influence buyers: Differentiation, switching costs
Suppliers	Higher prices Reduced quality and services	To reduce switching costs To encourage competition To threaten backward integration
Substitute products	Limited potential return A ceiling on prices	To improve price and performance To redefine products and services
Traditional rivals	Competition on price, product, distribution, and service	To improve cost effectiveness To control market access To differentiate product and company

should consider the potential impact of IOSs on the competitive environment and on the implementation of competitive strategy. Following are examples of how a company can use IOSs to implement competitive strategy.

1. OVERALL COST LEADERSHIP. Interorganizational systems can improve efficiency and scale in production and distribution. A number of these systems have reduced costs through electronic purchasing and ordering. The fashionable just-in-time delivery systems are examples of such electronic links among organizations. In one plant, General Motors has experimentally tied its CAD/CAM and order-entry systems to its suppliers' production systems. A supplier's computer communicates directly with its robot-based assembly line to provide "flexible" manufacturing.

2. DIFFERENTIATION. In support of a differentiation strategy, an IOS can be used to add value to products and services. The IOS may be coupled with a special service that differentiates the product or company. For example, a company that manufactures maintenance chemicals gave to its largest customers microcomputers linked to its host computers. Customers could thus use an application that helped them make decisions on product mix, order frequency, and maintenance schedules (as well as the obligatory direct order-entry capability). Over time, the chemical company changed the basis of competition from price alone to a range of services. Interestingly, once its customers had accepted the microcomputers, they were unwilling to take similar systems from the chemical company's competitors.

An IOS may serve as a means of differentiation by a radical modification of access and distribution channels. American Airlines' SABRE and United's APOLLO reservation systems, developed from the late 1960s to 1983, illustrate interorganizational links that control market access in their industry. Travel agencies that use automated reservations systems will, on average, use one of these two systems in 65% of the reservations they make.[5]

3. FOCUS. This strategy usually combines low cost and differentiation. In addition, the business entity chooses to address a particular niche of one industry. An example of this strategy is a consortium of small stock brokerage and investment firms with various specialties. They are sponsoring the development of an application similar to Merrill Lynch's Cash Management Account. Access to the system will be by a home banking network offered by a major West Coast bank. The target customer for this product is the investor with a portfolio of $40,000 or more. The consortium will attempt to offer a flexible range of integrated services at a much lower cost than its competitors.

INFLUENCE ON INDUSTRY STRUCTURE

When the basis for competition changes, restructuring can occur: shifts in buyer, supplier, and intraindustry rivalries take place together with the introduction of new or substitute products and new entrants. Good examples of this can be found in the financial services industry, where IOSs have permitted small savings and loan companies to provide insurance and discount brokerage services.

Heavy equipment manufacturers have required their major suppliers to link directly into their CAD/CAM systems while also providing ancillary services such as order tracking to their customers via an IOS. In this case, the IOS sets the stage for redefinition of organizational boundaries and competition patterns in their industry segments.

Organizations may unite under a common set of standards and protocols, which can set up entry or exit (mobility) barriers. For example, General Motors now requires its primary suppliers to adhere to computer hardware standards and communication protocols recommended by the Automotive Industry Action Group, of which GM is a part.

In other instances the IOS stimulates new entrants, as happened when small savings and loan institutions started providing the insurance and brokerage services just mentioned.

Similarly, an IOS may protect or amplify the status of a given market as in the several consortiums for nationwide networks of ATMs. Some industry observers believe participation in this system for some banks is a defensive maneuver to protect their retail banking markets from potential new entrants (for example, Sears) that already have in place computer and communication infrastructure to offer interstate banking services.

Clearly, interorganzational links will bring changes in the pattern of competition within industries. Further, we can expect that industry boundaries will adjust and reshape themselves as new relationships emerge and traditional organizational boundaries become blurred.

ORGANIZATIONAL IMPACT

Interorganizational systems appear to have a range of impacts on participants. The first changes generally occur in business processes. The particular process (such as order entry and production) must change to conform with the standards of the IOS or to take into account various procedures in internal control, report formats, planning systems, and communication patterns. In turn, the shift in the underlying business process and communication pattern brings changes in the skills of employees and, in some cases, even new employee categories. Examples are independent insurance agencies that now illustrate products through a computer network and do their back-office accounting through links to the airlines and to the home offices of large insurance companies.

The customer service representative in large travel agencies has evolved from the clerk who simply flipped pages in airline guidebooks to the sophisticated computer user who can access numerous data bases on hotels and car rental agencies. In the insurance industry, the growth of IOSs has enabled brokers to become "estate planners" and to sell much more complex, but customized, products than were feasible a decade ago.

When an IOS is used for a key business function such as market access systems (for example, shared ATMs in retail banking), the IOS may force changes not only in skills required and organization structure but even in business strategy. The order of internal change appears to vary depending on whether an organization is reacting to an IOS implemented by another company, as in the case of the large travel agency, or whether it is the initiator or implementer of the IOS. If a company joins in an IOS proposed by another organization, general management frequently does not participate in the decision-making process, and it neither explicitly plans nor considers the implications of the system. Thus the evolution just described may take place; that is, changes will occur in business process (first-order impact), skills and staff requirements (second-order impact), and organization structure and business strategy (third-order impact).

When an organization is the initiator or implementer of an IOS, the order of these impacts changes. This is primarily attributable to more effective planning for the system. The IOS is the enabling vehicle for changes in organization structure and strategy. Changes in the business process occur last because of the planning for the introduction. Thus the order of changes becomes strategy and organization structure (first), training and selection of employees (second), and business process (third).

The degree of change that an IOS necessitates is directly related to the significance of the competitive forces that it affects. General managers should ensure that the organization makes an appropriate commitment to such changes.

IOS Participation Profiles

Managers reacting to or contemplating the implementation of an IOS should also understand the range of alternatives for involvement in an IOS. If they decide to participate in an IOS, they must first consider the extent of investment and management of information systems technology they want to be involved in. A second consideration is how much influence they want over access and the design of the IOS. Technologically, participation in IOSs falls into three levels.

1. Information entry and receipt.
2. Software development and maintenance.
3. Network and processing management.

As the level of involvement increases, responsibility, cost commitment, and organizational and technical complexity also increase.

INFORMATION ENTRY AND RECEIPT

At the first level, the IOS participant performs no application processing and merely acts as an information entry-receipt node. The user generally has access only through restricted protocols. The IOS simply provides standard messages, as, for example, when an independent travel agency uses one of the major airline reservation systems with no additional in-house processing capability. The majority of current IOS participants are operating at this entry level. Employees using these systems include shipping clerks, order clerks, salespersons, and fund and credit managers—all of whom are involved in information retrieval, authorization, and validation activities.

At this first level of participation, higher-level participants determine the standards and procedures and retain control of the application. For example, in the airline reservation system just mentioned, the travel agent must follow the policies and procedures embedded in the computer programs written and maintained by the major carrier. At this stage, interconnections exist only at the basic data exchange level and the switching cost is low (for example, the cost of moving from one automated reservation or home banking system to another, if simple inquiry is the only use).

Compatibility requirements generally exist, but initially exact protocols are rarely needed. In some situations, the higher-level participant will increase the dependence of lower-level participants (for example, some home banking systems permit automatic payment systems after the customer keys in a large amount of data, which dramatically increases the cost of changing to another system). The level 1 participant can become increasingly dependent on the higher-level participant as tasks or processes require more coordination across organizational boundaries.

Although level 1 participation is not complex, the relationships established with other organizations over time can help restructure the industrial marketplace in which the participant operates. For example, IOS brokerage networks have permitted savings and loan (S&L) organizations to offer discount brokerage services. In the larger S&Ls, this innovation has given rise to a new customer segment, and the resulting increased transaction volume has forced improvements in the software and communications systems.

This improvement in turn has had the effect of bringing about economies of scale, driving unit costs down, and introducing other products and services (such as insurance). This chain of events illustrates why the distinctions among brokerage houses, insurance agencies, and banks have become blurred from consumer perspective and how structural change in one element of an industry can cause industry or marketplace changes. Such a change is not piecemeal; rather, when one element changes, changes occur in other areas.

SOFTWARE DEVELOPMENT AND MAINTENANCE

Companies participating at level 2 develop and maintain software used by other IOS participants. Usually, the developer of the IOS has absorbed the cost of this development and maintenance to gain exclusive control over decisions on access, price, and design of the application and the network. In the airline reservation system examples already mentioned, American and United Airlines are level 2 participants. They are primarily responsible for developing their SABRE and APOLLO systems, respectively. Data Resources, Inc., an economic modeling and information resource firm that permits customers to access its data and applications, is another example.

Administrative overhead increases for level 2 participants as coordination across organizational boundaries becomes necessary. For example, in planning the system, an organization may need input from other participant or facilitator organizations, such as estimates of transaction volume for capacity planning, which generally increases the time required to develop the plan.

NETWORK AND PROCESSING MANAGEMENT

The level 3 participant serves as a utility and usually owns or manages all the network facilities as well as the computer processing resources. Examples include public information networks such as the Bell operating companies, The Source, and CompuServe. Costs increase dramatically at this level.

In addition to network development and maintenance costs, the level 3 participant accepts considerable internal control responsibility for the integrity of information exchanged. For example, consider the CIRRUS network that permits ATM transactions nationwide. CIRRUS must accept a great deal of responsibility for the reliability, availability, integrity, security, and privacy of its system.

Control and Influence

Following the technology involvement question, the major consideration in IOS participation is the degree of control or influence a participant or a facilitator exerts over key management decisions about the IOS. The chief control lies in access and participation—that is, in determining who can or cannot participate in the IOS and under what conditions.

Owners of major airline reservation systems have been able to exclude schedules of regional carriers and other airlines from their systems until forced to include them. Likewise, some airlines have established guidelines that require travel agents to execute minimum numbers of transactions on their systems to remain "qualified" to use them. Companies also determine entrance and exit guidelines that include timing and characteristics of use.

United Airlines and American Airlines are at present fighting an antitrust suit that 11 other U.S. airlines have filed against them for limiting competition. United and American are accused of charging inordinate fees for competing airlines' participation in information systems, stringently limiting that participation, and displaying competitors' flights in an unfavorable light on the computer screen.[6]

Pricing and cost decisions are also a critical part of exploiting the system. In many instances, companies have used pricing to erect access barriers. For example, one major air carrier prices the use of its reservation system high enough that low-cost, long-haul carriers would find becoming participants impractical. The specification of transaction pricing to achieve cost recovery is an important consideration in IOSs. From the perspective of an IOS participant, the cost of using an IOS should be directly related to the amount of use.

The final category of control involves the mechanism for establishing, maintaining, and changing the application, standards, protocols, and internal control procedures. Some companies at levels 2 and 3 have found that although higher investments in technology can result in great expense, they also bring greater control.

In considering IOSs as a strategic possibility, managers should weigh internal and industry aspects, participation issues, and social impact and public policy.

The key internal issue is the readiness of the organization to deal with changes in business process, personnel, and structure that it may face as a result of IOS participation. It must also have the ability to adapt to the competitive pressures that may arise.

The industry issues involve the strategy and position of the organization in its market. The Porter framework for assessing the potential impact of an IOS in an industry provides a perspective for this analysis. Companies must also determine the appropriate level of technology investment and the level of control they expect to exert over an IOS. The organization becomes a participant in a new entity that presents new problems as well as opportunities.

The social impact and public policy issues, though not obvious, are critical. What impact will the continued rapid introduction of IOS systems in the buyer-supplier chain, for example, have on the large portion of our work force involved in direct sales? At what point is the consumer paying an inappropriate price because of biases built into dominant systems, such as those in the airline industry? When should regulatory guidelines be introduced so they do not discourage creativity, innovation, and risk taking but do prevent unfair business practices via these systems?

To assess the potential impact of an IOS, managers should first identify and assess key competitive forces for given strategic business units. Next, they should explore potential uses and the impact of an IOS on these forces. Since a short-run, ROI focus may obscure opportunities for adding value through electronic links, managers must think broadly. Next, they should develop a plan for evaluating the possible current and future effects of an IOS. Finally, the company should monitor and track IOSs generally, especially in regard to public responses to these systems, such as the congressional hearings on airline reservation systems, so that they will be in a position to adapt to and perhaps even influence the trends.

Notes

1. Felix Kaufman, "Data Systems That Cross Company Boundaries," *Harvard Business Review*, January-February 1966, p. 141.

2. F. Warren McFarlan, "Information Technology Changes the Way You Compete," *Harvard Business Review*, May-June 1984, p. 98. Article is Chapter 2 in Part II of this collection.

3. The definitions in this section are partially based on the following work: S. Barrett and Benn R. Konsynski, "Inter-Organizational Information Sharing Systems," *MIS Quarterly*, Special Issue, Fall 1982, p. 93.

4. Michael E. Porter, *Competitive Strategy* (New York: Free Press, 1980) and "How Competitive Forces Shape Strategy," *Harvard Business Review*, March-April 1979, p. 137.

5. *Report to Congress on Airlines Computer Reservations Systems* and addendum to the report, prepared by the Civil Aeronautics Board in consultation with the Department of Justice, Spring 1983.
6. "Rivals Sue United, American," *New York Times*, November 11, 1984.

4
Rattling SABRE—New Ways to Compete on Information

Max D. Hopper

I have built my career, and American Airlines has built much of its business, around massive, centralized, proprietary computer systems. Developing these systems consumed millions of man-hours and billions of dollars, but their marketplace advantages were huge. As a result, our experience underscored the competitive and organizational potential of information technology. At the risk of sounding immodest, we helped define an era.

That era is over. We are entering a new era, one in which the thinking that guided "best practice" as recently as five years ago is actually counterproductive. In this new era, information technology will be at once more pervasive and less potent—table stakes for competition, but no trump card for competitive success. As astute managers maneuver against rivals, they will focus less on being the first to build proprietary electronic tools than on being the best at using and improving generally available tools to enhance what their organizations already do well. Within their companies, they will focus less on developing stand-alone applications than on building electronic platforms that can transform their organizational structures and support new ways of making decisions.

Who, by now, cannot recite the computer-based success stories of the 1970s and 1980s?

SABRE, American Airlines's reservation system, which eventually became a computerized reservation system (CRS), and Apollo, the other leading CRS, transformed marketing and distribution in the airline industry.

American Hospital Supply's ASAP order-entry and inventory-control system generated huge sales increases for the company's medical products and turned it into an industry leader.

United Service Automobile Association used its Automated Insurance Environment—a collection of telecommunication systems, data bases, expert systems, and image-processing technologies—to consistently outperform its insurance industry rivals in service quality, premium growth, and profitability.

Mrs. Fields Cookies relied on its Retail Operations Intelligence system, an automated store management network, to build and operate a nationwide chain of 400 retail outlets without a costly and stifling headquarters bureaucracy.

These and a handful of other well-known computer systems (the Information Technology Hall of Fame, if you will) represent an important chapter in the application of electronic technologies to build competitive advantage and enhance organizational effectiveness. But it is time to turn the page. In 1984, F. Warren McFarlan published an influential article in the *Harvard Business Review* on the competitive potential of information technology (see Part II, Chapter 2, of this collection).[1] He asked managers to consider how information systems might benefit their companies. Could the technology build barriers to competitive entry? Could it increase switching costs for customers? Could it change the balance of power in supplier relationships? He went on to argue that for many companies the answer was yes. By being the first to develop proprietary systems, pioneers could revolutionize their industries.

Increasingly, however, the answer is no. While it is more dangerous than ever to ignore the power of information technology, it is more dangerous still to believe that on its own, an information system can provide an enduring business advantage. The old models no longer apply.

The Information Utility

The new era is driven by the greatest upheaval in computer technology since the first wave of modern computer development 30 years ago. We are finally (and just barely) beginning to tap the real potential of computer functionality. As we change what computers can do, we must change what we do with computers.

Think of it as the emergence of an "information utility." Using superfast RISC architectures, hardware suppliers are delivering enormous processing power at remarkably low costs. UNIX and other software and communications standards are bringing unprecedented portability among different vendors' products and among different classes of products. Software tools like relational data bases, expert systems, and computer-aided software engineering are helping create powerful applications that meet specialized needs at reasonable costs. The ultimate impact of these and other technical developments is to give end-users greater power to shape their computer systems and manage their information needs. Increasingly, technology is allowing groups and individuals within companies to perform many of the functions once reserved for data processing professionals.

It is hardly news to most managers that technology is changing faster than ever. Yet I wonder how many appreciate just how radical and rapid the changes are. Over the past two decades, price/performance ratios for computer technology improved at an annual compound rate of roughly 10%. In recent years, those ratios improved at a compound rate closer to 40%. This massive acceleration in performance will have profound implications for how computers are used and how useful computers are. Three features of the new environment will be particularly important.

Powerful workstations will be a ubiquitous presence in offices and factories, and organizations will use them far more intensively and creatively than they do today. One of the paradoxes of the information age is that computers become easier to use as they become more powerful and complex. That's what is so important about dramatic hardware advances like microprocessors with a million transistors on a chip. Personal workstations running at near supercomputer speeds will finally be powerful enough to be simple and thus truly useful. Meanwhile, new graphical user interfaces are creating screen environments (electronic desktops) that make it quicker for employees to become skilled with their workstations, to move between systems without extensive retraining, and to develop the confidence to push the functionality of their machines.

In the not-so-distant future, computers will be as familiar a part of the business environment as telephones are today. They will also be as simple to use as telephones, or at least nearly so. As a result, companies will find it harder to differentiate themselves simply by automating faster than the competition. It will be easier for every organization to automate and to capture the efficiency benefits of information technology. This leaves plenty of room for competitive differentiation, but differentiation of a new and more difficult sort.

Companies will be technology architects rather than systems builders, even for their most critical applications. The widespread adoption of standards and protocols in hardware, software, and telecommunications will dramatically recast the technology-management function. At American Airlines, for example, we have spent 30 years handcrafting computer systems. We like to think we're better at this than most and that our skills in hardware evaluation, project management for software development, and systems integration have given us an important leg up on the competition. But we look forward to the day when we can buy more and more of our hardware and software from third-party vendors capable of tailoring their systems to our needs—and that day is rapidly approaching.

InterAAct, our major new initiative for organizational computing, is a good example. Unlike SABRE, which incorporates a vast amount of AMR-developed technology, InterAAct is built around hardware and software provided by third-party vendors: workstations from AT&T, IBM, and Tandy; minicomputers from Hewlett-Packard; HP's NewWave presentation software and Microsoft Windows; local area networks from Novell. We play a role in systems integration (in particular, merging the networks), but outside suppliers are capable of delivering more value than ever before.

Of course, if we can buy critical hardware and software from outside vendors, so can our competitors. Our skills as electronic-tool builders, honed over decades, will become less and less decisive to our information technology strategy. This may sound like bad news, but we welcome it. We're not in business to build computer systems; our job is to lead in applying technology to core business objectives. We don't much worry if the competition also has access to the technology; we think we can be smarter in how we use it.

Economies of scale will be more important than ever. We have entered the age of distributed computing, an age in which a young

company like MIPS Computer Systems delivers a $5,000 worksta-
tion with processing speeds comparable to those of a $3 million
IBM 3090 mainframe. Yet the amount of information required to
solve important business problems also keeps growing, as does the
capacity of telecommunications systems to transmit data quickly
and reliably between distant locations. More than ever, then, the
benefits of distributed computing will rely on access to vast
amounts of data whose collection and storage will be managed on
a centralized basis. The proliferation of desktop workstations will
not erode the importance of scale economies in information processing.

Consider the airline industry. American Airlines began working
on a computerized reservation system in the late 1950s as the
volume of reservations began to outrun our capacity to handle them
with index cards and blackboards. In 1963, the year SABRE de-
buted, it processed data related to 85,000 phone calls, 40,000
confirmed reservations, and 20,000 ticket sales. Today there are
45 *million* fares in the data base, with up to 40 million changes
entered every *month*. During peak usage, SABRE handles nearly
2,000 messages per *second* and creates more than 500,000 passenger name records every day. As we enhance SABRE, we are aggressively replacing "dumb terminals" in travel agents' offices,
airline reservation offices, and airports with workstations capable
of intensive local processing. But as a system, SABRE still works
only in a centralized environment. The level of data collection and
management it must perform dwarfs the demands of the 1960s just
as thoroughly as the performance of today's computers dwarfs the
performance of their ancestors.

The continued importance of scale economies has at least two
major implications for information technology. First, truly useful
computer systems are becoming too big and too expensive for any
one company to build and own; joint ventures will become the rule
rather than the exception. Second, organizations (like AMR) that
have developed centralized systems will eagerly share access
to, and sometimes control of, their systems. For companies to remain low-cost providers of information, they must tap the
enormous capacities of their systems. Tapping that capacity requires opening the system to as many information suppliers as
possible and offering it to as many information consumers as
possible.

From Systems to Information

I do not mean to diminish the pivotal role of information technology in the future or to suggest that technology leadership will be less relevant to competitive success. Precisely because changes in information technology are becoming so rapid and unforgiving and the consequences of falling behind so irreversible, companies will either master and remaster the technology or die. Think of it as a technology treadmill: companies will have to run harder and harder just to stay in place.

But that's the point. Organizations that stay on the treadmill will be competing against others that have done the same thing. In this sense, the information utility will have a leveling effect. Developing an innovative new computer system will offer less decisive business advantages than before, and these advantages will be more fleeting and more expensive to maintain.

The role of information technology has always been to help organizations solve critical business problems or deliver new services by collecting data, turning data into information, and turning information into knowledge quickly enough to reflect the time value of knowledge. For 30 years, much of our money and energy has focused on the first stage of the process—building hardware, software, and networks powerful enough to generate useful data. That challenge is close to being solved; we have gotten our arms around the data-gathering conundrum.

The next stage, and the next arena for competitive differentiation, revolves around the intensification of analysis. Astute managers will shift their attention from *systems* to *information*. Think of the new challenge this way: In a competitive world where companies have access to the same data, who will excel at turning data into information and then analyzing the information quickly and intelligently enough to generate superior knowledge?

On Wall Street, there are stock traders who wear special glasses that allow for three-dimensional representations of data on their screens. They need three dimensions to evaluate previously unimaginable quantities of information and elaborate computer models of stock patterns. Manufacturers Hanover has developed an expert system to help its foreign-currency traders navigate through volatile markets.

In our industry, powerful new tools are helping us answer faster and more precisely questions we have struggled with for years.

What is the best price to charge for each perishable commodity known as an airline seat? How do you reroute aircraft after a storm disrupts airport operations? How do you distribute your aircraft between airports? How do you meet the special needs of each passenger without pricing your basic service out of reach? As the process of analysis intensifies, decisions we once made monthly, we'll make weekly. Those we made weekly, we'll make daily. Those we made daily, we'll make hourly.

Consider yield management, the process of establishing different prices for seats on a flight and allocating seats to maximize revenues—that is, calculating the optimal revenue yield per seat, flight by flight. Yield management is certainly one of the most data-intensive aspects of the airline business. Computers review historical booking patterns to forecast demand for flights up to a year in advance of their departure, monitor bookings at regular intervals, compare our fares with competitors' fares, and otherwise assist dozens of pricing analysts and operations researchers. During routine periods, the system loads 200,000 new industry fares a day. In a "fare war" environment, that figure is closer to 1.5 million fares per day.

The initial challenge in yield management was to build software powerful enough to handle such demanding analyses. We spent millions of dollars developing SABRE's yield-management software, and we consider it the best in the world. Indeed, we believe our pricing and seat-allocation decisions generate hundreds of millions of dollars of incremental annual revenue. For years, we guarded that software jealously. Since 1986, however, we have sold SABRE's revenue-management expertise to any company that wanted to buy it. One of our subsidiaries—called AA Decision Technologies, many of whose members built our original yield-management applications—is knocking on the doors of airlines, railroads, and other potential customers. Why? Because we believe our analysts are better at using the software than anyone else in the world. Whatever "market power" we might enjoy by keeping our software and expertise to ourselves is not as great as the revenue we can generate by selling it.

Similarly, Mrs. Fields has begun marketing to other retail chains the sophisticated networking and automation system with which it runs its cookie operations. Price Waterhouse is helping companies like Fox Photo evaluate and install the Retail Operations Intelligence system, the backbone of Mrs. Fields's nationwide expansion.

This is the competitive philosophy with which American Airlines is entering the new era: we want to compete on the use of electronic tools, not on their exclusive ownership.

Computers and Competition: SABRE Reconsidered

Perhaps no case study better illustrates the changing competitive role of computer technology than the evolution of the system that helped define the old era—SABRE. According to conventional wisdom on SABRE, the fact that American Airlines developed the world's leading computerized reservation system generated substantial increases in traffic for us by creating market-power advantages over the competition. This has always been a difficult proposition to document. Analysts once pointed to so-called "screen bias" as a source of marketing advantage, even though the government-mandated elimination of such biases in 1984 produced no appreciable decline in bookings for American Airlines. Others argued that American's access to CRS data regarding the booking patterns of travel agents gave us an incalculable information and marketing edge over our rivals—an argument that has proven groundless. Now the experts speak of a halo effect that by its very nature is impossible to identify or document.[2]

We are proud of what SABRE has achieved, and we recognize that it represents a billion-dollar asset to the corporation. But I have always felt the folklore surrounding SABRE far exceeded its actual business impact. SABRE's real importance to American Airlines was that it prevented an erosion of market share. American began marketing SABRE to travel agents only after United pulled out of an industry consortium established to explore developing a shared reservation system to be financed and used by carriers and travel retailers. The way American was positioned as an airline— we had no hubs, our routes were regulated, and we were essentially a long-haul carrier—meant that we would have lost market share in a biased reservation system controlled by a competitor. SABRE was less important to us as a biased distribution channel than as a vehicle to force neutral and comprehensive displays into the travel agency market.

My concerns about the conventional wisdom surrounding SABRE, however, go beyond the issue of market power. SABRE has evolved through four distinct stages over the past 30 years. In each stage, it has played different roles within American Airlines, and each role has had a different impact on the industry as a whole. Unfortunately, most analysts mistake the CRS distribution stage for the entire story. To do so is to invariably draw the wrong lessons.

SABRE took shape in response to American's inability to monitor our inventory of available seats manually and to attach passenger names to booked seats. So SABRE began as a relatively simple inventory-management tool, although by the standards of the early 1960s, it was a major technical achievement.

Over the years, the system's reach and functionality expanded greatly. By the mid-1970s, SABRE was much more than an inventory-control system. Its technology provided the base for generating flight plans for our aircraft, tracking spare parts, scheduling crews, and developing a range of decision-support systems for management. SABRE and its associated systems became the control center through which American Airlines functioned.

American installed its first SABRE terminal in a travel agency in 1976, inaugurating its now familiar role as a travel-industry distribution mechanism. Over the decade that followed, we added new services to the data base (hotels, rail, rental cars), built powerful new features to help travel agents offer better service, increased the installed base of SABRE terminals, and created a training and support infrastructure. SABRE now operates in more than 14,500 subscriber locations in 45 countries. Largely as a result of the proliferation of such systems, travel agents now account for more than 80% of all passenger tickets as compared with less than 40% in 1976. SABRE and its CRS rivals truly did transform the marketing and distribution of airline services.

Today, however, SABRE is neither a proprietary competitive weapon for American Airlines nor a general distribution system for the airline industry. It is an *electronic travel supermarket,* a computerized middleman linking suppliers of travel and related services (including Broadway shows, packaged tours, currency rates) to retailers like travel agents and directly to customers like corporate travel departments. Speak with any of the 1,800 employees of the SABRE Travel Information Network, the system's marketing arm, and you will hear that their division doesn't treat American Airlines materially differently from the other 650 airlines whose schedules and fares are in the system. American pays SABRE the same booking fees as other airlines do. SABRE's capacity to write tickets and issue boarding passes works similarly on other large carriers as it does on American flights. Although limited performance differences remain (largely as a result of SABRE's technical heritage as an in-house reservation system), SABRE programmers are working to overcome these limitations and put all carriers on an equal footing in the long term.

I don't deny that there is some halo effect from SABRE that benefits American Airlines in the marketplace, although we have never been able to determine the magnitude or causation. But the core identifiable benefit American Airlines now receives from SABRE is the revenue it generates. This is not an inconsequential advantage, to be sure, but it is difficult to argue that the SABRE system tilts the competitive playing field in ways that uniquely benefit American Airlines. This is not necessarily how we would prefer it, but it is what the technology, the market, and the U.S. government demand. There is no compelling reason for a travel agency to accept a CRS that does not provide the most comprehensive and unbiased system for sorting through thousands of potential schedules and fares. If SABRE doesn't do the job, another system will. SABRE's industry-leading U.S. market share of 40% means that rival systems account for three out of every five airline bookings.

I receive weekly reports on our "conversion wars" with Covia, whose Apollo reservation system remains our chief competitor, and the other U.S.-based CRS systems. Subject to contract-term limitations that are established by the U.S. government, it takes only 30 days for a travel agent who is unhappy with SABRE to pull the system out and install a competing system. If a CRS can be replaced within a month by a rival system, can it really be considered a source of enduring competitive advantage? The old interpretations of SABRE simply no longer apply.

As a group of *Harvard Business Review* authors argued, "Early developers of single-source or biased sales channels should plan for the transition to unbiased electronic markets. That way, they can continue to derive revenues from the market-making activity."[3] The alternative, they might have added, is for the biased channel to disappear altogether in favor of unbiased markets offered by other suppliers.

This is the future of electronic distribution. It is increasingly difficult, if not downright impossible, for computerized distribution systems to bind customers to products. Smart customers simply refuse to fall into commodity traps. (Indeed, American Hospital

Supply has opened ASAP to products from rival companies.) It is increasingly difficult to design information systems that locked-out competitors or coalitions of locked-out competitors can't eventually imitate or surpass. It is increasingly difficult for one company to marshal the financial resources to build new information systems on the necessary scale.

We are applying these new rules outside the airline realm. AMRIS, a subsidiary of AMR, is developing a computerized reservation and yield-management system for the hotel and rental car industries. Its power and sophistication will exceed anything currently available. We expect that the introduction of the Confirm system, scheduled for 1991, will affect pricing strategies and marketing techniques in the hotel and rental car industries in much the way Apollo and SABRE transformed the airline business. But we are not approaching the system itself in the same way we approached SABRE—at least three major differences stand out.

For one, we are not going it alone. AMRIS has formed a joint venture with Marriott, Hilton, and Budget Rent-A-Car to develop and market the Confirm system. Moreover, there will be nothing biased about Confirm's reservation functions—no tilted screen displays, no special features for the sponsors. Finally, the management aspects of the system, such as the yield-management software, will be generally available to any hotel or rental car company that wants to buy them. Confirm's sponsors are participating in the creation of the most sophisticated software in the world for their industries; but the moment the system is operational, they will offer its tools to their competitors around the world.

Not all companies will benefit equally from this new system. As is true with marketing or finance or employee development, some organizations will excel in manipulating, analyzing, and responding to the data Confirm generates. But no company will be locked out of access to the data or the opportunity to use it to compete. As in airlines and so many other industries, competition shifts from building tools that collect data to using generally available tools to turning data into information and information into knowledge.

Building the Organizational Platform

As with competition between companies, technological change will have profound consequences for the role of computers within companies. Until recently, I was not a champion of office automation. Workstations were simply not powerful enough nor affordable enough nor easy enough to use nor capable enough of being integrated into networks to justify large investments in organizational computing. Indeed, a visitor to my office would be hardpressed to find more than a handful of personal computers on the desks of the information technology professionals.

In the last few years, though, as a result of the technology changes I have outlined here, my caution has given way to genuine enthusiasm. But in this area too, it is time for new thinking. Understandably, given the earlier limitations of the technology, most companies approached office automation with an "applications" mind-set. They developed discrete systems to make administration more efficient, to improve planning and control, or to deliver particular services more effectively.

We are taking a different approach. AMR has embarked on a multiyear, $150 million initiative to build an information technology platform modeled directly on the utility concept. This platform, called InterAAct, provides for the convergence of four critical technologies: data processing, office automation, personal computing, and networking. InterAAct will provide an intelligent workstation for every knowledge worker at AMR and will guarantee that every employee, no matter the rank or function, has easy access to a workstation. These workstations will be part of local area networks connecting work groups and a corporatewide network linking every location in the company, from departure gates in Boston to the underground SABRE facility in Tulsa, Oklahoma to the CEO's office in Dallas/Fort Worth.

The goal of InterAAct is *not* to develop stand-alone applications but to create a technology platform—an electronic nervous system—capable of supporting a vast array of applications, most of which we have not foreseen. InterAAct is an organizational resource that individuals and groups can use to build new systems and procedures to do their jobs smarter, better, and more creatively. It should eliminate bureaucratic obstacles and let people spend more time on real work—devising new ways to outmarket the competition, serve the customer better, and allocate resources more intelligently.

InterAAct began to take shape in 1987, and rollout started last June. It will take at least three years to extend the platform throughout the AMR organization. We are approaching the project with four guiding principles.

1. The platform must give each employee access to the entire system through a single workstation that is exceptionally easy to use and that operates with a standard user interface throughout the company.
2. The platform must be comprehensive, connecting all managerial levels and computing centers within the company, and be connectable to other companies' platforms.
3. The project must generate hard-dollar savings through productivity gains that are quantifiable in advance, and it should be rolled out in stages to ensure that it is delivering those hard-dollar savings.
4. The project must be managed as much as an *organizational* initiative as a technology initiative. Installing a powerful electronic platform without redesigning how work is performed and how decisions are made will not tap its true potential.

Installing InterAAct is partly a matter of faith. But $150 million projects cannot be justified on faith alone. After extensive study (including in-depth analyses of how 300 AMR employees from different parts of the company actually spend their time), we estimated that extensive automation could produce enough hard-dollar savings to generate a 10% return on the InterAAct investment. AMR's standard hurdle rate is 15%, so corporate directors with a pure financial mind-set would not have approved this project. That's where faith comes in. We are confident that the "soft-dollar" benefits—better decisions, faster procedures, more effective customer service—will boost returns on InterAAct well above the hurdle rate. Still we are rolling out the project in stages and testing its impact along the way to be sure the hard-dollar savings materialize first.

I don't know how InterAAct will change our company's organizational structure and work practices over the next five years. But I guarantee there will be major changes. Most large companies are organized to reflect how information flows inside them. As electronic technologies create new possibilities for extending and sharing access to information, they make possible new kinds of organizations. Big companies will enjoy the benefits of scale without the burdens of bureaucracy. Information technology will drive the transition from corporate hierarchies to networks. Companies will become collections of experts who form teams to solve specific business problems and then disband. Information technology will blur distinctions between centralization and decentralization; senior managers will be able to contribute expertise without exercising authority.[4]

We are currently at work on a series of InterAAct applications to reduce common sources of frustration and delay within AMR. Why should employees remain in the dark about the status of resource requests? On-line forms and electronic signature control, to be introduced later this year, will help speed such approval processes. Why should an employee's personnel file remain locked away and inaccessible? A pilot project at the Dallas/Fort Worth airport allows baggage handlers to use a workstation to check how much overtime they have accrued. Eventually, employees should be able to file their own insurance claims or check on their reimbursement status. With respect to bureaucratic procedures, the potential of an electronic platform is obvious: eliminate paper, slash layers, speed decisions, simplify the information flows.

Other organizational possibilities are even more far-reaching. InterAAct standardizes spreadsheets and data bases, provides direct access to the corporate mainframes, and will eventually support automatic report generation. The new ease and speed with which analysts will be able to accumulate and disaggregate data, conduct "what if" scenarios, and share information should accelerate the planning and budgeting process. It's not our job to design a new planning process. InterAAct gives our analysts the potential to redesign systems to best suit their needs.

Finally, and perhaps of greatest importance, InterAAct will allow senior executives to make their presence felt more deeply without requiring more day-to-day control. Eventually, executives should be able to practice selective intervention. The information system, by virtue of its comprehensiveness, will alert senior managers to pockets of excellence or trouble and allow them to take appropriate action more quickly. Over time, the role of management will change from overseeing and control to resolving important problems and transferring best practices throughout the organization.

Who Needs the CIO?

The ultimate impact of the hardware, software, and organizational developments I have described is to proliferate and decentralize technology throughout the organization. Piece by piece and brick by brick, we and others are building a corporate information infrastructure that will touch every job and change relationships between jobs. Much work remains to be done. We need better tools, more connectivity, and richer data that reflect the real business needs of our companies. But in all these areas, momentum is moving in the right direction.

As technology reshapes the nature of work and redefines organizational structures, technology itself will recede into the strategic background. Eventually—and we are far from this time—information systems will be thought of more like electricity or the telephone network than as a decisive source of organizational advantage. In this world, a company trumpeting the appointment of a new chief information officer will seem as anachronistic as a company today naming a new vice president for water and gas. People like me will have succeeded when we have worked ourselves out of our jobs. Only then will our organizations be capable of embracing the true promise of information technology.

Notes

1. F. Warren McFarlan, "Information Technology Changes the Way You Compete," *Harvard Business Review,* May-June 1984, p. 98. Article is Chapter 2 of Part II in this collection.

2. For a comprehensive review of CRS technology in the airline industry, see Duncan G. Copeland and James L. McKenney, "Airline Reservation Systems: Lessons from History," *MIS Quarterly,* June 1988.

3. Thomas W. Malone, JoAnne Yates, and Robert I Benjamin, "The Logic of Electronic Markets," *Harvard Business Review,* May-June 1989, p. 168. Article is Chapter 4 of Part I in this collection.

4. For a good overview of the organizational possibilities, see Lynda M. Applegate, James I. Cash, Jr., and D. Quinn Mills, "Information Technology and Tomorrow's Manager," *Harvard Business Review,* November-December 1988, p. 128. Article is Chapter 3 of Part I in this collection.

PART

III

IT and the General Manager

1
How Executives Can Shape Their Company's Information Systems

Thomas H. Davenport, Michael Hammer, and Tauno J. Metsisto

A big bank headquartered in New York had to make a decision about its information technology. The bank was expanding its London operations and needed a new computer system there. Technical specialists in London were certain that only one particular vendor could meet the requirements. The information-systems people in New York were equally certain that another vendor's system was the best choice.

When, after several months, the technical managers still hadn't chosen a vendor, they took the issue to a senior management policy committee. New York and London each stated its case in terms like "instruction set architectures," "file system performance," and "transaction throughput rates." The policy committee, confused by these technical issues, kept postponing the decision. Meanwhile, the head of the London office complained that the stalemate threatened the unit's growth.

How should the policy committee choose a vendor?

In the past, managers simply delegated technology decisions like this to the in-house computer wizards and attended to other matters. But managers can no longer easily avoid the process of making decisions about information technology (IT). IT affects the entire business—from organizational structure to product market strategies. Delegating such important decisions doesn't ensure that IT

Authors' note: We would like to thank PRISM, whose sponsors supported the research in this article.

investments will further the company's business strategy. In fact, it practically guarantees that they won't. The technical experts just don't have a deep enough understanding of where the overall business is going.

General managers, however, usually don't know much about computers. They may like the idea of using information technology strategically, as companies like American Hospital Supply and American Airlines have done. But they seldom know how to translate their wishes into specific IT investments. They may not even know what questions to ask, and the technical jargon can sound like a foreign language. So they tend to delay IT decisions or avoid them altogether.

Yet the consequences of postponing or mishandling IT decisions can be severe. The company might lose out on important competitive opportunities, it might waste money on relatively unproductive technologies, and it might have to spend heavily to get its IT on the right track later.

One industrial-products company learned this lesson the hard way. As part of its business strategy, senior management eliminated administrative tangles by cutting the number of distributors carrying its products. Meanwhile, it delegated hardware and software selections to the information-systems groups in each division. The IT groups were unaware of what top management was trying to accomplish, and top management was unaware of the decisions each IT group was making. By the time senior management realized that it would be much easier to consolidate the distributors if all divisions were using the same order-processing system, it was too late. The divisions had already bought or built applications that were incompatible. It took the company years to redo the ordering systems so distributors had access to all the products.

A division of a large chemical company learned a similar lesson. Technical managers consulted their product-manager peers and became convinced that a customer data base integrating information from all four product groups would be useful for cross-selling and coordinating customer orders. But neither the technologists nor the product managers knew that senior management planned to move several product groups into different divisions and to sell off others. The senior managers also had no idea that the integrated data base did not allow a product group's information systems to move with the group. The company had to undertake an expensive and disruptive crash project to separate the systems.

Clearly, many companies need a new approach to IT decision making, one that blends the technical knowledge of the computer experts with the vision of senior management.

Simple Truths

We have studied the IT decision-making processes of more than 50 large organizations, many of whose IT efforts were lacking direction. A few companies, however, had articulated their basic philosophies about IT, and they seemed to be using technology more effectively. They expressed these philosophies through a set of IT management principles that summarized how the company would use IT to achieve its goals. Those principles then guided any technology decisions that arose over the next few years. If the decision was in keeping with the principles, it was also in keeping with the corporate strategy.

Principles are simple, direct statements of an organization's basic beliefs about how the company wants to use IT over the long term. By translating the main aspects of a company's business strategy into the language of technology managers, these principles bridge the communication gap between top managers and technical experts. This way, business strategy drives technical strategy, as conventional wisdom says it should.

Think again of the opening example of the bank that was expanding in London. The debate was not about technical issues at all. The tension was between operating-unit autonomy and global consistency. The London office wanted to penetrate a new marketplace as quickly as possible; packaged software on its preferred computer would allow it to be up and running quickly. Headquarters in New York had a different concern: to give top management a complete and instantaneous view of the worldwide business. If the company had established a principle like "Computing hardware should facilitate global information consistency," there would have been no conflict. The technical experts in both New York and London would have been working toward the same end, and their decision would have been easy to reach and consistent with the organization's most important goals.

The industrial-products company whose top managers wanted to consolidate distributors would have benefited from a principle like "All product data should be accessible through a common order-processing system." The IT groups at the divisions would have known from the start that their ordering systems must be compatible, since the principle conveys the important relationship between business strategy and technology.

The chemical company whose information systems couldn't move with the product groups could have used a principle like "All product groups should be self-sufficient in their information-systems capabilities." This would have ensured that specific technical decisions would not interfere with senior management's need for flexibility.

Sometimes decision makers have trouble sifting through the details to the more enduring connections between IT investments and strategic goals. Principles can help the decision maker keep long-term strategic issues in perspective and give a clear basis for the decision. A marketing manager who needs better market research may select the local area network (LAN) that can run a certain software package, even though the LAN precludes a later shift to regional marketing. A principle like "Marketing data and applications should be easily movable to field sites for regional and local market analysis" would make it easier for the manager to choose the right LAN.

Similarly, a chemical research director wanting to speed product development might choose the star scientist's favorite high-powered workstation—only to discover later that it cannot communicate with other computers in R&D. The statement that "Research computing should be integrated with computing in development and testing" would help the research director make a better choice.

The First Move

The "principles" approach to IT begins when someone—generally the head of information systems (IS)—takes the initiative to introduce the idea to the organization and begins to assemble a task force. Senior managers must be involved, so getting their cooperation is often the first hurdle.

The number of people on the task force and the mix of backgrounds varies from company to company. Generally speaking, the key is to gather a handful of people who deeply understand either the business or the technology and who are committed to the process. One good way to assemble such a team is to think of it in

two parts: five to ten senior managers, including a senior information-systems person, who know the organization well and can
get people throughout the company to endorse the principles later;
and a small group of IS managers who will create the initial set of
principles.

Before writing the principles, the task force should identify the
topics it wants to consider and make plans to interview those senior
managers not on the study team. The interviews should draw from
senior executives as much information as possible about broad
strategic or organizational issues. The idea is not to ask top managers to discuss computers or to reveal company secrets but simply
to understand their views on where the business is headed.

Among other things, the interviews should focus on issues of
risk, user autonomy, and the role of IT. How much risk is the
company able to take? Some organizations are perfectly willing to
accept technology-related risk, while others want to avoid it at all
costs. As one senior manager at a money-center bank commented,
"We'll accept any reasonable technology risk that has significant
business payoff but that will not compromise our name in the
industry." Some companies believe their users and user-managers
can make intelligent decisions about technology, while others prefer central control. Finally, many businesses—though certainly not
all—have accepted that IT can play a strategic role rather than
simply displace costs. Such basic attitudes toward technology tend
to be deep and persistent. The company's technology principles
should reflect these attitudes—not try to change them—so the task
force must identify them.

The overall direction the business is taking is also an important
consideration. A principle supporting common application systems,
for example, is inappropriate if the company's strategy involves big
acquisitions and divestitures in the near future. In such a turbulent
business environment, divisional systems should usually stand
alone yet be capable of communicating with those in other divisions.

The team should gather information on the existing systems
portfolio to unearth unresolved technology problems and to note if
existing systems make proposed principles unrealistic. If, for instance, a company discovers that several dozen LANs are already
in use, it would be unwise to draft a principle that discourages
LANs and instead favors minicomputers. And the team should scan
available and forthcoming technologies. The IT experts probably

know the technology landscape, but other participants need to understand it too.

Although the interview and information-gathering process can be time-consuming, especially when there are many people to talk to, the bigger problem is scheduling. The task force should be sure to make the rounds quickly so that it finishes the process in weeks, not months. Things tend to move faster if one person takes on the role of expediter. Some companies have completed the whole process—including drafting and refining the principles—in three months.

Once the interviews are done and transcripts of the responses have been distributed to team members, the task force can reconvene to discuss and summarize the results. With a synopsis of the company's business plans, IT problems, and values in hand, the team is ready to tackle the principles. The subgroup of IS managers usually takes over from here to draft an initial set.

Good Principles

While the process of establishing the principles is itself constructive because it forces managers to think things through and make their ideas explicit, the principles are the real goal. If the principles are good, general managers and technical experts will turn to them time after time for clarification and guidance. If, however, the principles are vague, managers will ignore them.

It's not a matter of coming up with the "right" principles. It's more a matter of creating principles that are helpful and appropriate for the particular company and its environment. They should reflect the organization that created them. Most companies need just 20 or 30 principles to capture their approach to technology management. Normally, this approach is deeply rooted in the company's culture, management style, and business strategy, and since those things change slowly, principles should remain valid for a few years. Only when the organization changes its basic business direction or undertakes widespread restructuring would it need to reconsider its principles more often.

The principles themselves should hold clues about the industry and the corporate strategy. If they don't, they may be too general. It is tempting to state principles like "Data is an asset." Consensus will be easy to reach. But when isn't data an asset? Such a statement is of no help at all when it comes to decision making. It is a cliche—not a guide for action. If a principle has any power at all, its opposite should also be a meaningful statement. The principle "We are committed to a single vendor environment" is contradictory to "We will select the best technology for each business situation, regardless of vendor." Either one is a useful guideline.

It helps to divide the work of drafting the initial set of principles by category of IT investments. Most companies' IT decisions fall into one of four areas: hardware and communications infrastructure, applications, data, and organization.

Infrastructure includes the number and types of computers the organization uses, the operating software that runs on them, and the communications networks that allow individuals and computers to talk to each other. *Applications* are the function- or process-specific computer programs the organization uses and also the process by which they are created, maintained, and managed. *Data* is of course all of the company's information. *Organization* is the often overlooked human support for IT, without which departments may receive the technical equipment they need but no help using it. By dividing the technology this way and creating five or six principles for each category, the team can be sure that the guidelines apply to nearly all technology decisions. The following examples illustrate principles for each type of resource.

Managers of an office-products company knew that the business was changing fast and were often frustrated by their inability to get current data. To fix this situation, they came up with the principle that "IS will develop only real-time applications so that data bases reflect the current state of the business and information is available when needed to affect decisions and actions."

The executives of an electronics company felt the need for various functions to act more like one company rather than independent operations. They established this principle, which fit into the applications area: "IS will provide applications that support cross-functional integration of business processes." This principle made cross-functional systems the priority and empowered IS to manage the complex issues that arise in their implementation.

One insurance company wanted users to choose IT products from the list of approved vendors and equipment. It felt, however, that users might rebel if they were prohibited from making their own selections. Moreover, there was little means to enforce such strict control. The company thought it best to offer a carrot instead of a stick, to offer support instead of threatening control. One of its principles in the infrastructure category captured this philosophy: "The IS department will maintain a short list of supported products in each technology category. Users may purchase other products at their discretion (subject to spending approval limits), but IS will not support them."

The IS organization in a different insurance company had responsibility for constructing computer systems, but it was not in a good position to implement the business changes needed to make the systems successful. The user who sponsored the system almost always had ultimate control over the resources and business processes in the department or function. A principle in the organization area put this fact on the record: "The user-sponsor of a systems project will be responsible for the business success of the system."

A consumer-products company wanted to make its telecommunications network more efficient. It had one voice-communications network and 24 separate data networks, many of which were incompatible. It wanted the data networks to be compatible not only with each other but also with the voice network. The company established a principle that said, "We will strive to achieve integration of voice and data communications for purposes of efficiency and increased functionality."

Fine Tuning

When the smaller groups have finished their work, the entire task force should meet again to resolve any inconsistencies and to agree on the rationale for and implications of each principle. These are also put in writing. Take, for example, the following principle: "Data created or obtained within the company belong to the corporation—not to any particular function, unit, or individual. They are available to any user in the company who can demonstrate a need for them."

The rationale behind it might be: Data are an important resource and often have greatest value when shared across the corporation. No particular part of the organization should be able to restrict the flow of data except for reasons of corporate information security or the integrity of the data base. To obtain access to data, a potential user generally needs only to request it from the data base custodian.

The implications would likely include: (1) Data custodians should respond favorably to reasonable requests for data access; (2) the technology infrastructure should make it possible to share data across functions and units; (3) IS needs to furnish data custodians with criteria for assessing concern about data security and integrity; (4) if the need for access is disputed or if the custodian feels that the security or integrity of the data are threatened, the technology policy committee will resolve the dispute.

The set of principles, with their rationales and implications, is not a finished product. The task force should present it to senior managers in a workshop setting and encourage everyone to discuss and modify the principles. Although this might seem like an invitation to undo a lot of hard work, more often than not, managers strengthen and refine the principles—they don't tear them apart and try to start from scratch.

The task force should encourage workshop participants to test the principles by applying them to recent decisions or to unresolved issues. One company, for instance, had just decided to bring in an external vendor to manage its telecommunications network. It found this decision consistent with the principle that nonstrategic, utility-oriented aspects of IS would be purchased externally. A company in the financial services industry found, however, that technology investments that business units had recently made on their own were proof that a principle mandating central coordination of investment decisions was not realistic.

Only after senior management has tested and endorsed the principles is the process complete. The task force can then publish and circulate them, and managers can begin to use them. Shortly after it developed its principles, a pharmaceuticals company needed to select its primary data base management software. The principle "Data base design should emphasize effectiveness in the business environment rather than efficiency in the technical environment" was the deciding factor in choosing between two of the final software alternatives.

Some companies find it useful to keep narrowing the guidelines for decision making. They can do so by following the principles with a set of models. A model might specify such things as how computers should be linked or how a divisional IS group should be structured. Technology standards make the guidelines even more detailed by stating the particular vendors or equipment the company favors. The standards must conform to the models, and the models must conform to the principles.

Whether or not models and standards accompany them, principles simplify the lives of managers who face one tough technology decision after another and of executives who would otherwise be consulted in each instance. The time and effort spent to discover the common ground between the IT manager and the business manager put the company on firmer ground when it comes to making IT investments that truly reflect business priorities.

2
Beyond Chief Information Officer to Network Manager

John J. Donovan

Decentralized computing is sweeping business like a wave rolling onto a beach. Its advance is unstoppable—and for some powerful reasons. Economics is one important factor. On a mainframe computer, the average cost per mip (millions of instructions per second), a benchmark of hardware performance, approaches $200,000. On a personal computer the cost is only about $4,000. A similar cost comparison applies to software. Individuals and small groups can develop computer applications faster and less expensively than large teams can. To avoid diseconomies of scale in programming, companies disperse the software development process.

Strategic and organizational factors are also driving the decentralization of computing power. By definition, information systems that link companies with distant customers or suppliers—the much-heralded use of information technology as a competitive weapon—cannot be restricted to a headquarters computer facility under tight central control. Within companies, the emergence of confident and capable computer users creates a powerful constituency favoring decentralization. Employees want to operate their own systems, in their own way, and when it's most convenient for them.

The migration of computing power from corporate headquarters to divisions, plants, and desktops promises to reduce costs, enhance competitiveness, and renew organizational creativity. But it also poses profound technological and political dilemmas for senior executives responsible for computer operations. If they try to exploit the favorable economics of PCs and locally developed software, they may wind up with hundreds of isolated applications—what I call information islands—unable to share data. If senior executives focus on avoiding these information islands by resisting decentralization, they may not only forfeit attractive business opportunities but also invite mutiny among users wanting to develop systems of their own.

There is no shortage of cautionary tales about the perils for managers of decentralized computing. For example, the senior executive in charge of computer systems at a lawn-equipment company allowed its two major factories to develop their own information systems for tracking work orders and inventory. Both used stand-alone IBM System/36 minicomputers, but their application teams wrote incompatible programs customized to their factories' operations. This created problems when the CEO asked for regular consolidated reports on shipments and inventory. The chief information officer's staff had to collect data from each factory separately and combine the information by hand. Responsiveness to the individual needs of each factory interfered with corporate-level data collection and analysis.

These problems are not confined to the private sector. One state government's information center allowed individual agencies like public welfare and finance to purchase their own computer hardware and specify the most urgently needed applications. To avoid connectivity problems, software engineers in the information center wrote the programs and made sure they conformed to standards. But long backlogs developed, and frustrated users began squeezing free applications from their hardware vendors or burying the acquisition of unauthorized software in equipment purchase orders. Ultimately, the government wound up with dozens of data bases and spreadsheets that could not feed into its central computer. It still has not unraveled the mess.

In the world of business computing, the 1980s has been the decade of the chief information officer. Company after company has named a senior executive, reporting to the CEO, to preside over its strategic information agenda and data-processing operations. CIOs and their staffs have been busy managing enormous hardware and software budgets, designing strategic applications, training new users, and building and running vast computer systems.

I believe the 1990s will witness the emergence of a new breed of senior information executive—the network manager—whose priorities and challenges will differ in many important respects from the CIO's. Unless CIOs successfully transform themselves into network managers, they will be ill-equipped to confront the user dissatisfaction, organizational squabbles, and technological roadblocks invariably triggered by the advance of decentralized computing.

What's the difference between a CIO and a network manager? Network managers understand that in a world of accelerating decentralization, the most effective way to oversee a company's computer resources is to relinquish control of them and instead focus on the networks that connect them. Network managers won't merely accept the inevitability of decentralized computing. They will encourage it by surrendering authority over hardware purchases and software development while seizing control of communications systems and policies. These areas will grow increasingly complex as hardware and software migrate down the organization, and the business relies more heavily on electronic links with customers and suppliers.

In practice, network management means evaluating hardware technologies with as much emphasis on telecommunications capabilities as on sheer processing performance. It means developing systems-level software tools that guarantee network security and create consistent, easy-to-use interfaces between workstations of different power built around different architectures. It means implementing connectivity standards throughout the organization so that users are free to revise their applications without jeopardizing the company's entire network. In short, it means setting technological and organizational ground rules to guide self-directed computer users.

Up to now, CIOs have governed computer use in decentralized environments using several distinct policies. (See Exhibit I, "The Four Stages of Decentralized Computing.") The logic of this framework is quite simple. CIOs make centralization/decentralization choices on three levels. The three dimensions of the framework correspond to these choices. The x-axis traces the degree to which companies distribute hardware to factories and offices. The y-axis reflects the decentralization of development functions like writing new applications and updating software. The z-axis tracks the location of decision-making authority over information systems — for example, who approves hardware purchases, or who determines what applications to develop.

The point on the framework where the three axes meet repre-

Exhibit I.

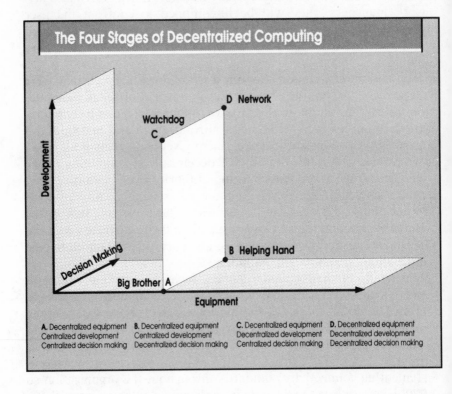

The Four Stages of Decentralized Computing

A. Decentralized equipment   B. Decentralized equipment   C. Decentralized equipment   D. Decentralized equipment
Centralized development   Centralized development   Decentralized development   Decentralized development
Centralized decision making   Decentralized decision making   Centralized decision making   Decentralized decision making

sents the set of centralized policies with which virtually every company entered the computer age three decades ago. Here, the corporate information staff wields absolute control: large mainframes available only to data-processing professionals run programs designed and written by centralized software teams. Today this set of policies is an organizational and technological dinosaur. To be sure, some companies still maintain administrative systems, like payroll and accounts payable, under rigid central controls. But the proliferation of minicomputers, technical workstations, and PCs has rendered extinct policies based on highly centralized hardware.

Point B, on the other hand, represents the "helping hand" method of managing computers in the current era of distributed hardware. Mainframes, minicomputers, and PCs are located in and are operated by the factories or branch offices that use them. But these departments do not write, update, or service the application software that powers their equipment. A central technical staff performs all development work in response to priorities set by the users. The state government information center described earlier operated under such policies.

None of these points represents a natural home base for an organization. The competitive demands of the industry, the organizational structure of the company, and the technological competence of the work force all influence the pace and method of decentralization. But virtually every company is moving (although at different rates) toward Point D, the "network" model. Let's look at each of these policies in turn.

Big Brothers and Powerless Users

Big brother policies usually govern transaction-oriented systems where users have limited technical expertise—applications like point-of-sale scanners in supermarkets or hand-held terminals that help truck drivers track billings and deliveries. One distinguishing feature of big brother systems is their simplicity. Applications in this environment are specialized, with users choosing from no more than ten possible transactions. Moreover, since users of big brother applications tend to be line personnel, they usually lack clout within the organization to voice or act on any dissatisfaction they feel about the system.

The simplicity of the applications and the lack of expertise and organizational standing among end users allow the information systems (IS) department to maintain a tight grip on computing systems. It trains and supports users and distributes single, centrally developed versions of all software. Rather than give users source code that might permit them to tinker with an application, the IS staff distributes only binary machine code—a string of ones and zeroes that even experts might find difficult to alter and that unsophisticated users certainly couldn't revise. In deciding how to meet users' needs, the CIO often keeps an eye on controlling costs instead of trying to minimize response time.

This environment suffers from several built-in tensions. For example, though the users may spend the bulk of their day working with the computers, they have little control over how they operate. Companies that base service on minimizing costs often create long backlogs for users who seek to have programs updated or modified.

Even if cost is not an issue, the IS staff in big brother environments often resists upgrading its responsiveness to users for fear that too many versions of an application may undermine software consistency. Backlogs and lack of responsiveness breed resentment.

That's what happened at the department of motor vehicles in a large southern state. The department processed automobile registrations and title applications on dedicated IBM Series 1 computers located in 187 tax offices throughout the state. To facilitate data feedback from these offices to a powerful Amdahl computer in the state capital, the IS department insisted on absolute control over the details of every application.

But its 12 programmers couldn't make even minor changes fast enough to satisfy users. Some local offices wanted to enter names in an order different from standard. Others wanted touch screens to speed data retrieval. Still others wanted more efficient search routines for updating vehicle information on existing files. These disenchanted users began tinkering with the programs and acquiring unauthorized software. State legislators, worried about applications overload of the IBM equipment, pressured central IS to clamp down.

The motor vehicles department has not yet devised a solution. Ultimately, however, it will have to face up to a classic information systems dilemma. Should the department expand its programming staff to make it more responsive to user needs? Or should it accept the users' growing confidence by loosening control over applications while requiring conformity to data communications standards? Whatever the department decides, the central lesson is clear. Once users in the big brother environment reach a critical mass of restlessness, the status quo is almost impossible to maintain regardless of the users' lack of power to act on their grievances.

A Helping Hand for Indirect Control

Helping hand policies govern complex applications used by executives who have a deep understanding of their operation's competitive strengths and weaknesses. The manager of an insurance company's regional office, for example, will have unsurpassed knowledge of that territory's risk profiles, regulatory structures, and customer preferences. It's unlikely that computer professionals at company headquarters could generate programs that meet the needs of this regional office without its close involvement. In this case, unlike the big brother model, the central IS staff writes and maintains programs to meet specifications set by branch offices, divisions, or subsidiaries. And computer users often have direct access to senior management—a political reality that can complicate the CIO's control over computing resources.

But maintaining control is still the CIO's basic objective. The IS staff develops software that is based on user specifications, but that also conforms to standards set by headquarters. The IS department selects programming languages, development procedures, and operating systems that maximize network connectivity. It uses its authority over departmental purchases of hardware, software, and peripherals to maintain consistent hardware architectures. Finally, the IS office trains and supports the technically unsophisticated end users.

The control tactics in the helping hand model are more indirect than in big brother policies. The CIO and the IS staff play supportive instead of authoritarian roles. Developers work closely with users when writing programs and discourage features that might interfere with the company's broad computing goals. Central IS often acts as a software librarian, maintaining tapes of programs and swapping applications between offices and departments. A financial analysis program developed for one branch office might be offered as a bonus to other branch offices. In this way, software becomes a bartering chip with which the CIO maintains user harmony.

Central IS must also play a mediating role as offices and divisions vie for limited resources. Indeed, scarce programming resources—particularly for maintaining existing applications—are the greatest source of instability in the helping hand environment. Analysts estimate that every dollar a CIO spends developing a program requires an additional $4 in maintenance costs over its life. So as customized applications proliferate, IS budgets skyrocket.

Consider how changes in federal tax laws affect computer systems at a real estate development firm. The IS group may have to alter dozens of customized financial, marketing, and accounting programs that contain now-obsolete assumptions about tax rates and depreciation schedules. Then it must distribute the changes to possibly thousands of PCs simultaneously—an expensive and time-consuming operation.

While central IS defines development procedures in principle, in practice frustrated users can threaten program consistency in several ways. Consultants hired without authorization can develop chunks of programs or entire applications that don't follow IS guidelines. The availability of low-cost, off-the-shelf software can also give rise to elaborate spreadsheets and data bases outside IS control. If they're incompatible with existing programs or network software, these pockets of information can introduce inaccuracies into corporatewide data and jeopardize the smooth functioning of strategic applications.

A real estate company owned by a major entertainment conglomerate illustrates these risks. The company's local offices relied on customized sales and marketing support systems tied into a central mainframe to track their primary resources: homes, condominiums, and raw land. The CIO wanted to maintain an accurate inventory of all the company's holdings by ensuring smooth data flow between local computers and the company mainframe. To this end, the IS department required local offices to run the core applications on a brand of personal computer chosen for its ease of connection with the mainframe. Within these hardware and software constraints, IS programmers modified and enhanced the sales and marketing applications based on local specifications.

The backlog of unmet modifications kept growing. Central IS tried to buy time by offering users remote access to other popular programs on the corporate mainframe. But local managers appealed to the company's senior executives and got permission to hire consultants to make the much-delayed software changes. Before long, information began to migrate from the mainframe corporate data base to these new PC programs—not all of which fed smoothly back to the mainframe. The company could no longer maintain an accurate inventory of its properties; and, because users often failed to back up data on their new programs, information on some properties disappeared altogether during hardware failures.

The CIO called for audits to root out troublesome programs and withheld mainframe services from the renegade offices. The political struggle became corporatewide and tempers ran high. There still is no long-term resolution to this situation. A carrot-and-stick approach based on rewards for good behavior and software audits may provide incentives to maintain the integrity of the data base. Otherwise, the CIO may have to allow local offices to take charge of their own software modifications as long as the changes meet strict mainframe-to-micro communication standards.

Watchdogs Can't Watch Everything

The factors that give rise to watchdog policies are often the reverse of those that lead to helping hand principles. Watchdog policies most often govern large, inflexible bureaucracies with clear lines of authority and hierarchy. Military installations almost always operate this way, with teams of engineers writing programs specified by higher ranking officers. In general, end users in the watchdog environment are technically proficient, but lack the business insights to specify the applications they need. As a result, central IS controls all major decisions, from hardware and software purchases to application development priorities. The IS staff standardizes operating systems, programming languages, sometimes even programming style, and the CIO enforces directives through frequent and rigorous audits. It's not unusual for auditors to visit departments on a weekly or even daily basis to search through computer files for unauthorized programs.

Within these tight constraints, however, independent development teams essentially run their own technical shops. The local staff handles day-to-day operations like setting passwords and correcting hardware and software failures. These local teams develop and distribute software to users. Still, they must requisition the hardware and development tools from central IS and obtain permission to develop applications.

The watchdog environment has the most severe built-in tensions of any of the models I've studied and is therefore the least stable. Despite the elimination of programming backlogs (local developers write and update their own software), purchase orders and requests for permission to develop applications can pile up and slow the programming process. Bright, capable engineers resent development delays even more than their business-minded counterparts in the helping hand framework or the line personnel in the big brother environment. Moreover, strict policing by central IS can be interpreted as interference or harassment—another potential source of frustration. So it's not unusual for talented local programmers to spend a good deal of their time developing and hiding unauthorized software or otherwise skirting IS controls.

The government of a large northern California city recently experienced this problem. Each of the city's 24 departments had two or three programmers responsible for loading, integrating, and debugging software on the department's private branch telephone exchange (PBX). One important application tracked outgoing telephone calls and billed the offices that made them. In turn, each of the PBXs was connected to a citywide network through a communications program controlled by a central computer services group. But the communications software had weaknesses that the central group was slow to correct.

Long accustomed to the hierarchy of city government, local programmers wasted no time in going over the CIO's head to voice their frustration. They simply developed their own communications software, which eventually created inconsistencies in the network. Moreover, the time local programmers devoted to communications software was time they should have spent on other projects. This is a clear example of a CIO losing control of a vital resource—in this case, programmers' time—by neglecting the technical concerns of subordinates who were fully capable of addressing those concerns themselves.

The Challenges of Network Management

There is a structural elegance, based on simplicity and self-direction, that distinguishes the network model from its counterparts. End users in the other frameworks are under the control—direct or indirect, respected or circumvented—of the corporate information staff. As we've seen, such control can lead to struggles over scarce resources. This turmoil not only undermines the CIO's authority but also jeopardizes the computing goals the policies were designed to serve.

Control over day-to-day computing is not an issue for network managers. Technical staffs under the direction of the company's departments or divisions handle every aspect of their information systems. They purchase hardware and peripherals, develop and write applications, load operating systems, and respond to equipment failures. Development backlogs and approval delays are a thing of the past.

Beneath this decentralized simplicity, however, lurk imposing technological challenges. Completing the transition from CIO to network manager requires implementation of the three levels of connectivity—physical, systems, and applications—that link computers and enable them to share information. The computer industry's failure to adopt multivendor standards in so many areas— operating systems, data storage and exchange, mainframe-to-micro communications—immeasurably complicates the network manager's job. But the development of effective, customized solutions to all three levels of network connectivity is a prerequisite for evolution to the network model.

Let's consider each level separately. A single noisy telephone line or a faulty chip at a component installation can cripple a system that depends on exchanging information between factories, or between a mainframe computer at headquarters and microcomputers in branch offices, or between a company and its customers. So a network manager's most basic responsibility is to build and maintain a robust data communications infrastructure—the physical network—that minimizes interruptions and downtime. This means paying closer attention to the selection and maintenance of telecommunications equipment and services like long-distance data transmission, modems, multiplexers, and controllers, and evaluating these technologies on the basis of reliability and accuracy, as well as cost.

Today data transmission at many companies is the responsibility of a director of telecommunications who focuses mostly on selecting telephone companies, purchasing equipment, and cutting long-distance phone bills. These managers almost never give data networks the attention they deserve. Some forward-looking companies have assigned special responsibility for data communications to a manager who reports directly to the CIO. This is an improvement, but it doesn't go far enough. The CIO must become personally and deeply involved in communications decisions—perhaps to the point of spending several hours a day on the design, maintenance, and expansion of the physical network. Otherwise, it's unlikely that the company will make the investments or devote the staff resources necessary to build a high-performance communications infrastructure.

Systems-level connectivity is the second major challenge. A smoothly functioning network should allow the corporate information staff to monitor and address the performance of every computer on a particular network. For example, the network manager's staff should be able to assign or modify passwords quickly to block unauthorized access to new applications on a network that contains sensitive data. Likewise, the IS staff should be able to distribute new applications to whatever computers in the network need it, regardless of their operating systems or locations.

Several major vendors, including IBM, Digital Equipment, and AT&T, as well as a few independent software companies, offer systems-level tools that perform some connectivity functions. But these third-party solutions have grave shortcomings. Most of them provide security and manage remote terminals, but they generally don't integrate these capabilities under a consistent, easy-to-use interface. And as with the physical network, the absence of industry standards means that no single product can address more than a fraction of the hardware and communications protocols scattered throughout the organization. Effective systems-level connectivity may require a large investment of staff time to develop customized solutions to vexing technological problems. These investments won't be approved unless the senior executive in charge of information systems makes them a priority.

Building a reliable communications infrastructure whose performance can be monitored by the central IS staff is valuable only if the hundreds of applications running on the network can freely exchange information. True applications connectivity is a formidable challenge—even for a network composed of nearly identical computers and software—because applications are constantly changing. And modifications can interfere with an application's ability to feed data into other software.

The technical obstacles to relationship banking, a highly prized application in the competitive financial services industry, are a case in point. A single marketing representative analyzes, evaluates, and recommends changes in a customer's entire portfolio. To do this, the representative must be able to summon on command a comprehensive profile of the customer's activities in all the bank's services. That requires pulling information from the separate computer systems that manage, for example, home mortgages, certificates of deposit, checking accounts, and car loans. But each system's evolution can affect the entire network. Something as simple as reversing the order in which checking-account operators record first and last names threatens the integrity of a network unable to adjust to that change.

At this level, maintaining applications connectivity requires strict procedures to guarantee that departments notify the network manager of all software modifications. Under this system, the role of the central IS staff evolves from approving or developing applications to adjusting the interface between modified applications so they can continue to exchange data.

Applications connectivity becomes even harder when the network is supporting incompatible computer systems. For example, a bank that acquires a competitor and wants to offer relationship banking may have to gather data from two vastly different computing environments. Likewise, a network that links a company with its suppliers almost invariably must support several operating systems. Perhaps a decade from now the computer industry will adopt connectivity standards for easier exchange of data between computers built around different architectures. Until then, however, it's up to network managers to devise customized solutions.

These solutions require the development of what I call "application filters" that translate between different systems on the network, hide each computer's particular characteristics, and adjust for application changes. Several organizations, including Covenant Insurance, the American Red Cross, and Maryland National Bank, have implemented such filters in large strategic applications. Their experiences to date have been quite encouraging. In the near future, expert systems may be able to detect and adjust automatically for application changes affecting the rest of the network. Prototypes of such expert systems have been developed, although the technology required for full-scale implementation is still several years away.

The transition from CIO to network manager will be neither immediate nor easy. But it must be made if senior executives want lower costs and enhanced strategic advantage from their computer systems. The CIO who faces the challenges of network management head-on can overcome the perils of decentralized computing and tap its vast potential.

3
E Pluribus Computum

J. Daniel Couger

Although computers have spread into every corner of the organization, although people have become more knowledgeable and enthusiastic about them, many of their promises have not been fulfilled. End-user computing, which enables users to develop their own applications, has potentially the greatest impact of any development in the computer field. But for many organizations it has been far less effective and more costly than anticipated. Others have had good results. Despite the varied experiences, end-user computing is proliferating. Computing is now available for all—but at what price?

Several forces have led to the end-user computing phenomenon. Beginning in the early 1970s, users with so-called "dumb" terminals could retrieve centrally located information, but because the forerunners of today's English-like languages were not widely available, the users had to learn complex commands to perform the simplest functions. When they encountered problems, they called the central information systems (IS) group. By the mid-1970s, many companies had established information centers to give people some freedom from IS departments. The new centers encouraged autonomy through a variety of services—training, technical assistance, and limited access by terminals to corporate files, like customer data bases either in retrieval-only mode or as copies that could be altered.

Personal computing emerged in the early 1980s, primarily outside IS departments, as users independently purchased their first low-cost hardware and software. The new systems were easy to learn, so the gap widened between users and the central IS function—but at a price. The lack of communications capability on the first micros meant that they couldn't exchange data with other PCs, nor could they freely access and manipulate data on company mainframes. When PCs cropped up on the desks of so many non-technical managers, it was inevitable that people would tailor their own applications independently of IS departments. Companies have responded in different ways to these initiatives, but most have embraced some form of what has come to be called end-user computing.

For example, IS departments may encourage maverick computing efforts through end-user computing support groups or corporate information centers. Support ranges from training in new English-like development languages and promoting good computing practices to unlocking the corporate data base through sophisticated PC-to-mainframe links. Regardless of the form it takes, end-user computing enables technically unsophisticated managers not only to circumvent IS backlogs (they often average three years) but also to act as autonomous problem solvers, while enjoying the ease and power of inexpensive, off-the-shelf PC programs.

Hopes versus Reality

When studying end-user computing in 17 large companies with strong IS operation experience, I found 11 that had serious problems. Six of them enjoyed high ROIs, however, which proves that managers can overcome the obstacles. The companies I studied represented a variety of industries and locations in the United States, and each had had more than 15 years' experience in mainframe computing. Their net annual incomes varied from $100 million to $500 million, with total numbers of employees ranging from 3,000 to 45,000. Success in end-user computing did not correlate in any way with the size of the company, however.

The 11 troubled companies showed ominous symptoms from the start. And 4 of them laid out large sums for end-user computing services before they had even drawn up separate budgets for it. Tallying these companies' losses revealed avoidable problems in the way end-user computing had evolved.

One financial services business had bought micros from no fewer than eight vendors. Further complicating compatibility problems, the company signed maintenance contracts with five sources. Only one of the agreements specified same-day response to service calls; service delays from the other vendors could stretch into weeks and leave about 10% of the installed machines inoperable.

A manufacturing organization installed seven spreadsheet packages, making it difficult for separate work groups to share spreadsheet data. Moreover, because the logic built into each spreadsheet was unique, one executive's request for financial projections from three departments produced disparate sets of numbers. Only then did the seven-package problem come to light.

After this problem surfaced, the company reviewed all its PC software and found nine word processing packages. Because the end-user support team provided training and assistance on only one of them, the company had sustained a loss of 8,000 person-hours while employees learned other programs through trial and error.

A bank bought three fourth-generation language packages. They used English-like commands for application development and information retrieval and cost more than $200,000 in software licensing fees. One $50,000 package could have handled all department needs effectively. Making matters worse, maintenance agreements on the two unnecessary packages committed the bank to spending $35,000 a year for two years beyond the year of purchase.

An insurance company tripled its training budget in one year because of the support needed for more than 20 PC software packages. The training group alone invested more than $30,000 in labor to support them. An IS department analyst estimated that five packages could have easily handled the company's needs.

Most of the troubled companies missed the benefits of end-user computing because they didn't estimate their costs, much less anticipate subtle increases like those from increased use of communications links. Lack of careful cost-benefit analysis led to inaccurate budgets and operations that ran deeply into the red.

CLIMBING COSTS

The mistakes these companies made were largely avoidable. Corporations must pay for any rewarding new program, but they can predict many costs fairly easily. For instance, independent users often become headstrong about their purchases and buy a lot of hardware and software, so products proliferate in companies with end-user programs. Obviously, training budgets also must grow to encompass new courses in applications development.

But more apparent on the bottom line are the hidden costs. As they climb on the computing bandwagon, inexperienced users can place big demands on computer resources. More information is generated in companies with end-user programs, and that inevitably means more computer-related expenses.

Even when wary executives take the time to project end-user costs, their estimates can fall short. For example, in more than half of the 17 companies I surveyed, the IS departments' three-year plans to support end-user computing called for an extra shift—eight more hours—of corporate mainframe time every day. But in these nine companies, new end-user traffic so mushroomed that it clogged normal processing. Ultimately, all nine had to acquire a new mainframe dedicated to end users. That was an unbudgeted expense in the $100,000 range.

This unexpected surge in computer usage is easy to understand. Costs are higher when end users develop their own applications because much of their learning is trial and error. The fourth-generation languages that nontechnical staff can use quickly to generate reports also consume far more computer capacity than "procedural" languages that professional developers use, due to the expense of translating English commands into machine-readable form. One fourth-generation command reads, "Print profit broken down by customer from year 1982 through 1984." Before the manager can get the report, however, software must translate this English statement into 23 machine-language statements. Because of the deceptive simplicity of the fourth-generation tools, a user who is developing an application can write hundreds of fourth-generation statements and still remain ignorant of the huge demand this effort puts on computer resources.

The need for duplicate or "shadow" corporate data bases insidiously soaks up an organization's computer resources. Because these information stores must be protected, most companies restrict user access to retrieval-only mode, so data can be altered only by the central IS group. Any user who wants to manipulate data or perform analyses, therefore, must get a copy of the data base. This method still produces inconsistent sets of figures, however, and the resulting mistakes can be expensive. The only feasible solution is a shadow data base—a copy of a live data base—set up by the IS group every day from corporate mainframes. Although this approach maintains consistency of information throughout the organization, the multiplying data bases quickly devour computer storage space.

Moreover, maintenance costs, which usually comprise about 50% of the IS department's budget, can skyrocket when end users develop their own applications on their various machines. Nontechnical staff often pass on to the IS staff the maintenance of inefficiently written applications. In one case, a financial planner turned over to IS a program consisting of 14,000 lines of fourth-generation statements. This far exceeds the 500-line cutoff point beyond which many IS departments recommend development by IS professionals.

In addition to these strains on the IS budget, end-user computing creates conflicts within the IS organization. A support team may form closer working relationships with end users than the ties other IS people enjoy. The end-user support team is not usually trying to usurp central IS authority; the closeness results naturally from spending more time with the end users as they learn. The other IS members, responsible for large transaction-processing applications, complain about this, though, because they rely on feedback from end users to know their work is appreciated.

HARD CONTROLS

In addition to budgeting, careful planning is necessary to steer companies clear of certain pitfalls. Two sources of difficulty arose with startling frequency in the less successful companies: a lack of formal cost justification and the failure of "hard" controls—those rigid policies for policing end users.

Though it's traditional to cost justify computer use, only a few of the companies I surveyed applied formal models to their end-user applications. In policy development, each organization fell into one of three phases involving cost justification and chargeback. Not surprisingly, these stages match the three-phase evolution associated with all types of IS implementation.

In the first phase, the IS department, eager for acceptance of its new services, picks up the tab for end-user computing, with predictable results—a dramatic rise in usage as people take advantage of free goods. Unfortunately, since there's no charge for services and thus no cost incentive, efficiency is low.

When costs exceed expectations in this phase, most organizations are forced into phase two. The IS department now bills users for services, and efficiency improves as users become more cautious in their computing habits. At the same time, effectiveness sags as departments avoid using services whose advantages they can't measure.

In the final stage, IS departments include cost-benefit analysis with their chargebacks, identifying reduced clerical costs or improved quality of company information. This method increases computer usage, and the efficiency and effectiveness factors begin to coincide.

In trying to limit computer costs, many companies institute hard controls. It's not surprising that of the 11 problematic companies, the 4 that established no controls suffered the worst results. But curiously, the 7 companies that resorted to rigid or hard controls also encountered huge cost overruns. Many tried to police users by requiring IS approval for all PC-related purchases and for access to company data files.

The users in these businesses devised ingenious ways to circumvent the controls. For example, purchase control specified IS approval for items that cost more than some threshold amount—usually about $3,500 (the cost of a PC with useful business features). To avoid having to get approval, users unbundled their purchases, buying the basic processor on one order, the printer on another, software on a third.

Some of them embedded PCs in an existing minicomputer budget, listed them as terminals, and renamed software "program documentation." When one IS organization conducted an audit a year after implementing hard controls, it was surprised to discover more than 1,500 unapproved PCs. Nor did the control on IS files prove worthwhile. Users just built their own files from scratch or by entering data from the regular computer output that IS provided.

Obviously, the circuitous approaches hurt company budgets. IS departments couldn't fully exploit quantity discounts, and failure to employ IS expertise in writing contracts produced inadequate maintenance agreements. Worst of all, the multitude of unauthorized data files cost the companies dearly, not only in labor as users duplicated data-entry efforts but also in accuracy of information. The reentered files were full of errors and out of date. False data circulated, often influencing important decisions.

Hopes into Realities

Because some companies didn't predict or control end-user costs, they missed certain advantages that the six successful companies realized. With end-user computing in place.

1. Measures to boost productivity and cost saving are implemented more quickly than by the traditional IS route in which users translate their needs to IS and wait years for their application to emerge from the backlog.
2. Users can tailor computer applications to their needs.
3. The quality of information throughout the company can improve as more people have access to corporate data bases as well as to each other's PC-based data and programs.

Ironically, the companies with good end-user computing operations spent no more—and often spent less—than the businesses that had serious problems. The successful companies planned for efficiency and effectiveness and applied standard cost-benefit analyses to determine ROI. In each example that follows, user-developed applications yielded measurable benefits.

After developing a report-generator software package, one company's personnel and facilities management departments stopped turning out reports by hand and saved 18 person-months the first year of use. The company said its personnel department realized an ROI of 2:1 and the facilities department, an ROI of more than 3:1.

Using a fourth-generation language, a purchasing department developed a system for handling purchase orders that saved $12 million a year.

In two days, a maintenance company developed fourth-generation software to automate tracking service contracts and the work performed. The annual labor saving is $15,000.

One manufacturing business used a statistical analysis package to select and manipulate information from several sources for monthly reports. Created in three days, the application produced an ROI of 6:1.

Another company offered training on a query package and a related graphics package to several divisions. A redistribution of the workload in the organization—relieving it of the necessity of hiring contractors—accounted for a large part of the net benefits exceeding $4 million.

All the companies in these examples did two things: they were proactive rather than reactive when developing end-user policies and support teams, and they used soft rather than hard controls.

TAKING CHARGE

Managers in the six successful companies took charge—establishing end-user policies to prevent PC-related cost overruns. As a first step, companies set standards for all PC-related purchases. For hardware this is quite simple—PC selection is limited to compatible machines. But several software issues come into question.

A company should choose one operating system that supports many users and provides high-level links, so PCs and mainframes can interact easily. Many of the most popular systems, like IBM's MS/DOS and Apple's CP/M, are incompatible. Moreover, keeping several operating systems updated is expensive. The most successful companies supported just one PC operating system. They also standardized their applications packages, for instance, selecting a single integrated spreadsheet and a single word processing package.

Settling on a single fourth-generation software package is a tougher decision. Users seek two capabilities: flexible information retrieval that lets them pull data from central files in various formats that package data as a report generator would; and a strong, easy-to-use modeling capability, permitting nontechnical people to fashion their own applications. No one fourth-generation package excels in both areas, and the effective IS groups chose one in each category.

The successful companies also gave users substantive technical training. While such training won't transform first-time developers into efficient software engineers, it can teach them new tricks and shortcuts to help them squeeze the most from company resources, especially when dealing with spreadsheet development or fourth-generation tools.

A critical goal—and one that's not easily attainable—is motivating the end-user support group to work well with nontechnical users. The attitude many technicians display toward computer neophytes interferes with this delicate relationship. Although IS personnel complain if their contact with end users dwindles, they seldom find intensive activity with them challenging. They use words like "nursemaiding" and "hand-holding" in describing work with new users. A study of more than 6,000 computer professionals revealed that they have little need for social interaction and a great need for challenging work.[1] These technically savvy types would rather burrow into complex issues back at the IS department than help others.

Staff problems don't have to detract from end-user computing, though, because it needs support from only a few IS people. Executives can choose the right people to help from those who have the highest need for social interaction.

Successful leaders of the end-user teams orient assignments to appeal to their employees' need for challenge. The leaders stressed two points that motivated their staffs: end-user programs center around state-of-the-art tools like fourth-generation languages, so a support team is using new technology; and user support is crucial to the whole company because it affects high-level managers, particularly in the information they draw from decision support systems. Only by combining a motivated technical team with aggressive policy making can a company shape an effective end-user program.

SOFT CONTROLS

Unfortunately, planning and policy making are fruitless unless companies can induce users to adopt IS guidelines. "Soft" controls work well. They can provide gentle incentives for adhering to IS standards and guidelines. Support of user freedom yields subtle but valuable rewards. Replacing the us-versus-them mentality that hard controls generate is an environment that encourages users to experiment, and important breakthroughs can happen.

For example, naive users left to develop their own applications drift naturally toward a method called prototyping, where a simple model is computerized, then tested, enhanced, and retested. Despite its rough state, the model often produces useful results quickly. This contrasts with standard IS procedure in which developers labor for months to produce a sophisticated, near-flawless version of a program, the goal being to install software that may require little or no change for one to two years. Prototyping has proven so effective that many IS departments are now adopting it for developing transaction-processing programs.

The successful companies I studied applied the following soft controls.

Selected hardware—the IS team maintains only certain machines.

Centralized purchasing—quantity discounts on the selected PCs, with savings passed on to user departments.

Limited training—instruction only on software that meets IS standards.

Consistent software distribution—a central agency distributes new releases, which diminishes the possibility of incompatibility and inconsistencies.

Distributed development—teaching leaders of end-user programming projects about good development methodology; if their applications meet IS standards, long-term maintenance will be easier and less expensive.

Software bonuses—an electronic mail system for communications-compatible PCs.

Even though soft controls often involve offering extras as incentives, they don't cost more. On the contrary, as they limit proliferation, incompatibility, and maintenance problems, they foster a creative environment based on mutual cost-reduction goals.

The micro invasion has decentralized computing, making inexpensive information tools available for everyone. Experts project a 1987-installed PC base of more than 20 million. As the pattern continues, by 1989 the number of workstations in U.S. business should exceed the number of white-collar workers.

But management use is far below predictions. Executives still tend to delegate computing-related tasks other than information retrieval to clerical and technical staff. An accompanying lag in predicted rewards—improved white-collar productivity, for instance, and better information for crucial management decisions—is also noticeable. To change this pattern, companies need to provide more functions with more user-friendly access in an integrated manner. That is, they need to improve the system to enable managers to accomplish all computational and data retrieval functions through English commands.

As IS departments gradually unleash end users, computer professionals must still teach cost control and careful planning as well as cultivate new methods to prod gently rather than police inexperienced users. Liberating end users from the IS grip is inevitable. The challenge lies in more precise planning of this decentralization.

Note

1. J. Daniel Couger and Robert A. Zawacki, *Motivating and Managing Computer Personnel* (New York: John Wiley, 1980).

4
Make Information Services Pay Its Way

Brandt Allen

It's no secret that companies can use information technology as a key to competitive advantage. But the computer key can't unlock the competitive door if information services (IS) functions—or rather malfunctions—as it does today in many companies. Top managers routinely rate their computer departments dead last among staff functions. Not only is IS slow and inefficient, they complain, but it's also expensive and unresponsive to inside customers.

If IS is to achieve a strategic end, companies must manage it as a productive part of the organization. The best way to do this is to run IS as a business within a business, as a profit center with a flexible budget and a systematic way to price its services. In companies that have already turned their IS systems into profit centers, the results have been impressive: the top management complaints are greatly reduced, and the expected efficiencies have materialized. When organizational shackles are lifted, IS can and does serve a strategic purpose.

Many managers are openly skeptical about the profit-center concept. They continue to view IS as a drain on, rather than a contributor toward, corporate resources. These managers are wedded to a past in which computer departments were part of the controller's organization; they were treated as cost centers with fixed budgets and were not expected to generate revenues. Many managers thus dismiss the computer department as part of overhead, the company's deadweight.

I find it helps to understand the importance of the profit-center approach if you look at the spectrum of ways that companies control and manage IS. At one end of the spectrum, IS is just another corporate staff function, and its strategic importance is usually nil. At the other end, IS is managed as a division or operating unit and plays an integral part in the corporation's strategic plans.

The *classically centralized* computer department is completely subsumed in corporate overhead. Companies in which decisions about applications, priorities, and technical solutions are made only at the top prefer this approach. IS does not allocate costs (chargeout) to customers but may still publish them to make users aware of their magnitude.

Under *bureaucratic* control, IS managers and users of IS services share decisions about everything from applications to budgets, usually through a steering committee. IS operates as a fixed-budget center with established measures of service; chargeout is a matter of costing, not pricing.

The *profit-center* department is different. Budgets are variable. The center sells services to users at a price. Users assume most of the responsibility for decisions about computer use and choice of technology.

I have broken down these three approaches into eight levels, based on how costs are allocated. Levels I and II are centralized approaches; levels III through VI, bureaucratic approaches; and levels VII and VIII, profit-center approaches. Each approach has its advantages and disadvantages. The first section of this article details the eight levels and their differences. The second section answers the questions about the profit-center approach most often asked by management skeptics. Those managers who wish to understand the logical progression to the profit-center approach should start with the first section. Those who wish simply to understand the theory and practice of profit centers should begin with the second.

Levels of Control

In a chargeout system, computer department costs are assigned to users—the various departments and divisions within a company that benefit from or consume computer services. There are almost as many approaches to cost allocation, or chargeout, as there are companies, but they all essentially fit into one of the following eight basic levels.

LEVEL I

No chargeout: "We don't believe in it." Some organizations simply do not allocate computer department costs, either for applications development (design, programming, and maintenance) or for processing (computer operations); instead, they simply treat these costs as part of corporate overhead. Users are never billed for their share of the computer charges.

LEVEL II

Charge included in corporate overhead allocation: "It's in your G&A." Some companies allocate the costs of corporate overhead, including computer department costs, to divisions or departments, based on some criterion such as revenue, assets, or head count. Although a portion of these allocated costs includes computer costs, the allocations aren't related to use.

LEVEL III

Memo record: "We don't do it, but if we did." A memo-record system has no interdepartmental accounting entries, and users don't have to budget for computing. Companies do, however, prepare estimates of what the cost would have been. This system is sometimes called "let's pretend chargeout" or "show-back accounting." It gives users cost information, even though they don't pay the costs. Companies can use memo-record accounting for both operations and systems development. It is an essential first step toward implementing a chargeout system. Some companies take this step by treating the computer charges as "noncontrollable" or "below the line"—charges that appear on users' operating statements but for which they're not held accountable.

LEVEL IV

Classic chargeback: "We'll let you know at the end of the year." Companies commonly make a first stab at computer costing by end-of-period cost allocation, or book balancing. If a department consumes 37% of the computer resources and 40% of the development and maintenance hours, it is assigned these shares of each cost. Sometimes the corporate office may subsidize a certain proportion of the costs. The chief drawback of this classic system is that companies make no charge until the year is over. Users rightly complain that they never know what the charge is until it's too late to do anything about it. They must guess at the cost implications of their decisions. This approach is also called zero-balance cost recovery; I call it bookkeeping run amok.

LEVEL V

Break-even rates with year-end adjustments: "We reserve the right to adjust everything in December." Some companies go beyond the classic system and predict the rate of consumer use from budgeted costs and forecasted volumes; they bill for usage at estimated rates. Unfortunately, such forecasting results in under- or overbooked costs at year's end. Leftover funds go back to the users in proportion to their computer charges over the year—hence the name "the Christmas present" method of chargeout. Development costs are handled the same way: users get estimates of a project's total cost but developers are not bound by the estimates. By adroitly combining frequent rate changes and end-of-year accounting shuffles, companies break even using this system—more or less.

LEVEL VI

Budgeted rates: "Our rates are set for the year." With this approach, companies may actually set the rates they charge users so that the system will theoretically break even. At year's end, the company neither allocates leftover costs back to users nor rolls them forward to the next period. Typically, they treat them as an overhead expense. The estimates made for development projects are like contract prices; the user and IS department often share cost overruns.

LEVEL VII

Standard rates and negotiated prices: "We use standard costs." This is the first level in which companies explicitly recognize that cost and price are two different things. For applications development, IS charges contracted prices (perhaps with penalties or savings sharing). For computer operations, a company either takes a break-even approach or bases rates on standard costs, costs plus a markup, outside market prices, or some negotiated rate. Charges at this level operate in a fashion similar to other interdivisional transfer prices in the company.

LEVEL VIII

Functional pricing: "We use transaction pricing." In levels III through VII, companies divide IS charges into cost pools (processor, disks, printers, tapes). Companies using functional pricing base prices on a completed task or attribute rather than the machine units necessary to produce it and attach the charge to what the user sees, receives, or causes—a report or a transaction, for example. Thus a user might be charged $3.25 for a report, $12.50 for a payroll check, $17.00 a transaction for order processing, or $27.80 per month per employee. Companies choose tasks or attributes that are meaningful to the user while at the same time approximating the cost of the service provided. The users readily understand what they're buying.

With functional pricing, the computer department still needs a system to know just what each of its tasks costs, and some applications must still be costed in the traditional machine-rate fashion, but much of what is produced in computer departments today can easily be task priced. For example, banks charge their branches so much per month for customer checking accounts as well as so much per item (a check or a deposit).

Why Do Chargeout?

In theory, companies have four objectives in doing cost allocation, or chargeout; in practice, however, they may adopt only one or two.

1. Cost assignment. Although you often hear that "chargeout recovers costs," it really assigns the cost of information processing directly to the departments and divisions that used the services. Departments can analyze the full costs of their own products and services, including IS costs, and the company can do better departmental profit-and-loss accounting. If the trust department of a bank consumes $1 million of IS resources, for example, the organization must find some way to assign that million to the department. The department must know what each of its services really costs, and the bank must have some way to measure the overall performance of the trust department. Chargeout costing methods (levels IV through VI) all accomplish this objective.

2. Control. The company either wants users to act responsibly when consuming IS resources or would like to hold both users and IS management accountable for their actions, typically by using a chargeout figure other than actual cost, like standard rate or negotiated price (level VII).

3. Incentives. To steer the organization toward certain technologies or methods and away from others, a company may subsidize an emerging technology while penalizing the use of outmoded options.

4. Budgeting. Organizations taking a variable-operating-budget approach use chargeout to determine the overall level of IS spending. The chargeout (transfer price) serves to clear or level supply and demand between IS and the users. Under centralized and bureaucratic control, a company sets computer rates after predicting the volume and setting the spending budget. Under a variable budget, a company sets a chargeout price first; that price then determines the demand or volume. Flexible-budget IS centers are sensitive to demand; the price or rate for computer services indirectly determines spending (levels VII and VIII).

To be effective, a chargeout system must: (1) be understandable to the user, not couching their charges in technical terms few managers understand, (2) be predictable so that managers know the cost consequences of their decisions in advance, and, above all, (3) reflect economic reality. Chargeout should lead managers to make the right decisions about computer use—from the perspective of their own department and when judged by the interests of the whole company. An advanced chargeout system, designed to encourage both the users and the providers of computer services to make wise decisions, lays the groundwork for the smooth operation of IS as a profit center.

Profit-Center Potential

Despite the commonsense appeal of the profit-center approach, managers often resist adopting it in their corporation. Their main objection is that information-processing costs are fixed. In their view, chargeout is simply a bookkeeping exercise; it's funny money. Besides, since IS serves internal company users, it should be a cost center. Managers believe running the computer department as a profit center is impractical if not impossible and probably unfair. In fact, the profit-center approach is decidedly fair, unquestionably possible, and undeniably practical. To show how and why, I will deal in turn with some of the issues raised by skeptics, beginning with the basis of their skepticism.

AREN'T COMPUTER COSTS FIXED?

Years ago, computer costs behaved much differently from the way they do today. Departments were smaller, and growth rates lower. Hardware was the big cost item. Orders for new capacity were usually large and took a long time to fill. Companies could achieve significant economies of scale in processing. Understandably, many managers saw the computer department as one big fixed cost; at anything less than full capacity, the incremental costs were next to zero.

In today's environment, computer reality has shifted. Annual growth rates in processing capacity can run as high as 30%; disk storage rates are even higher. Data-center managers have limitless options and don't have to wait long to implement new ideas. Economies of scale in processing no longer exist; two small mainframes can produce job costs lower than one large mainframe. Even though average computer use is often considerably lower than a company's theoretical capacity, it is still a cost that should be borne by the users.

To appreciate the variability of the costs of a typical computer department in a large company today, it helps to look at its budget and capacity summary (see Exhibit I). Company A, a $3 billion company, operates 78 plants, is a leader in its industry, and is widely respected for its computer management expertise. With 971 employees, the company's IS department operates large IBM mainframes and a substantial telecommunications network; its computer processing capacity is growing by about 35% per year. The Exhibit shows the annual budget, current capacity, cost of additional capacity, and expected delivery time.

Only $1.3 million, or 2% of the company's costs, are truly fixed, including costs for software, particularly operating systems, as well as costs for data-base managers and compilers. Another $8.3 million, or 15%, are for occupancy, or "managed costs," and are a function of space requirements for the staff. More than $25 million of the total budget, or 45%, is for people; that, together with the costs of terminals and communication lines, brings the total for clearly variable costs to 64%. The speed of delivery for new capacity is also striking. The company can add disk and tape drives and printers within four months. The item with the longest lead time is a mainframe processor, which requires a six-month order cycle. The additional processor would add 15% to processing capacity, but only .7% to the total budget.

In short, IS costs are not really fixed: they can be made to vary with volume or demand over as short a time frame as one quarter. They can be managed even if there are constraints on their manageability. To succeed in this environment, IS managers must get closer to their customers (the users), anticipate their needs, and plan for contingencies.

HOW DOES A PROFIT CENTER WORK?

A profit center must have:

A way to price or value computer services at some figure other than cost.

The authority to incur costs and to acquire resources to meet demand. Senior management must delegate responsibility for selecting what level of computing users may request. User demand drives a flexible, or variable, operating budget.

Exhibit 1. Company A's Computer Budget and Capacity Summary

Cost pool	Annual budget thousands	Current capacity	Type of cost	The next increment			Delivery time months
				Capacity	Cost		
Staff	$25,400	971 people	Variable over short term	<1%	<1%		2
Terminals	2,010	1,304 terminals	Variable over short term	<1	<1		1
Communication lines	9,694	795 circuits	Variable over short term	1	1		3
Disk storage	1,508	218 spindles	Variable over short term	1	1		4
Tape storage	271	33 drives	Variable within six months	3	2		4
Printers	163	4 printers	Variable within six months	4	13		4
Communications equipment	619	11 units	Variable within six months	20	29		5
Mainframe processors*	5,254	2,243 units	Variable within six months	15	8		6
Equipment maintenance	2,195	n.a.	Mostly variable	–	–		–
Occupancy, overhead	8,351	n.a.	Managed cost	–	–		–
Software†	1,315	n.a.	Fixed	–	–		–
Total	$56,780						

*Processing capacity is measured using industry standard units wherein the IBM 370/158-3 equals 45 units. The next increase in capacity would be to upgrade an IBM 3083J to a 3081K.

†Software includes IBM operating systems, utilities, and third-party packages.

An objective that its revenue must equal or exceed cost. The center must measure both its input (cost) and output (revenue) in financial terms. Implied is a customer who purchases the information services and an IS management that encourages products whose revenues will exceed costs and discourages those whose revenues don't. Managing the difference between these two figures is the essence of profit-center control.

By the same token, the profit center need not become an independent service bureau with outside customers. Nor does the center need to make a big profit or for that matter any profit at all. As a practical matter, most data centers will continue to have expenses and revenues that are more or less equal because they lower prices to keep revenues in line with costs. Actual levels of profit or loss won't change the way IS functions or is viewed by the organization; the combined controls of variable budgets, chargeout prices, and profit-center measures will.

Finally, the profit center does not imply a lack of control over IS spending; it implies only that budget and financial controls work much differently than they would in a cost center. The computer department must still compete for capital funds, but its operating budget is no longer fixed by management fiat. It is indirectly set by the users. Profit-center budgets reflect management's plans to meet demand under various forecasts.

WHO CONTROLS SPENDING?

When IS is run as a cost center, senior managers control the funding for computing and are responsible for monitoring the efficiency of the IS department. Most find this a tough assignment; few have much confidence in their ability to do it well. Because the computer department's overall performance is difficult to measure, senior managers periodically cut the budget to force IS management to be careful about spending.

Establishing the computer department as a profit center transfers control of funding to those who use the services. Users are the source of funds, and they judge IS efficiency. When the data center is efficient and responsive, it gets more work. When it is not competitive, users are free to seek alternate solutions like departmental computers, micros, purchased packages, and service bureaus—or they can simply pressure IS for rate reductions and service enhancements.

WHAT ARE THE ADVANTAGES?

A profit-center approach benefits the organization and encourages the use of information processing when the overall value to the department of using the service exceeds the cost of the service and when the price received by IS for the service exceeds its cost.

IS profit-center management has five key advantages over cost- or service-center control. First, when managed as a profit center, IS provides better service because it is rewarded for successfully responding to the demands of users. When companies manage data centers as fixed-budget cost centers, the departments have neither the budgetary flexibility nor the performance measures necessary to be truly responsive to customers, and the computer service erodes. A profit-center approach encourages responsiveness, high-quality service, innovation, and cost control.

Second, the IS budget-setting problem disappears for the corporation because users determine their own budget limits. Users, not the hapless IS director, must justify the IS budget.

Third, the IS function becomes more efficient because the profit-center approach provides a basis for measuring both its efficiency and its effectiveness. The chargeout price reflects the cost of a service and what it "ought to cost." It really is the wholesale value of the service. The application may have retail value to the user but that's for the user to decide. To the user an application may mean greater sales, better market analysis, or a quicker product introduction, but to the computer department it represents so much disk storage used, so many computer cycles turned, and so on. When IS is set up as a cost center, its managers act as if they were selling a commodity. The emphasis is not on efficiency. Rather, if they can turn over their actual costs to users, they will—whether these costs represent great efficiency or outrageous extravagance on the part of IS.

Think of IS as a manufacturing division; companies don't let individual plants charge their actual costs to the plant that uses their components. Instead, companies use standard costs (what the cost should be) or standard cost plus a markup or a transfer price (reflecting perhaps a market price). You can treat information services in the same way. Once management has a dollar figure to associate with the results of IS (other than cost), it can compare the costs of IS with its results.

Fourth, users make better decisions about how to use and acquire information services. Typically, a cost-based chargeout system results in distorted "funny money" figures. You often hear an IS justification like "Yes, I know that we charged you $400,000 for that job last year and, yes, you could probably do it on your own model X machine for $250,000, but that doesn't mean the company would save $150,000. Actually, we figure switching to the local machine would cost the company an extra 50 grand." Such statements quickly destroy the confidence managers might otherwise have in both the chargeout system and the IS organization and drive them to alternate computing services, even when no one knows whether such alternatives would be in the company's best interests. When IS is a profit center, the transfer price becomes *real money*—IS is willing to provide the service at that figure. If the user has a better alternative that still meets the corporation's security and strategic policies, it is best for all parties (the user, IS, and the company) for the user to pursue it.

Fifth, companies introduce new technology sooner and with better results. Users can better evaluate and acquire new systems, software, and information-processing technology than can a central IS function. In general, companies using a profit-center system have more advanced technology and fewer failures than those using cost centers. One reason is that the managers who benefit from the new technology can justify the expense and pay for the service. They don't have to depend on central budget approval. There's less game playing, greater trust, and a more harmonious relationship between IS and the users.

The most common failures with the profit-center approach occur when management overrides the variable budget with caps or constraints. Under profit-center control, it is the users who can best decide, application by application, where to cut costs. Companies also have problems when data centers sell services both inside and outside. Unless the data center is especially well run and efficient, the inside business subsidizes the outside contracts, and the situation becomes intolerable. Insiders then seek alternatives.

DO COMPANIES REALLY DO THIS?

Several sophisticated companies have instituted profit centers, although each has a different twist. The complex approach of a U.S. automotive manufacturer, in which several data centers provide services, gives data-center managers two budgets instead of one. A net budget covers the planned activities for which there is to be no cost allocation, such as corporate-office systems support, computing activities for research and development, or any purpose with no single, clearly defined owner. All other information processing is sold or charged to the users at a fair price. A total spending, or gross budget, is not fixed but is instead a function of what the users require. The demands of users change during the year as the level of activity in their plants changes and as decisions about micros, plant computers, service bureaus, and software purchases change. IS operates as an internal service bureau (actually, as several because each data center operates this way).

The IS division of a large electronics company has a profit objective and an ROI target. The IS division, which provides services only to other company divisions and headquarters departments, is run just like any other profit-center division. The reasoning is that if component divisions produce and sell various components to other divisions within the company and the company treats those component divisions as profit centers, why not treat computer services the same?

One of the most advanced and best managed U.S. government agency data centers operates as a variable-budget, full-chargeout profit center, although the agency downplays its profit-making dimension. While the agency calls it a "cost-recovery center," it behaves as a profit center. No central authority approves or appropriates the funds. The profit-center managers can change their plans and the budget as needed; they can spend what they sell. The excess of revenues over expenses just isn't called profit. (Actually, the center shows little profit because it keeps lowering its rates.) The center aims to increase revenues and reduce expenses. Additional expenses are expected to result in additional revenues. The center has been run this way for 20 years and is known for having the lowest costs and the highest service levels of any government data center.

At the profit center of one of the world's largest chemical companies, the IS budget divides all expenses into two categories:

budgeted, which includes costs for administration and related over-head, and forecasted, which includes computer rentals, operations and systems development, and other demand-sensitive expenditures. IS management must live within the budget authorization but does not have to adhere to the forecasted guidelines, although it must recoup those funds through user charges. Small end-of-the-year variances are expected and absorbed into a corporate over-head account.

A European corporation has set up IS as a separate corporation owned by the company's subsidiaries. As a profit center with a flexible budget, IS charges for its services at competitive rates, while a headquarters committee approves pricing policies. The company chose an independent legal entity to separate the concept of ownership from use. Some subsidiaries felt strongly about the advantages of a shared data center and provided the starting capital. These subsidiaries realize the profits and losses of the IS company in proportion to their ownership; users buy services and pay a competitive price in proportion to their use.

Ironically, companies using a cost-center approach have more problems with unfair charging than do companies with profit centers. Users can negotiate with profit-center management if they believe the prices are out of line and, in general, have a good sense of what a reasonable charge would be. In cost centers, arguments about cost never stop.

The increasing decentralization of computing to divisional and departmental data centers and the growth of end-user computing will not make the corporate data center obsolete. In fact, as micro-computers proliferate, corporate data centers will house corporate data bases or at least keep track of data bases throughout the organization. They'll be busy supporting the users' micros and workstations with networking capabilities, data subsets, and other support tools. Even in decentralized organizations, companywide or global systems will exist for which costs must be assigned to users. As large companies operate 5 or 6 times the computing capacity and perhaps 10 to 20 times the storage capacity in their central computer departments, they will need a well-conceived approach to data-center control.

WHERE DO PROFIT CENTERS FIT?

The requirements for controls like chargeout and profit centers vary over the experience cycle of a technology. Chargeout can inhibit a company in the early phases of a new technology but become more advantageous in the later stages when effective controls are essential.

Profit-center control fits best when users decide how much computing to use, how to use it, and in what form. Because users have funding responsibility they must have the experience and judgment to assume such responsibility.

The most important requirement for a successful profit center is that senior management believes that control over computing belongs with the users. If executives view computing as a specialist's task best controlled by corporate IS with top management oversight, then profit-center control isn't for them.

The profit-center approach is not a panacea for technologically backward, costly, and poorly managed departments unless the company wishes to spark a wholesale flight to decentralized or outside computing. It fits those operations that are already competitive with outside service bureaus. Indeed, many large corporate data centers claim cost levels half that of the well-known national service bureaus; the only reason these centers are not competitive internally is that they lack a service orientation.

Profit-center control can dramatically improve the way information services are provided within a corporation. It may not be an appropriate technique for all organizations, but when it fits, the results are dramatic. Given the size and growth of information systems spending, the increase in end-user computing and decentralization, and the changing economics of computing, most companies can use and benefit from a profit-center approach.

Computer managers often understand this and are aware of the need for changes but lack the authority to make them. Adoption of profit-center controls requires top management backing and some organizational changes. To perform as most managements wish, IS should not only have development and operations responsibilities but must also market and sell, conduct research, and manage its human resources. Without a profit center, many companies will find their IS function becoming their primary strategic weakness rather than their strength.

PART
IV
Managing IT Applications

1
Telecom: Hook Up or Lose Out

Eric K. Clemmons and F. Warren McFarlan

The new technologies of communications have the power to change the competitive game for almost all companies of all sizes. Many companies already use telecommunications to gain a competitive edge, yet many others fail to see how they might use these new possibilities in their strategic planning.

With the breakup of AT&T and the restructuring of communications, both local and long distance, some companies have seen opportunities for cutting telecommunications costs and this has made new arrangements attractive. In this new environment, companies have begun to explore their options. Some have established electronic links with their customers; others have tied in to their suppliers.[1] Such new relationships can change a company's position in its market, can change its market, and in some cases can even create new product markets.[2]

If costs are lower and opportunities so inviting, why have we not seen a rush to make use of the new promise of telecom (as insiders have quickly dubbed it)? Not least among the problems is the daunting range of possibilities. Where to go for the best equipment, how to be sure of its reliability, and what kind of hardware and software to choose from the myriad offerings are among the tough questions managers face. Further, making these choices depends on technical considerations and a better understanding than now usually exists between technical and general managers.

Even before they answer these nitty-gritty questions, however, companies must make decisions about what telecommunications can do for them. Since uncovering the best potential uses is not a simple task, we will examine what some companies have already done in order to draw lessons for managers. To give the best notion of the variety of available opportunities for companies of different types, we present a wide range of possible uses.

Company Experience

A major international bank has devised one of the most promising ways to use the new telecommunications technology. It puts terminals on the desks of the chief financial officers of its big European customers to allow them to transfer funds directly to the U.S. accounts of their suppliers. The bank provides all hardware, software, and communications networks. The customers are delighted with the speed and control these arrangements offer. But the big winner is the bank: not only has it scored a marketing coup with this service; it has also off-loaded onto the customer both the data-entry costs and the responsibility for data-entry errors.

This is an attractive kind of telecom application. The customer is happy, and the bank has less expense and liability. Perhaps most significant, though, the bank has created heavy switching costs for the customer, since extricating itself from the bank's network and starting over and learning to work with a competitor's system would require a long time. Moreover, with each new service and each new data base the customer uses, the greater these switching costs become.

In another type of application, companies make their offerings impossible to copy or duplicate. For example, most major airlines have frequent-flyer bonus plans of some sort, so it is not clear that any airline has gained a significant, sustainable advantage. Applications in which customers will ignore second or third entrants, however—for example, hospital purchasing terminals in which a hospital is linked to one supplier and airline reservation systems operated by one airline—offer much more promise to the first developer.

In today's deregulated environment, air carriers have taken advantage of the rapid feedback that they receive from their electronic links to travel agents. They use this information in pricing and marketing their flights and in making quick adjustments of their route structures to abandon unprofitable cities and coordinate feeder flights into their hubs.

Insurance companies that anticipated the changes in their competitive environment due to changes in banking regulations have fared far better than those that did not. In developing communications networks with their agents in the field, these companies have introduced new products as well as better customer services.

ENHANCED SERVICES AND PRODUCTS

For a company that wants to explore applications that add value to its product lines, examples from other companies can point the way.

TAKING UP SLACK. Telecommunications has the potential to smooth operations. A good case in point is the auto industry. Since companies in this industry never know what they will need downstream or when they will be cut off from their suppliers, they keep enormous safety stocks of components and ready-to-ship subassemblies. Through electronic links to suppliers and dealers, they can substitute information for surplus inventory, capital, or production facilities.

COORDINATION. In some instances, the use of telecommunications to enhance coordination is fairly informal—voice mail for messages to officers or consultants when they are out of the office, videotex to update instructions to sales personnel in the field. But means of increasing coordination are often much more formal, making extensive use of data retrieval and computer processing.

For example, at least one U.S. air carrier uses a network to monitor the location of all its aircraft, essentially in real time. By knowing its planes' locations and passenger lists, the passengers' connections, and the connection schedules, it can instantaneously make decisions about speeding up late flights or delaying connecting departures. The opportunities for controlling fuel costs and preventing revenue loss due to passengers' continuing on competitors' flights after missing connections may amount to tens of millions of dollars a year. Trucking companies and trains use similar methods to track cargoes and optimize schedules.

CUTTING EXPENSES. Though it didn't work, Citibank attempted to require all customers with account balances below $5,000 to use automated teller machines rather than human tellers, tried to offload clerical work to users, and encouraged banking by mail. Because of the cost advantages, banks will probably persist in the effort to promote ATM use.

HIGHER VISIBILITY. We have seen numerous examples in which a communications-based service permits a company to maintain constant contact with customers, providing information, advice, or the ability to place orders and receive confirmation rapidly. The company that has a terminal on a customer's premises gets many additional orders by default. It can usually preempt a competitor from putting in a second terminal and provide additional services that both increase value and raise the customer's switching costs. Often the secure and comfortable feeling customers enjoy will produce the benefits of greatest significance to the company.

CUTS IN TRAVEL COSTS. Telecommunications enables companies to move information rather than people. Although video teleconferencing has been slow to catch on, experience in some companies suggests that it effectively takes the place of some meetings and permits others to take place that could not be justified in any other way. Various technologies are available to avoid face-to-face meetings or to reduce their frequency. Full-motion video teleconferencing is the most complete replacement; slow-scan or freeze-frame video, voice mail, and computer conferencing afford progressively less realism but increasingly lower cost.

EXTERNAL LINKS. Telecommunications can provide better integration via interorganizational exchange of information. To eliminate rekeying and to expedite delivery, some companies have integrated a customer's purchase-order system with the vendor's order entry. Tying word processing to Telex eliminates rekeying and produces clean, well-formatted messages. By tying an inventory management system to the suppliers' systems, a company can order rapidly and ensure maintenance of adequate stock for just-in-time delivery.

FASTER COMMUNICATIONS. By replacing a Telex system with electronic mail on a more sophisticated system, a company can obtain speedy service. Another way of expediting communications is to replace telephone conference calls with the more effective video teleconferencing.

NEW PRODUCTS.   In addition to making operations more efficient and effective, telecom can lead to innovative products and services. Examples are the first bank-by-phone services and the first cash management account product. Another new product is a facsimile mail service for one- or two-hour cross-country delivery of documents, including text, hand annotations, and illustrations.

Value Chain

So far, we have been discussing the new uses of telecommunications in terms of improved services and new products. An effective way to think about telecommunication opportunities is to analyze a company's value chain—the series of interdependent activities that bring a product or a service to the customer. Exhibit I shows a typical value chain, drawn from Michael Porter's analysis, which briefly defines the meaning of a company's activities.[3] Telecommunications technology can profoundly affect each one of these activities, sometimes simply by improving effectiveness and sometimes by fundamentally changing the activity. In the process, the value chains of key customers and of competitors may change as well.

INBOUND LOGISTICS

Telecommunications technology has already shown its important effects in expediting materials to the point of manufacture. One major distribution company, for example, has installed a sophisticated series of terminals on customer premises to permit implementation of just-in-time on-line ordering. The company requires its suppliers to keep adequate inventory and to make the figures on available stock accessible to the distribution company's computerized purchasing system.

This system has cut down on incoming materials warehousing needs and reduced disruptions due to inventory shortfalls. The need to maintain inventory safety stocks, and the associated holding costs, have been passed along to the suppliers. The purchaser's computer can also rapidly scan several suppliers' data bases and order from the one offering the lowest price. This new efficiency has sharply eroded suppliers' margins. Because the distribution

Exhibit 1. The Value Chain

Support activities	Corporate infrastructure
	Human resource management
	Technology development
	Procurement

| Primary activities | Inbound logistics | Operations | Outbound logistics | Marketing and sales | Service |

Margin

Reprinted from Michael E. Porter and Victor E. Millar, "How Information Gives You Competitive Advantage," HBR July-August 1985, p. 151.

company just mentioned has great purchasing power, it has reaped most of the system's benefits. To change vendors has, however, become more difficult for the distributor.

A large department store chain is hooked directly to several of its textile suppliers. This hookup has not only improved delivery and permitted inventory reduction; it has also provided flexibility to meet changing demand almost immediately, which in turn, by making it easier to deal with local American suppliers rather than remote foreign suppliers, has offset the price differentials.

OPERATIONS AND PRODUCT STRUCTURE

Telecommunications technology information systems affect a manufacturer's operations and its product offerings. When one financial services firm, for example, wanted to go after more small private investors (with portfolios of about $25,000), it introduced a flexible financial instrument. It gave investors immediate on-line ability to move their funds among stocks or out of stocks, and it provided money market rates on idle funds as well as liquidity equal to that of a checking account.

This company, which was the first to introduce this service, captured huge initial market share. Continued product enhancement has ensured that investors have no incentive to switch services. In the first two years, this original provider achieved six times the volume of its nearest competitor. Five years later, it retained a 70% share of the market.

A news wire service company reconceptualized its business as being essentially a bit-moving operation (getting data from one place to another). This new concept led it to offer a new line of financial services, such as instantaneous financial information (up-to-the-second foreign exchange rates, for example) and was the key to its developing new services. The company had to make no important changes in its technology. With growing sales and profits from the new product line, the company recently went public, and the offering was very successful.

A major insurance company thought of its business as being a diversified financial services and bit-moving company. It improved services to policyholders by allowing immediate on-line checking of status for claims and claims processing. The company provided on-line access to new services and products for customers. These included modeling packages that enabled corporate benefits officers to determine the costs of various benefits packages so as to tailor them to costs and employee requests. It responded to clients' needs by selling software for claims processing, or claims-processing services, to corporate clients who elect to be self-insured. The company credits these initiatives with keeping it firmly in place at the top of its industry, despite tremendous competition from other diversified financial services companies.

OUTBOUND LOGISTICS

Telecommunications has a great impact on the way services and products are delivered to customers. To take one well-known example, the reservation system links to travel agents, provided chiefly by United Airlines and American Airlines, have affected their business relationship so profoundly that the smaller airlines that do not furnish this service have found it difficult to match. For example, prominent screen placement, which has strongly influenced purchasing behavior, in December 1984 prompted the Civil Aeronautics Board to issue a cease-and-desist order against the practice.

Further, this close cooperation with travel agents allows faster pricing and scheduling adjustment as well as disciplinary action against uncooperative agents (offering reduced access on tightly booked flights). The arrangement also contributes to revenues through the ability to charge the competition for listings, reservations, and tickets written. Obviously, each of the examples just cited as inbound logistics for one company represents outbound logistics for the other partner.

MARKETING AND SALES

Opportunities to use telecommunications profitably in marketing and sales are diverse. American Hospital Supply, a large medical supplier, provides remote order entry. The purchasing agent at a hospital has a terminal tied to a computerized order-entry system. This electronic link facilitates placing orders and speeds delivery.

It also offers inventory management software, which works only if the hospital purchases from this supplier, and a discount system that also encourages sole-source supply.

Once customers begin to rely on this inventory management, they usually stop dealing much with competitors. Not surprisingly, AHS quickly came to dominate the U.S. hospital medical supply market. Moreover, competitors have found it difficult to respond, since hospital purchasing agents have been unenthusiastic about accepting a second terminal and learning to work with a second set of order-entry and inventory management services. At least one of AHS's major competitors has been forced into corporate reorganization.

A large pharmaceutical company offers on-line order-entry services to pharmacies for itself and a consortium of allied but not competing companies. Not only has it increased market share, but it has also derived sizable added revenues from its consortium partners. Some companies excluded from the bundle have threatened legal action because of damage to their market shares.

In the industrial air-conditioning industry a major corporation has built a microcomputer-based modeling system to help architects model the heating and cooling system requirements for commercial properties, measurably reducing design time. The model often leads an architect to consider this company's products more favorably than others'.

A competing corporation subsequently made a similar model available to remote users via communications links, providing rapid support and allowing the architect to get detailed costs and parts listings quickly to complete the design. Because the system is on-line, this company was able to neutralize the damage produced by the competitor's earlier product.

An agricultural chemicals company has obtained similar results through a sophisticated on-line crop-planning service for its chief agricultural customers. From a personal computer, using a standard telephone connection, a farmer can call up agricultural data bases containing prices of various crops, necessary growing conditions, and the costs of various chemicals. The farmer can then call up various models and decision support systems and can tailor them to his fields' requirements, after which he can experiment with the models and examine the implications of various crop rotations and timing for planting. The model then helps him to select fertilizer and chemical applications and to group purchases to achieve maximum discounts. Finally, the farmer can place an order for future delivery by hitting a few keys.

In a different vein, a major bank trying to strengthen its marketing of agricultural loans has offered a similar crop-planning service. Two previously noncompetitive companies are now competing in the same software arena.

AFTER-SALES SERVICE

An elevator company has installed on its new line of elevators flight-recording devices such as airlines use. It has done so because customers often place service calls without indicating how the elevators have malfunctioned. The recording device permits the service representative to connect it to the elevator company's computer, discover the cause of the malfunction of two hours before, and then do the necessary repairs on the spot.

A large manufacturer of industrial machinery has installed an expert maintenance system in its home office computer. When a machine failure occurs on the customer's premises, the machine is connected over a telephone line to the manufacturer's computer, which does the fault analysis and issues instructions to the machine operator. Not only are direct service visits down by 90%, but customer satisfaction is also up markedly.

INFRASTRUCTURE. A major travel agency uses an on-line link to provide support to small, outlying offices. Because the travel industry still needs to deliver paper documents—passports, visas, tickets, itineraries—satellite or remote offices near big corporate customers are highly useful for pickup and delivery. These offices must have the full support capabilities of the home office. The on-line links have changed the organizational structure from a large, central office to many small, full-service offices. This change appears to have produced a 27% growth in sales.

PERSONNEL. An oil company has given all its corporate management committee members desk terminals. Through these machines, the committee has full on-line access to the detailed personnel files of the 400 most senior members in the corporation, complete with such data as five-year performance appraisals and lists of positions each person is backing up. The company believes this capability has facilitated its important personnel decisions.

TECHNOLOGY DEVELOPMENT.   On-line access to large computing facilities inside and outside the company has allowed a heavy industrial manufacturer to increase technical productivity by more than half. Senior technical management now would not want to operate without this support.

To guide its drilling decisions, a large oil company processes large amounts of infrared data gathered from an overhead satellite. The company believes this information, which is used in all aspects of searching for petroleum deposits, is essential to its operations, from deciding on which tracts to bid to determining where to drill. Similarly, CAD/CAM technology has fundamentally changed the quality and speed with which the company can manufacture its drilling platforms.

PROCUREMENT

With a series of on-line electronic bulletin boards that make latest spot prices instantly available around the country, a manufacturing company directs its nationwide purchasing effort. The boards have led to a tremendous improvement in purchasing price effectiveness.

A retailer, by virtue of its large size, has succeeded in its demand for on-line access to the inventory files and production schedules of its smaller suppliers. This access has permitted the company to manage its inventories more tightly than before and to pressure suppliers on price and product availability. This is another dimension of the earlier cited inbound logistics example.

We have found systematic examination of a company's value chain an effective way to search for profitable telecommunications applications. This analysis requires keen administrative insight, awareness of industry structure, and familiarity with the rules of competition. Companies need to understand their value chains and those of key customers and suppliers in order to uncover potential new service areas. Similarly, understanding competitors' value chains provides insight on the likely source of competitive attack. Finally, careful thought is needed to identify potential new entrants to an industry. These are companies whose value chains make expansion into a particular area attractive.

Management Questions

To make full use of the opportunities that telecom presents, managers will need some help from experts. Bridging the gap between specialists in telecommunications technology and general management for purposes of strategic planning is, however, an enduring problem. Since general managers are often uncomfortable with technology, many are unaware of new options the technology provides and the ways in which telecommunications can support strategy. On their part, information systems and telecommunications professionals are often not attuned to the complexities and subtleties of strategy formulation. They are generally not part of the strategy development process.

Their partnership is necessary, however, to bring general management and telecommunications expertise to the problem. Telecommunications experts understand the economies of the technology and know its limits. And they can help the organization anticipate and capitalize on tomorrow's technologies. For example, very rich and dense data bases may, today, be hard to work with because they are slow to give results. Having them in place, however, will permit companies to take advantage of new technologies that will be faster and easier to use.

General managers bring insight to overall business priorities. They have detailed knowledge of the various value chains and their potential in the real world and can find the paths of least staff resistance in implementation.

Synthesis of the two worlds is essential. As a way of starting the process, task forces to address the following questions have proved valuable.

1. What business are we really in? To answer that question, the task force may ask: What value do we provide to our customers? Does widespread, cheap, high-volume data communications change this? Are we an insurance company, or should we think of ourselves as a provider of diversified financial services? Are we a news wire service or a mover of electronic bits? A provider of spare parts or of parts and parts status reporting?

2. Who are our biggest competitors? What new competitors in the future does this technology make possible? Who else does, or can, provide the same products or services? If we see ourselves in the future as an insurance company, our competitors will be companies such as Aetna and Travelers. If we see ourselves as a financial

services company, our competitors will be firms such as American Express/Shearson Lehman, Merrill Lynch, Sears financial services, and Citicorp.

3. Can we integrate our clients' operations with our own through telecommunications and offer them faster, easier, or cheaper service? In particular, how can we lock them in—by introducing significant switching costs?

4. Can we lock competitors out through aggressive use of telecommunications?

5. What has changed in our overall competitive environment? Does this new world permit us to gain or sustain competitive advantage through telecommunications technology?

   Has our operating environment been changed by deregulation of our industry? Can technology help us compete for marketing, scheduling, control, and coordination?

   Has our environment changed due to deregulation of a related industry? Again, can technology help us compete? How can we add new products and services to retain our existing customer base?

6. Can we get there first? Should we attempt to make this move? These two may be the most difficult questions of all. They require foreseeing what's going to happen to the marketplace and to relationships with clients, customers, competitors, and regulators. Also, the company must determine which innovations will provide sustainable advantage and which competitors can readily copy, adding to the costs of all industry participants or shaving all margins.

The company must also decide what it wants to change and how technology makes that change possible. It helps greatly if in addition a company sees all this before its competitors do. The difference between an effective strategic initiative and a harebrained scheme in this area is razor thin and requires tough general management analysis.

Opportunities and Risks

Telecommunications technology affects companies of all types and sizes. It has altered services, changed relationships with suppliers and customers, brought new competitors to the forefront, and opened new distribution channels. In many instances the effect is synergistic, and both parties in a transaction have improved value chains. Electronic commercial banking gives an example of such synergy.

The value to the large corporate user comes from better service: speed in completing transactions with remote providers and recipients of funds, control over its transactions and their timing, access to additional data bases and information services, and continuing support from its omnipresent electronic banker. Benefits to the bank come from internal cost reduction, principally through decreased clerical expense and reduced liability for delays caused by transcription errors. Additional benefits to the bank accrue, of course, from the value its customers perceive.

The advantage gained can be defended since, as the customer comes to depend on a particular software interface, changing sourcing involves heavy switching costs. Further, the large cost of continuing software development and network procurement helps prevent all but the largest banks from matching these offerings.

Telecom brings both an opportunity for some and a risk for others. The industry reorganization that will come as a result of these new relationships between companies will put many wholesalers under pressure. Now regional wholesalers and local distributors may fall out of the distribution chain if they are offering only an order-entry service. An electronic capability enables manufacturers to receive orders without any prospect of competitors' sales. Moreover, the margin advantages the manufacturers enjoy can preclude competitors' regaining share by cutting price.

Competitors must deliver comparable electronic services or buy into those of the initial developers, increasing the pressure on the members of the traditional delivery chain. It is too early to predict the end result, as the middleman plays many roles simultaneously. Clearly, however, structural and service level changes lie ahead.

From our work in a wide variety of industrial settings, we conclude that every element of the value chain is subject to the major impact of telecommunications. However, most companies that have had successes to date have fallen into the opportunities or have taken an ad hoc approach to problems rather than carefully planning their strategies.

The external linkage patterns have already been recast in a number of industries, while they are just beginning in others. More flexibility exists, of course, in introducing internal telecommunications linkages. The lesson for corporations is that it is better to seize the opportunity on one's own terms than to be driven by others. The rules are complicated, however, by the fact that we are dealing with a floating crap game that changing cost and performance of the technology continually redefines. The economics of telecommunications will continue to evolve over the next decade as applications not feasible today become cost effective and competitive.

Notes

1. For a discussion of various structures, see James I. Cash, Jr., and Benn R. Konsynski, "IS Redraws Competitive Boundaries," Part II, Chapter 3, of this collection.
2. F. Warren McFarlan, "Information Technology Changes the Way You Compete," Part II, Chapter 2, of this collection.
3. See Michael E. Porter and Victor E. Millar, "How Information Gives You Competitive Advantage," Part II, Chapter 1, of this collection.

2
Information Technology Puts Power in Control Systems

William J. Bruns, Jr., and F. Warren McFarlan

It's time to turn another page in the chronicle of the computer revolution. Imaginative companies are creatively applying the speed and flexibility of low-cost data processing and communications systems to the control function, and the results have been astounding. Managers once stymied by the languorous flow of information from the work force or from customers can now grab data from the most remote corners of their companies in an instant. Key facts—from the slowing inventory turnover of an offshore plant to the sudden burst of sales in a distant territory—that were previously filtered out or obscured can now be presented in whatever form makes decision making easiest. The new computer systems permit companies to speed up changes in corporate policies by getting revised financial plans or new incentive programs to the work force rapidly. And managers can test those changes ahead of time by quickly running and comparing a dozen "what ifs."

The obvious benefit of this fast, more flexible data management technology at reasonable cost is that it can revitalize the three traditional purposes that control systems serve. It can help managers use resources more effectively, align disparate parts of the organization with companywide goals, and collect data for strategic and operating decisions.

But information technology—PCs, spreadsheets, telecommunications, and data-base management software—has done more than just enhance existing processes. It has created a whole new set of options for gathering, organizing, and using information. The broadened realm of possibility has sparked some progressive companies to rethink their information needs and wants. Those that selected wisely from the new list of options have seen their control systems and structures transformed. They have found ways to channel the power of information to the muscles of their corporations. As a result, they have boosted their efficiency and overall competitive position.

A Ride with the Mavericks

So far, only the most progressive companies have fully leveraged the new technology, perhaps because only they could bridge the gap between the control department and the IT group. It is well worth the effort for other companies to try to close that gap. The following examples show the kinds of benefits a business can obtain when it uses information technology to overhaul its control processes. Each of the enterprises described has capitalized on the technology by organizing information in one of three ways: consolidating, centralizing, or decentralizing it.

CONSOLIDATING DATA TO SELL AN INSURANCE PORTFOLIO

New systems permit managers not only to get information more quickly but also to shape data files into new forms as needed. This means that if the rules of the game change, managers can reshuffle material into whatever form will meet the challenge. By consolidating reports and raw numbers, companies in essence create new information from old, and new data can stimulate solutions to nagging problems or point to unexploited opportunities.

A prominent insurance company recently spent a lot of money to reorganize its computer files by customer rather than by policy number. The old filing system meshed with the company's longstanding incentive system, which paid salespeople commissions based on each product they sold. Salespeople were not penalized, however, when a customer dropped a product. The sales agent lacked not only the incentive but also the mechanism to review a customer's total holdings regularly and seek the right mix of products. The company had used several variations of people's names for purchase records—sometimes two initials, sometimes the full name, and so on. Even if salespeople had wanted to plow through mountains of product files for customer information, it's doubtful they could have caught all the varieties of each customer's listings.

Under the new system, salespeople regularly review a customer's entire product portfolio. They can use this information for suggesting replacement of outdated insurance or other financial instrument holdings. The company thus forestalls switching by a customer to other carriers and also continually generates new business. A new incentive system pays commissions to salespeople who build a long-term total relationship with customers rather than just going for short-term sales, thereby aligning each salesperson's goals with company goals.

Today many of that company's competitors are scrambling to install a similar setup to get a picture of the total financial relationship, but if they are just starting they face two or three years of costly systems programming to reorder their large, inflexible data files.

CENTRALIZING DATA TO IMPROVE THE ELEVATOR SERVICE CALL

Corporate headquarters can now promptly gather information from branch offices at low cost, getting a bird's-eye view of even the most remote branches in time to take corrective action. This permits close performance tracking and prevents problems from stalling in distant operating units.

One passenger elevator company used information technology to replace its decentralized service system with a centralized one in which trouble calls bypassed field service offices. Since service contracts are highly profitable in the elevator business and customers' switching costs are low, competition for such contracts is hot. For this reason, providing excellent service and spotting trouble before it gets out of hand were primary corporate goals.

Under the old system, branches fielded customer calls. But the monthly reports they sent to headquarters only summarized their activity. Moreover, important complaints often did not reach top management because the write-ups had to filter through four reporting levels. In fact, company executives suspected that some troubled branches regularly underreported their dirty linen.

The new system pumps out weekly service reports from a massive, centralized data base, helping management zero in on trouble spots. For instance, when the first service accounts rolled in, top executives discovered that certain elevators had been breaking down between 18 and 30 times each quarter. The problem had existed for years but had been buried in files at field offices.

Whether such difficulties stem from the inattention of service personnel or product design weaknesses, managers can now respond with quick action. Further analysis of such problems might lead executives to adjust staff levels or retrain service representatives, or if it's a design issue, to send the product back to engineering.

The new system improves the quality of each service call. The data base at headquarters contains the history of every elevator the company has installed. Before headquarters dispatches a service rep by beeper to answer a complaint about an elevator, he or she is briefed on its service history. The service person learns whether the elevator is due for any preventive maintenance and saves the extra trip later. Under the old system, the company had to rely on the service rep's memory and often incomplete branch files.

The improved system has increased the company's market share while cutting service costs.

DECENTRALIZING DATA TO TARGET SUPERMARKET INVENTORY

In transmitting important data from headquarters to the work force, progressive control systems give people the information they need to do their jobs right and, when tied to incentive programs, provide the motivation to do so. Whether funneling new price information to the PC in a salesperson's briefcase or monitoring customer buying patterns in retail outlets, companies can use IT to tighten corporate control.

A big supermarket company, like many others, has applied the speed and flexibility of the new technology to its decentralized inventory monitoring system. The old setup demanded that employees count stock, then translate the numbers into buying and merchandising plans. If sales of an item surged, store managers often learned about it too late. Furthermore, because suppliers had the only up-to-date facts on what was selling where, they acted as consultants and sometimes prodded stores to overstock slow-moving products. This consulting relationship also gave suppliers more bargaining power in price setting.

With the new system, scanners at the checkout counters log every item that leaves the store. The scanners post inventory records instantly and far more accurately than earlier methods. As a result, store managers have been able to lower inventory levels, boost turnover, and match product mixes to consumers' changing tastes. Managers can offer special promotions or merchandise items in a timely way. Moreover, because they possess the best information, they have more bargaining power over suppliers.

Redesign, Not Just Repair

Traditional control systems often fall short of serving their intended purposes. Failure can usually be laid to one of three reasons: people don't understand corporate goals, they understand them but lack the resources to meet them, or they simply are not motivated to fulfill them.

Sometimes people don't know what is expected because the corporate plan has changed but dissemination of that message is lagging. For instance, a cash-flow crisis may cause the vice president of finance to cut budgets. In a huge conglomerate that relies on old technology, management can take weeks to rework budgets and get new spending guidelines out to operating units. In the meantime, large amounts of cash may have already drained away.

Even after a message makes the long trip from headquarters to dispersed units, the work force may lack the information to act on it. Recall that the insurance company had directed salespeople to manage each customer's entire portfolio; had it not given them customer-oriented data files, however, salespeople would not have had the wherewithal to meet that company goal. And if performance is not measured accurately or promptly, people may lose motivation or retain bad work habits. A sales rep whose bonus is tallied only once a year has no way of knowing where she stands six months into the new year. She may not realize until too late that her techniques are off the mark.

New control systems arm managers with the tools to solve existing problems, but more important, they enable them to step back and rethink what they want a control system to do. Here are some of the new options.

MEANINGFUL BUDGETS

Because budgets identify individual and unit tasks in detail, managers use them to tell people what's expected of them, and when individuals help to develop them, budgets bind those individuals to organizational goals. Each blank in a budget form forces a question into a manager's mind. But with the old technology, the sheer time required to fill in the blanks prevented managers from trying out a number of answers and looking down the road to see the implications of each.

New spreadsheet technology not only speeds the budgeting process by allowing managers to plug in numbers faster but also improves the quality of those budgets by letting managers step through a wide range of "what if" scenarios and compare the outcomes. If a business is trying to project revenue, say, it can run through several iterations based on possible changes in the market.

The first run-through could assume a regulatory change that bolsters the sales of one product; in another, the absence of the new law causes sales to remain flat. By using computer models to test various assumptions, managers can think more carefully about plans and expenditures associated with them, and they follow these ideas through to their logical conclusions. In this way, the technology drives management to better anticipate and prepare for future contingencies. Also, since individual unit budgets can be almost immediately consolidated into overall corporate financial plans, the process helps companies to coordinate diverse activities.

In addition, the new technology lets managers continuously update budgets based on actual performance. Organizations are no longer wed to documents that are immediately out-of-date. They can quickly change plans in midstream based on performance data. For instance, a telecommunications network can quickly notify manufacturing to beef up inventory as actual sales exceed the forecast. Similarly, the effect of cost overruns on end-of-month profits can be projected as soon as they occur.

Information technology turns the budget into a meaningful set of instructions that optimizes the company's performance under changing conditions. One controller of a large U.S. corporation claims that quickly consolidated on-line spreadsheets for each department and business unit have improved tenfold his company's ability to coordinate action under various alternatives. Moreover, he needs less staff to meet budget deadlines.

ADAPTATIONS TO CHANGE

More powerful data architectures help companies adapt to regulatory or other environmental changes. When the 1986 tax law shifted the game rules for insurance companies, one competitor quickly capitalized on the change. Within weeks of the law's passage, the company launched a campaign to educate its agents and customers about the statute's ramifications. While enterprises whose customer files were policy-oriented scrambled to deliver a coherent message to their clients, this company's computer system produced thousands of individually tailored reports explaining in a few pages how the new rules would affect policyholders.

The point of the program was to persuade customers to pay back loans against their whole-life policies, since loan interest is no longer tax deductible and the cash-value buildup on a policy receives favorable tax treatment. (Customers, of course, were in the habit of borrowing against the cash value of their policies at a low rate, deducting the interest on those loans, and pouring the money into high-yield Treasury bills. The net effect was a huge drain on company coffers.) This innovative company is succeeding in convincing customers to repay millions of dollars on their loans and is at the same time generating massive new sales of single-premium life insurance, which is both liquid and nontaxable under the new law. The ability to respond to environmental change is paying a handsome dividend.

SOLUTIONS FOR PRODUCTION

The increased power and versatility of new control systems help managers identify trouble spots in their administrative, field, or factory operations. One of the widest uses of IT is in production facilities, where monitoring systems track errors per hour, flag equipment downtime, measure machine speeds, and assess worker productivity—allowing managers to remedy production problems before they become disasters. Conventional systems force managers to rely on someone spotting the variation in a machine's production, or to wait until a piece of equipment breaks completely. But the modern systems can detect even the slightest deviation in human or machine performance. Early detection allows early correction, thereby improving the economics of manufacturing.

Examples of this application abound. One cigarette manufacturer has installed an automated system that regularly pulls cigarettes off the line and puts them through 20 tests, noting the smallest inconsistency in quality. Paper companies use sophisticated monitoring devices to detect variations in paper thickness or color that are invisible to the human eye. The precision with which these machines detect slight flaws means that workers can quickly adjust equipment—or their own tasks—as needed.

FACTS TO MAKE THE SALE

Information technology can help management align control and sales-incentive measures with the realities of the market. Failure to use that ability can have embarrassing results. One prominent retail bank recently sent salespeople to call on upscale clients with the intention of selling new financial products. Unfortunately, the bank lacked data on each customer's total holdings. When through ignorance of these holdings, salespeople pushed products that were wildly inappropriate for the clients, their image as financial counselors was quickly undermined. The bank should have made the investment in its control systems first. The outmoded systems had thwarted efforts to better serve customer needs, and ultimately the bank had to cancel its well-conceived but poorly executed campaign.

Some companies have used IT to spread their sales tentacles ever closer to the customer without relinquishing coordination and control at the top. Banks and travel agencies, for instance, use computer systems to execute transactions at remote sites and instantly post them to centralized files. Automatic teller machines and travel agent terminals have allowed these innovative companies to shift the point of purchase nearer customers while retaining timely records that top management can easily access.

Consider the case of a trust officer who wants to court the beneficiaries of a trust so that when the trust initiator dies, the money stays at the bank. In a large bank that handles 10,000 trusts, information about the beneficiaries, many of whom are children, is likely to be buried in computer files or in paper archives. With the right information and an automated tickler system, the bank officer can send credit applications to them as they come of age, thereby founding early relationships with the inheritors. Opportunities to reshape customer relations take many forms.

TRACKING INVENTORY AND SALES

New inventory tracking systems let companies continuously trace an order, update account balances, monitor inventory, and alert manufacturing and suppliers to upcoming requirements. Companies have applied such systems to control in a variety of ways. One electric sign company installed a sophisticated production control system that pipes orders directly to manufacturing. Under the old arrangement, orders took a week longer to trickle down to the factory floor. The production manager never knew what was in the pipeline, so he could never prepare the materials and staff ahead of time. Production bottlenecks and huge inventories were a way of life. The new system drives down inventory costs by eliminating the need to overstock expensive materials, and it ensures that capacity is better used throughout the 22-step manufacturing process.

Some systems amplify the benefits of low inventory without shortages by linking the order-entry function to suppliers. An automobile manufacturer has electronic ties to its suppliers, which now receive up-to-the-minute information from the company's order-entry system. The supplier can then ensure that necessary materials arrive on time. The system has proved so successful that the manufacturer has reduced its investment in inventory and warehouses—and the saving more than offsets the system's cost.

An inventory monitoring system can also help managers get the product to the market where it is selling best. To be most useful, the procedure must be able to capture more information and manipulate it quickly. One variety-store chain bought a scanner-based inventory system for its outlets. The old system had used a punch card at the end of each stack of 12 products to signal the need to reorder. But while items were trickling out of stores, corporate management had no idea what was selling in which areas, or how quickly.

Today a wand at the checkout counter reads the bar code off each item sold, and headquarters polls every store across the country every night for inventory data. In this way, management can assess customer trends on a daily basis. An item that turns quickly in 32 upscale locations might stall in inner-city stores, and vice versa. The new system allows managers to tailor product mix to clientele and helps identify emerging market niches that demand new product designs.

Automated order entry and inventory tracking can help companies vary their sales and pricing strategies between regions or customer type and keep their sales reps informed of price changes. One national food company with its own truck fleet faced a tough problem: each sales region required its own pricing strategy, and each store its own product mix. What's more, the company wanted to base its strategy for each store on a combination of the items sold and the number of stale items left over from the previous day. Clearly, drivers couldn't sift through customer records every night or new prices from headquarters every morning and still be expected to make their rounds.

The company installed microcomputers in more than 1,000 delivery trucks. Every morning, each driver's PC receives from a headquarters mainframe computer the subregion's prices and recommended stock mix. Every night, the company receives from each driver what items were delivered and which stale items were removed from the shelves.

EFFECTIVE INCENTIVE SYSTEMS

Technology can help managers create more effective incentive systems—from corporate profit-sharing plans that eliminate internal rivalries to schemes that automatically pay factory workers bonuses for meeting deadlines.

A simple form of automated incentive system in one company continuously tallies sales commissions and allows salespeople to access their records. A salesperson's review of how far he is from meeting his quota may encourage him to push just a little harder to make it over the edge. One who finds her bonus surprisingly low may be shocked into picking up the pace.

Additionally, IT-based measurement systems can identify and track the contribution of a working unit that may otherwise go unrecognized. The automotive industry has found this capability attractive. The first dealer a customer visits usually invests a lot of time explaining the various models and demonstrating their features. But the customer may buy the car from a different dealer, who has done far less work but offers a slightly lower price. Knowing this pattern, the first dealer may do a hasty job of educating the customer and quickly try to close the deal. While automakers may not like this situation, the industry's commission structure, which measures only sales, supports it. One manufacturer is now considering a customer tracking system that would modestly reward a salesperson who makes an initial presentation even though another dealer makes the sale.

Some organizations use innovative systems to influence customers to buy more. With sophisticated on-line analysis, a company can base a customer's discounts on total volume rather than on each order. One contact lens company offers consignment inventory to dealers that can turn it over 13 times a year. Since opticians can fill 65% of their orders from that inventory and get paid on the spot, they're spurred to sell heavily from that manufacturer's line. Moreover, fast information tells the company and the opticians whether the stores are on schedule to meet their turnover quotas. This clever system boosted the lens company's market share.

Before You Go

Because control systems affect all areas of the corporation, changes in them inevitably affect strategy and organizational structure. For this reason, managers should think long and hard about how they want to apply IT to the control function, and they should press themselves to imagine all the implications.

Technology is organizationally neutral. It does not favor centralization over decentralization. It simply offers top managers choices they have not had before. For the elevator manufacturer, technology shifted ownership of repair records from branch offices to corporate headquarters. As a result, local managers lost some autonomy. On the other hand, the supermarket's automated control system gave store managers more information, which helped them make better decisions at the store level.

There is danger in failing to make such choices consciously, as there is in overlooking how any change will affect reporting relationships. Taking away or adding decision-making power may mean that a different type of manager is needed in some posts. And the blurring of operational and managerial control may also require restructuring and redefinition of managers' roles.

There is danger, too, in failing to consider all the strategic advantages to be gained from the creative use of information. One competitor in the elevator industry copied the other's move to centralize service records. But the copycat company went a step further: it identified elevators that chronically failed, then approached the clients with proposals to rebuild those units. The innovator now has, at least temporarily, a whole new market to itself.

Expensive data storage, sluggish retrieval, and complex systems that overwhelm their would-be users are all relics of the past. The technology now exists to transform the internal workings of the organization. Today is a good time to step back and ponder whether decentralized units really adhere to company goals and whether incentive systems are on the mark. Can technology offer new solutions to these issues? Are plans and budgets made quickly and are they well communicated? Are decisions made in the right place? And if something changes, inside or outside the company, as it invariably will, can the control system adapt to the new requirements?

3
Automation to Boost Sales and Marketing

Rowland T. Moriarty and Gordon S. Swartz

In the rush to automate, the marketing and sales function is the next frontier. As everybody knows, over the past decade information systems have been making great inroads in engineering and manufacturing. Automation has cut direct labor to a small fraction of production costs—an average of 8% to 12% in manufacturing companies. Therefore, wringing yet more cost reductions from production labor is increasingly difficult. In such technically advanced industries as computers, semiconductors, airframes, metalworking, and autos, incremental investments are now garnering diminishing returns.

On the other hand, investments in marketing and sales automation systems hold tremendous potential for productivity improvements. Marketing and sales costs average 15% to 35% of total corporate costs (not just production costs). So a focus on marketing and sales provides a welcome lever for boosting productivity. Moreover, the importance of marketing and sales services is growing. According to the U.S. trade representative and the National Association of Accountants, manufacturers' service activities account for 75% to 85% of all value added.[1] This means that the price a product can command is less a reflection of raw materials and labor than of marketing-related services like selecting appropriate product

Authors' note: We thank Professor Thomas V. Bonoma of the Harvard Business School and Charles A. Khuen, president of Adelie Corporation, for helpful comments on early drafts of this article.

features, determining the product mix, and ensuring product availability and delivery.

In cases we have reviewed, sales increases arising from advanced marketing and sales information technology have ranged from 10% to more than 30%, and investment returns have often exceeded 100%. These returns may sound like the proverbial free lunch, but they are real.

Because of the complexity of their marketing organizations, large companies are good prospects for what we call marketing and sales productivity (MSP) systems. Tangles of national account management, direct sales, telemarketing, direct mail, literature fulfillment, advertising, customer service, dealers, and distributors all offer opportunities for efficiency improvements. But even small companies that adopt MSP systems can expect impressive results.

Marketing automation investments by a $7 billion electronics manufacturer and an $8 million custom printing company each produced a first-year return of more than 100%. The electronics concern installed a sales support system for more than 500 salespeople. Sales rose 33%, sales force productivity rose 31%, and sales force attrition dropped 40%. The reduced attrition alone produced savings in recruiting and training costs that paid for the company's $2.5 million investment in less than 12 months. At the custom printer, an $80,000 investment in a minicomputer and telemarketing software returned a 25% increase in sales and attained payback in less than 6 months.

Increasing marketing productivity even a small amount can have a great impact on the bottom line. MSP systems have a double punch because they can reduce fixed costs and variable costs. Lower fixed costs mean lower breakeven points. So a given percentage increase in sales produces a correspondingly larger increase in operating profits. (See Exhibit I). Meanwhile, lower variable costs mean that every sale contributes more to the bottom line. Indeed, because lower variable costs make the slope of the new contribution curve steeper, the absolute size of the financial advantage continues to grow as sales rise.

Despite the proven worth of this technology, few companies have automated any part of their marketing and sales functions. Even fewer appear to understand the significant strategic benefits that can accrue from marketing and sales automation; most early adopters have automated as a matter of faith rather than as part of a strategy for gaining competitive advantage. A better approach be-

Exhibit I.

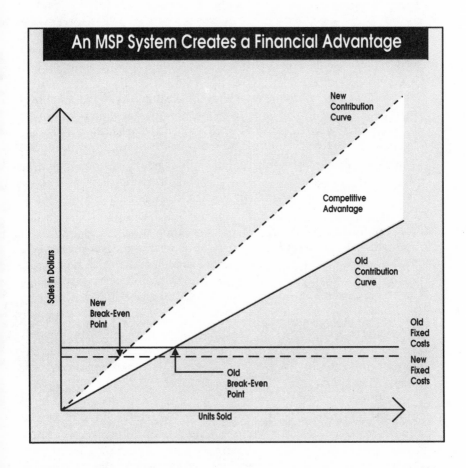

gins with an understanding of what marketing and sales automation can do, how it works, and how it can be implemented.

What the Systems Do

Distinct from general office automation systems, MSP networks are of course specific to marketing and sales. They support more intense product or service differentiation, improved customer service, reduced operating costs, and more streamlined operations.

Here are some MSP systems and the tasks for which they are customarily used.

Salesperson productivity tools—Planning and reporting of sales calls, reporting of expenses, entering orders, checking inventory and order status, managing distributors, tracking leads, and managing accounts.

Direct mail and fulfillment—Merging, cleaning, and maintaining mailing lists; subsetting lists (or markets); tracking and forwarding leads; customizing letters, envelopes, and labels; generating "picking lists" for literature packages; and managing literature inventory.

Telemarketing—Merging, cleaning, and maintaining calling lists; subsetting lists (or markets); tracking and forwarding leads; ranking prospects; and prompting scripts (sales, customer service, and support).

Sales and marketing management—Providing automated sales management reports (sales forecasts, sales activity, forecasts versus actuals, and so on); designing and managing sales territories; and analyzing marketing and sales programs by such criteria as market, territory, product, customer type, price, and channel.

MSP systems can automate the work of a single salesperson, a single marketing activity like direct mail, or a company's entire marketing and sales operation. MSP systems also cut across every type of information technology from single-user PCs to networks of PCs, minicomputers, and mainframes serving thousands of users.

A simple system meets the needs of one fast-growing $25 million producer of data communications equipment that sells its products through 65 distributors. To cut down on paperwork in handling sales leads, the company adopted a PC-based MSP system. (See Exhibit II showing its operation.) Compare this with the networks supporting the more than 5,000 direct salespeople of a major office automation vendor. (See Exhibit III showing its operation.) This vendor's system combines direct selling, distributor relationships, telemarketing, and direct mail to: generate, qualify, rank-order, distribute, and track sales leads; fill prospects' requests for product and price information; update customer and prospect files; provide sales and technical product support by telephone; and automate order entry and sales reporting.

While the scales of these two networks are obviously vastly different, both of them collect, organize, and update information

Exhibit II.

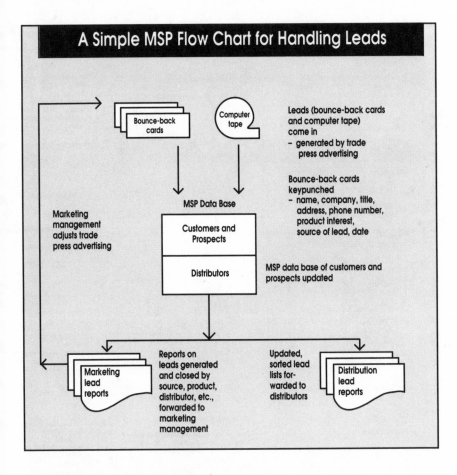

A Simple MSP Flow Chart for Handling Leads

Bounce-back cards

Computer tape

Leads (bounce-back cards and computer tape) come in
- generated by trade press advertising

Bounce-back cards keypunched
- name, company, title, address, phone number, product interest, source of lead, date

MSP Data Base

Customers and Prospects

Distributors

Marketing management adjusts trade press advertising

MSP data base of customers and prospects updated

Marketing lead reports

Reports on leads generated and closed by source, product, distributor, etc., forwarded to marketing management

Updated, sorted lead lists forwarded to distributors

Distribution lead reports

about every lead generated, every sales task performed, and every customer or prospect closed or terminated. What is less obvious, but no less important, is the basis both systems provide for improving marketing and sales executives' decision making.

Most MSP data bases contain essential information on customers, prospects, products, marketing programs, and marketing channels. Some systems supplement the essentials with industry data (growth rates, entries, exits, and regulatory trends) and data on competitors (products, pricing, sales trends, and market shares). For most businesses, the information incorporates a subtle but important shift from other data bases. Rather than focusing on products

Exhibit III.

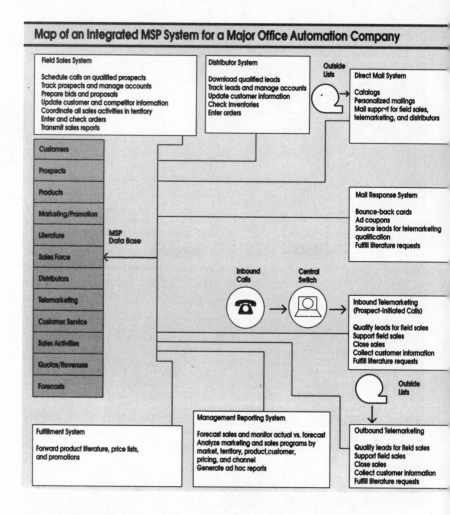

Map of an Integrated MSP System for a Major Office Automation Company

Field Sales System

Schedule calls on qualified prospects
Track prospects and manage accounts
Prepare bids and proposals
Update customer and competitor information
Coordinate all sales activities in territory
Enter and check orders
Transmit sales reports

Distributor System

Download qualified leads
Track leads and manage accounts
Update customer information
Check inventories
Enter orders

Outside Lists

Direct Mail System

Catalogs
Personalized mailings
Mail support for field sales, telemarketing, and distributors

Customers
Prospects
Products
Marketing/Promotion
Literature
Sales Force
Distributors
Telemarketing
Customer Service
Sales Activities
Quotas/Revenues
Forecasts

MSP Data Base

Mail Response System

Bounce-back cards
Ad coupons
Source leads for telemarketing qualification
Fulfill literature requests

Inbound Calls   Central Switch

Inbound Telemarketing
(Prospect-Initiated Calls)

Qualify leads for field sales
Support field sales
Close sales
Collect customer information
Fulfill literature requests

Outside Lists

Fulfillment System

Forward product literature, price lists, and promotions

Management Reporting System

Forecast sales and monitor actual vs. forecast
Analyze marketing and sales programs by market, territory, product, customer, pricing, and channel
Generate ad hoc reports

Outbound Telemarketing

Qualify leads for field sales
Support field sales
Close sales
Collect customer information
Fulfill literature requests

(What was the cost to produce each unit? How many units were made, sold, and shipped?), the MSP data base is customer driven.

Whenever marketing or sales activities are performed, the data base captures information that answers questions about customers and their needs. Who were the prospects? What were their interests? How were these interests generated? Which sales or marketing personnel performed which tasks? When were the tasks performed? Which follow-up tasks are required and when? Did any sales result? Gradually the data base becomes a rich source of marketing and sales information, enabling management to track marketing activities and measure the results of marketing programs.

How They Aid Productivity

MSP systems improve productivity in two ways. First, automation of selling and direct marketing support tasks boosts the efficiency of the sales and marketing staff. Second, automating the collection and analysis of marketing information improves the timeliness and quality of marketing and sales executives' decision making.

These networks make direct sales and direct marketing more efficient by automating highly repetitive support tasks, like answering requests for product literature and writing letters, and by reducing the time salespeople spend on nonselling tasks, like scheduling sales calls, compiling sales reports, generating proposals and bids, and entering orders. In 1985, Xerox installed an internally developed MSP system in its southern region. Xerox credits the system with a 10% to 20% gain in sales force productivity and with trimming $3 million off the company's 1987 marketing support and overhead budget. By automating sales administration and support tasks, Xerox has given its salespeople more time to sell.[2]

MSP systems for direct marketing also hone the efficiency of customer contacts. For example, a system for the telemarketing function can schedule and dial calls based on the prospect's priority, prompt the telemarketer with a sales script, and automatically update customer files. At Aratex Services, a $500 million uniform supply company based in Encino, California, telemarketers using the company's old manual system each made 35 to 40 calls per day and about one sale per month. Working with an automated system, each telemarketer now makes 50 or 60 calls daily and lands three or four sales per month.[3]

Automated networks also elevate the impact of each sales communication. Access to the central data base gives salespeople and direct marketers information to improve the quality of the contact, whether it is by mail, by telephone, or in person. A large financial services concern uses a telemarketing system to handle account inquiries. While responding to a customer's request or query, the telemarketer is prompted by the system to update the customer's profile information and to cross-sell other financial products.

At a division of Vanity Fair that makes women's and children's apparel, salespeople use laptop PCs to access the corporate data base for up-to-date inventory and order status information on 2,000 stockkeeping units. This step has trimmed the company's order cycle from more than two weeks to just three days. It also has made ordering more accurate, resulting in greater customer satisfaction, reduced order cancellations, and a 10% increase in sales.

In companies with many channels, MSP systems upgrade efficiency by using the central data base to track and coordinate all marketing activity. Without this coordination, independent marketing groups often unwittingly pursue conflicting goals. At one multibillion-dollar office automation company, a direct salesperson had just nailed down a big order by giving a key account the "maximum" price discount. Before the deal was signed, however, the telemarketing group reached this customer and undercut the salesperson's price by 10%. Aside from the damage to its reputation, this vendor lost much of its expected margin on the sale.

This company is now installing an MSP system that will collect and organize information on all marketing programs and activities, including: (1) all customer contacts, whether by mail, phone, direct salesperson, or national account manager; (2) the status of all sales efforts; (3) the origins of all leads; (4) all leads that are being qualified internally and by whom, and all leads that have been forwarded to distributors; (5) all customers who decided to buy; (6) what and when they purchased; and (7) any incentives or promotions that helped close the deal. Coordination of information through this system is expected to prevent further embarrassments.

A Management Tool

Creation of an MSP data base is an investment in astute management. The data base chronicles every one of a company's marketing and sales activities, from advertising that generates leads to direct mail and telephone qualification of the leads to closing the first sale—all the way through the life of each account. It enables marketing and sales management to relate marketing actions with marketplace results.

At the $25 million data communications company whose lead-handling system we diagrammed, marketing managers use this system to evaluate media placements on the basis of sales closed. Before this procedure was in place, the company had no way to link information on leads to sales and evaluated media placements solely on the number of leads generated, not closed.

MSP systems also reduce marketing inertia because they streamline the implementation of marketing programs. For example, after designing an in-house system to organize and manage its customer/prospect files, one $2.5 million industrial manufacturer let 70 manufacturer's agents go and replaced them with in-house direct mail and telemarketing functions. The results? The company raised its accounts by 50% and cut marketing costs from 18% of sales to 13%.

Systems for sales force automation also drive the rapid implementation of less drastic changes in marketing programs. By using telecommunications software and laptop PCs, Du Pont's Remington Arms division has trimmed the time requirement for a national rollout of pricing and promotional programs from two weeks to less than two days.

As marketing managers become accustomed to these systems, they find new uses for them, like analyzing and modeling the buying behavior of prospects and customers. The data base at Excelan, a $39 million marketer of circuit boards and software in San Jose, California, was essential in identifying a shift in customers' buying behavior from a very technical product focus to an office automation orientation. This discovery has influenced the marketing and sales managers' decisions about hiring and training employees as well as about selecting and developing new target markets.

Account histories also improve management's ability to devise and implement account management policies based on profits. By linking orders, services delivered, and prices paid with the actual costs of lead generation, preselling, closing, distribution, and postsale support, MSP systems furnish the tools for analyzing and adjusting the marketing mix. Grede Foundries, a Milwaukee producer of castings for original equipment manufacturers, has used the MSP system to develop a "perceived quality index" that yields a more complete and more accurate measure of customers' reactions than simply tracking returned goods. The system also provides pricing support. By tracking quoted prices and final selling prices, the system gives management a better idea of the price that will win a particular job.[4]

Moreover, automated networks coordinate and direct sales resources—including salespeople, distributors and agents, direct mailers, telemarketers, and manufacturers' representatives—toward the highest priority prospects and customers. Hewlett-Packard's Qualified Lead Tracking System (QUILTS) electronically transmits inquiries to a telemarketing center, which qualifies and ranks them and electronically returns them to H-P headquarters. The company has trimmed the turnaround time for leads from as much as 14 weeks to as little as 48 hours. "Hot" leads are handled even faster; they are telephoned to the field sales force from the telemarketing center.[5] Similarly, field salespeople in Chevron Chemical's fertilizer division in San Francisco use laptop PCs to access rank-ordered prospect lists in the company's mainframe. At any time, the salespeople have access to leads that are only 24 hours old. Before automation, new prospect lists were printed at headquarters and mailed to the field reps, which took one to two weeks.

Finally, the MSP data base is a management tool for making better use of marketing resources—that is, ensuring that they are employed to further corporate goals rather than the goals of individual marketing or sales groups. While this may sound like something management does without effort, our research shows that optimizing marketing resources is much more easily said than done. In several companies we've looked at, salespeople routinely discard hundreds or even thousands of sales leads, making little or no effort to evaluate or review them. In essence, they are dissipating the resources that generated these leads—budgets for advertising, trade shows, public relations, and other communications media.

In their defense, the salespeople complain that pursuing raw leads is a waste of time. And they are generally right. In one of these companies, salespeople who followed up the raw leads averaged only one or two sales per month, while those who followed their "instincts" averaged more than three. The cost of pursuing the raw leads was at least one lost sale per salesperson per month. To the salespeople, ignoring the leads was common sense. On the other hand, the advertising group, which was evaluated on the number of leads generated, was increasing its budgets to generate more and more leads. One company has solved this problem by implementing an MSP system that will use telemarketing to qualify leads before sending them to the salespeople. The system will also close the loop, allowing management to evaluate both the company's advertising placements and its sales efforts on the basis of their contributions to revenues and earnings.

Efficiencies gained through task automation and improved marketing management are interdependent and reinforcing. Task automation drives the collection of more complete customer and marketplace information, and more informed decision making targets marketing and sales activities where they are most effective. In this way, marketers get a bigger payoff from low-cost, low-impact selling methods, like direct mail and catalogs, as data bases customize the timing and content of mass-marketing campaigns. At the same time, high-cost, high-impact selling methods, like personal selling and national account management, become more efficient as MSP systems perform routine sales support tasks, reduce nonselling time, and synchronize the use of these resources.

When you combine low-cost, low-impact methods with high-cost, high-impact approaches to gain just the right amount of stimulus at just the right time, you can obtain hefty impact at minimum cost. Hewlett-Packard, for one, has taken advantage of this synergy and has discovered the savings made possible by orchestrating direct mail, telemarketing, and personal selling.

How to Get from Here to There

The cases we have reviewed show that companies implementing MSP systems encounter many of the same barriers they would confront adopting any new technology. From our observation, the process can be streamlined by following six guiding principles.

1. CLARIFY THE SCALE OF THE PROJECT AS WELL AS POTENTIAL ADDITIONS. An audit of the marketing and sales tasks will yield these categories: those that must be automated now, those that will or may be automated later, and those that will not be automated. This simple exercise will identify marketing and sales activities that must be coordinated and focus the automation effort on getting measurable results without sacrificing flexibility.

It is important to view the project not from the perspective of the marketing groups but from a corporate perspective. With a corporate view, the company can build a "battleship"—a system that takes advantage of information-sharing and task-coordination synergies. Without this strategic perspective, independent marketing groups are more likely to invest in a number of incompatible and wasteful "rowboats." And even a rowboat can cause problems. At a big high-tech manufacturer, eight salespeople had their own PC-based sales force automation system installed. By raising issues of compatibility, data entry, and "file structure definitions," they delayed the start-up of a companywide, 300-salesperson MSP system for more than a year.

2. CONCENTRATE ON TASKS THAT CAN ADD VALUE FOR THE CUSTOMER. As in other corporate activities, marketers can get competitive advantage in two ways: by lowering costs and by enhancing the differentiation of the product or service offering. At the custom printer we referred to, streamlined job-costing and order-entry processes enable customers to price and place orders with one phone call. The "real-time" order-entry and order-tracking capabilities of the Vanity Fair unit's salespeople have upgraded its customer service. In both cases, customers benefit from better service, and sellers benefit from lower costs.

Other companies add value by using automation to improve the exchange of information during sales calls. The 22 salespeople in Hercules's Fragrance and Food Ingredient Group use their laptop PCs and a computer program called Flavor Briefs to consult with prospects on applications. Otherwise, Hercules salespeople would be unable to provide such detailed advice on their product line's many applications. The system saves the customer and the salesperson time and also furnishes a valuable service.

3. IN THE BUDGET PROCESS, ACCOUNT FOR HIDDEN COSTS AND INTANGIBLE BENEFITS. Budgeting for an MSP system entails overcoming three principal obstacles: high perceived financial risk, poorly understood benefits, and biased capital budgeting systems.

First, automating marketing and sales is costly. A typical hardware and software outlay per salesperson ranges from $4,000 to $7,000—so automating the tasks of 100 field salespeople can cost between $400,000 and $700,000. In addition, if the MSP system must communicate with other corporate information systems, it is likely to require the development of specialized minicomputer, mainframe, or communications networking software.

Department-level telemarketing or direct mail systems range in price from $30,000 to more than $100,000. Sales or marketing management software may up the price another $30,000 to $100,000. Of course, the cost of tying all these pieces together depends on how many pieces there are, where they are located, and how they communicate. It would not be unusual for a company with 500 salespeople as well as telemarketing, fulfillment, and direct mail operations to spend between $3 million and $5 million on integrated MSP hardware and software.

But the budget process must anticipate and account for hidden costs too. In a number of cases we studied, in-house information was so scattered and communications equipment so incompatible that simply preparing a customer list required a major effort. Other hidden costs include system customization, expert consulting, and end-user training. Depending on the circumstances, these services can double or even triple the overall cost.

Because malfunctioning of an automated marketing system can threaten a business's revenue stream, it's advisable to budget for the cost of two systems—automated and manual—until the network has proved out. Naturally, all these expenses ratchet up the perceived financial risk of MSP automation.

On the other side of the equation, estimating the full financial benefit of an MSP system is extremely difficult. Tangible productivity gains, like increases in selling time and cost reductions on telephone campaigns, can be gauged fairly accurately. But intangible productivity gains, like better marketing decision making, more responsive customer service, and deeper understanding of customers, are much more difficult to track.

Still, it would be a mistake to ignore them, especially since capital budgeting processes are often biased against intangible productivity investments. Furthermore, few marketing managers and even fewer sales managers know much about their companies' capital budgeting processes—especially when huge investments in information technology are at stake. Senior executives have to take care that the process remains flexible enough to give MSP automation a reasonable evaluation.

An MSP system is a strategic investment for the whole corporation. But unlike other assets that are consumed over time, the more it is used, the more valuable it becomes. So it should be viewed as a long-term asset, not as the expense of a functional group. And, needless to say, senior management must match the scale of the company's investment to the scale of the project. Otherwise, fragmented marketing budgets will foster fragmented automation. The result, as noted above, may be many MSP rowboats with little or no coordination or compatibility.

4. MAKE ANY TESTS REALISTIC. Because launching a full-scale network can be tremendously risky, most companies hedge their bets first by piloting automation on small portions of their marketing operations. A single function, like telemarketing or personal selling, is usually the test site. If this pilot is successful, the company adds more functions.

This ramp-up strategy, however, has serious drawbacks. It permits no insight into the complexity of coordinating multiple marketing and sales activities. Though single-function solutions may yield gratifying returns, evidence of their true worth may also stay hidden until they are combined into a system that demonstrates synergy. Consequently, estimates of financial returns based on single-function pilots may be negatively biased.

Finally, critical performance limitations may remain hidden unless the complexity and scale of the test parallel the system's actual use. One big manufacturer's telemarketing pilot ran flawlessly, providing the telemarketers with a steady stream of calls and instant access to customer profiles and scripts. But eventual integration of telemarketing with other MSP networks seriously degraded the performance of the overall system. Every time the telemarketers asked for new information during a call, they were confronted by blank computer screens for more than 40 seconds. As the business manager put it, "That's a long time to talk about baseball."

A company with a multichannel, multimethod marketing system is better off with a pilot plan that automates a multifunctional subset of the marketing organization. In this type of pilot, an integrated system, encompassing all marketing and sales functions, is installed for a single division, region, product line, or customer group. This experience is likely to be more realistic than the single-function approach.

5. PINPOINT THE ROLES AND RESPONSIBILITIES OF THOSE SELECTING, DESIGNING, AND OPERATING THE SYSTEM. Even standard

MSP systems, though they may be touted as off-the-shelf products, require extensive customization. This necessity complicates the selection or design process in a number of ways.

The process requires expertise in technology (computers, data communications, and software) as well as in marketing and sales.

Naturally, a company's existing MIS systems are likely to constrain the choice (or development) of an MSP system.

Marketing professionals and MIS professionals rarely speak a common language, and they often approach marketing automation projects with different perspectives. While marketing thinks about functionality (e.g., Will the system help perform marketing and sales tasks?), MIS people often focus on technical considerations (e.g., Will the system interact with other corporate information systems? Who is responsible for ensuring the integrity of corporate data bases?).

It's senior management's job to make sure that the MIS and marketing professionals talk to each other and work together. It's not easy. An MIS group may automate its conception of marketing and sales only to discover later that the automated system does not actually work. Everybody knows of cases in which the MIS department loads the sales force down with reams of report forms to complete and return to headquarters. Of course, much of the requested information is irrelevant from the salespeople's standpoint, and the report forms end up in the same round file as the old lead cards.

During the long, complex process of designing and implementing a major MSP system, responsibilities sometimes become diffuse and project accountability gets blurred. In one case we know of, poorly defined responsibilities for MIS and marketing have caused big headaches. Bickering over cost allocations and data-base controls has made the company's $1 million MSP system useless. The MIS group will not allow marketing to access the corporation's data bases. But the marketing group's computer budget is too low to keep the marketing data base up-to-date. (Not surprisingly, headquarters viewed the entire MSP development process as a marketing expense instead of a corporate investment.)

6. MODIFY THE TECHNOLOGY AND THE ORGANIZATION TO SUPPORT THE SYSTEM. As in every instance in which management implements new technology, it must pay close attention to the attitudes of people in the organization. In successful MSP implementations that we have seen, both the organization and the MSP system have gone through an interactive process of change—altering the technology to fit the marketing and sales environment, then altering the environment to fit the technology.

To be useful, for example, the MSP data base obviously must contain accurate, up-to-date information. Because obtaining this information requires salespeople to use the system and to support the information collection process, they have to become adept at using the new technology. Problems can result, however, if the end-users lack computer skills or if they are uninterested in using the system.

Training can overcome skill problems (if enough money is budgeted and enough time set aside), but lack of interest is harder to deal with. Experience suggests that the best way to sell the sales staff on the network is to demonstrate that it can give every user something back. That is, by helping salespeople or telemarketers work more productively, MSP systems can boost not only the company's sales but also *their* sales and *their* compensation.

For many companies, postponement of automation of the marketing function may seem to be a good way of skirting a difficult decision, but this do-nothing posture condemns the organization to being a marketing laggard. It may also be a costly mistake. Early adopters of MSP systems have gained superior competitive advantage. Compared with their "manual" competitors, they perform selling tasks with greater economy and impact. They know their customers better and can tailor their sales communications to supply just the right amount of sales stimulus at just the right time. Overall, they craft and control their marketing programs more intelligently. In the long run, the competitive barriers they establish may change the nature of marketing in their industries.

In view of this impressive record, some marketers about to embark on automation may embrace unrealistically high expectations. But MSP systems cannot work miracles. They will not offset a poorly conceived or poorly executed marketing strategy. They will not compensate for an inferior sales force, and they will not sell inferior products. Complex MSP systems are difficult to implement, and the associated returns, like any other lasting accomplishment, have to be earned.

Notes

1. James Brian Quinn, Jordan J. Baruch, and Penny Cushman Paquette, "Technology in Services," *Scientific American*, December 1987, p. 50.
2. Thayer C. Taylor, "Xerox: Who Says You Can't Be Big and Fast?" *Sales & Marketing Management*, November 1987, p. 63.
3. Kate Bertrand, "Converting Leads with Computerized Telemarketing," *Business Marketing*, May 1988, p. 58.
4. Louis A. Wallis, *Computers and the Sales Effort* (New York: Conference Board, 1986).
5. Karen Blue, "Closing the Loop: Hewlett-Packard's New Lead Management System," *Business Marketing*, October 1987, p. 74.
6. Dorothy Leonard-Barton and William A. Kraus, "Implementing New Technology," *Harvard Business Review*, November-December 1985, p. 102.

4

New Gold Mines and Minefields in Market Research

Leonard M. Lodish and David J. Reibstein

The secret to a successful marketing career has usually been to have a good understanding of what the customer wants and doesn't want. Without this understanding, it is impossible to devise a suitable advertising, pricing, or product strategy.

How one gets the feel for the market has never been fully determined. Is it something a marketer is born with, or is it learned? How does one come by an ability to empathize with the customer? Whatever the answer, this talent is becoming less important as new technology provides the opportunity to obtain data-based insight into the pulse of the market. With this change in data and analysis comes change in practice and skills. The evolving technologies allow managers to revolutionize the practice of marketing. The usual assumption in buying behavior is that the customer operates as "a black box." But the box is being opened, and competitive pressures will make the new insights hard to ignore.

New Technological Options

Consumer packaged-goods industries, in particular, have benefited from the availability of new data and analysis methods for assessing markets. Two advances in data collection have been especially important: split-cable technology and uniform-product-code (UPC) scanners.

SPLIT-CABLE TECHNOLOGY

Television that allows different advertisements to appear on the same television program within the same geographic area is called split cable. In communities having split-cable systems, two neighbors separately watching NBC at the same time can see two different commercials that a research firm has chosen for their viewing. The firm intercepts the network feed and inserts certain commercials in the transmission to selected households.

In split-cable systems, household purchases (which brands at what prices) are recorded. Comparing the purchase behavior of households receiving one ad with that of households receiving another allows researchers to assess the more effective effort. By eliminating the impact of extraneous, uncontrollable factors, such a research approach also enables marketing managers to experiment with advertising strategies.

Most advertising field experiments rely on two or more budget levels (determined generally by number of ads shown) or ad copies (themes or executions) in separate test cities. Comparison of the test cities permits attribution of the variations occurring in the test areas to the different advertising implementations.

To find a match of all the characteristics of one community with another is, of course, very difficult. The alternative is to run each experiment in many cities. Aside from driving the costs up, however, each experimental treatment may get different results. This situation can lead to confusion since variations in the results have to be explained, usually by differences in city demographics, competitive environments, and product distribution.

The split-cable approach puts neighbors in different experimental cells, or treatment groups. In a large sample, the experimental cells are indistinguishable except for the ads they get. Consumers shop within the same group of stores, so that the distribution and effect of product displays and promotion on various cells do not vary.

The approach is most commonly used for budgeting decisions. Nestlé and AT&T have tested two budget levels within one community, approximately 100,000 households receiving each experimental ad campaign. Such tests can cost less than $100,000.

Split-cable systems can also be used for copy testing. For example, AT&T had been quite successful with its "Reach Out" campaign but was not content with the amount of long-distance calling of its light users.[1] Through an attitude survey, the company discovered that light users were overestimating the costs of long-distance calls by as much as 50%. In response, AT&T developed its alternative campaign called "Cost of Visit," which emphasized making use of the economy of "offpeak" hours.

To test this campaign as an alternative to the proven Reach Out theme, AT&T chose to conduct a split-cable experiment. Over 15 months, one group of cable TV subscribers received the Reach Out campaign, while the second group in the same community and watching the same television shows saw the Cost of Visit commercials. AT&T obtained records of telephone use from the telephone company's billing system.

The Cost of Visit strategy produced more long-distance calling during experimentation than the Reach Out strategy, especially among light users. The company estimated that the new copy could generate additional revenue of nearly $100 million over a five-year period—at no additional cost to the phone company.

Prior to using such a split-cable system, little was known about how and under what conditions advertising works or about how to test advertising effectiveness. Now, thanks to the advent of split-cable technology, marketers can assess the impact of advertising on a micromarket basis.

UNIFORM-PRODUCT-CODE SCANNERS

These devices read and register the prices of items as they are checked out in retail outlets. The scanners automatically track inventories, reduce clerical errors, speed checkout procedures, and ease price changes. They also automatically store a wealth of marketing information—prices, for instance, which make it easy to determine price elasticity. Scanner memories store information on coupon use so that marketers can quickly measure the consumer response to using coupons across product categories. Information about shelf space, end-of-aisle displays, use of cooperative advertising, and the like can be retained on these scanners and then measured with respect to impact on sales, item movement, and net contribution.

A growing number of small organizations specializes in analyzing scanner data to recommend optimal pricing levels to retailers. Primarily, these organizations examine historical demand at var-

Exhibit I.   *UPC-Aided Optimal Pricing for a Retail Grocer over 16 Weeks*

Retail price	Average weekly sales of boxes of Minute Rice	Unit contribution at $.69 cost	Actual total contribution at $.69 cost	Unit contribution at $.79 cost	Anticipated total contribution at $.79 cost
$ .89	80	$.20	$16.00	$.10	$ 8.00
.99	66	.30	19.80	.20	13.20
1.09	62	.40	24.80	.30	19.60
1.19	50	.50	25.00	.40	20.00
1.29	42	.60	25.20	.50	21.00

ious pricing levels and determine the prices at which retailers can maximize total contribution at retail stores.

One retail grocer, for example, offered Minute Rice at five different prices over 16 weeks. The average demand levels, shown in Exhibit I, ranged from 80 boxes to 42. With current costs of $.69 per box, the store maximized its contribution from this one item by charging $1.19. At this price, the store generated an average weekly contribution of $25.00 on this item. When the grocer offered Minute Rice at a special promotion price of $.89, the sales volume increased from 50 units at $1.19 to 80 boxes per week. The total weekly unit contribution, however, was only $16.00. The lower price, therefore, did not generate sufficient incremental volume and cost the store $9.00 ($25.00 minus $16.00).

There may, of course, be objectives other than maximizing item contributions. What the system provides is an automated means of quickly scanning the thousands of items in a retail store and, at a minimum, determining the optimal price to charge for each item or the cost of the other objectives.

If the cost of Minute Rice increases to $.79 per box, moreover, then the price that maximizes item contribution is no longer $1.19 but $1.29, as shown in Exhibit I. Thus, the system automatically detects optimal new prices to correspond with cost increases.

THE APPROACHES COMBINED

Other data-collection firms have gone a step further in integrating data from split-cable television and UPC scanners. They ask a large sample of consumers in several geographic areas that are simultaneously served by split-cable television to complete a questionnaire detailing a wide set of demographic and family characteristics. In return for lottery choices and gifts, respondents are given identification cards to use while they shop in cooperating supermarkets and drugstores, and their homes are connected with a split-cable network. The marketers can track who makes which purchases (via the identification numbers) and at which prices, how the products are displayed, whether coupons are used, and which television commercials are shown to which households.

It does not take a brilliant mathematician to use such information to identify how changes in marketing expenditures affect the purchasing behavior of market segments. The wealth of valuable consumer information is almost endless.

Methods and Technologies for Analysis

Aside from offering exceptional detail, the consumer research techniques of the 1980s have other useful attributes. They allow data to be gathered unobtrusively, to show details about individuals, and to be ready for analysis.

Another major advance is the marketing managers' accessibility to data via companies. No longer are the data relegated to the corporation's data processors. The special marketing-decision software that one can easily learn to use now provides managers a way to combine modeling, statistics, graphics, flexible report generation, and data-base management.

A combination of scanner panels, computer technology, and microanalysis is now available to consumer product companies so that they can improve their use of consumer coupons. From 1975 to 1981, the distribution of consumer coupons increased from 36 billion to 102.4 billion.

Most companies look at the redemption rates of coupons as a measure of their success. But what do redemption rates have to do with profit? And what would happen if the companies ran different coupon promotions or if they ran no coupon promotions at all?

There is a syndicated service that mails out coupons to one group in a scanner panel and that tracks a matched control group which receives no coupons. Analysts at the service then compare the sales volumes of the group that has been exposed to the coupons and of the group that has not. Exhibit II shows the sales effect of coupons for two different brands. It is quite easy to compare these sales with those of the no-coupon group. Notice how sharply sales rose after the mailing of the coupons.

The figures show only the short-term, obvious sales effects of coupon mailing. To determine the long-term effects, marketers need to apply mathematical models of consumer brand choice and loyalty. Do those who get coupons change their brand loyalty, and does it last? Is the use of a coupon for an established product by somebody who has not tried it for a while just like a new trial for a new product? These are questions such models are designed to answer.

The combination of computer technology and the new levels of data refinement (micro levels) have brought about a revolutionary development in marketing decision models. The models forecast choices of product and service purchases. Each choice the consumer makes is modeled as a function of all the variables that may be affecting the customer at that point. These include variables that the manufacturer and retailer control, such as shelf price, advertising, and promotion, as well as uncontrollable behavior like brand loyalty, size loyalty, and price responsiveness.

These micro-level choice models enable marketers to evaluate more decision variables than ever before and to predict more precisely the effect of marketing activities on sales and market share. For example, it used to be difficult to forecast the impact of advertising, promotion, and display variables on the retail market share of Coke and Pepsi. With the aid of a micro-level choice model, a scanner panel, and the appropriate computer technology, marketers can now make highly informed predictions.

No longer do marketing experiments require the manipulation of marketing expenditures in large geographical areas. The use of split-cable television and scanner panels or other micro-level data enables researchers to use much smaller experimental units, such as areas of a city or groups of households. The individual consumer can now be the unit of analysis, and every home the object of observation.

Getting statistically significant results with these smaller experimental units is much easier and cheaper than in the recent past.

Exhibit II.   Cumulative Test Minus Control

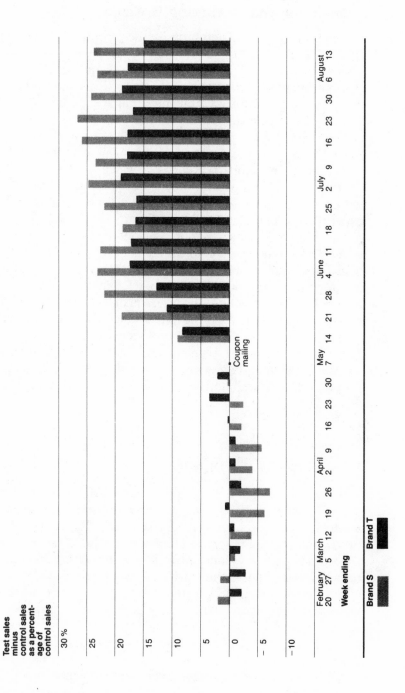

Test sales minus control sales as a percentage of control sales

Week ending

Coupon mailing

Brand S   Brand T

Dangers on the Marketing Horizon

Two problems could compromise the potential of the new micro-level experimentation and decision support software. The first is senior management's not putting the costs and benefits of the microexperimentation data into perspective. Even though manipulating marketing variables within these microexperiments costs less than do traditional experiments, the cost of the data is higher. Scanner panels and split-cable data are not cheap—they cost about $150,000 per year per product class per microtest market.

As long as the short-term focus prevalent in American industry dominates most companies, they cannot take advantage of the potential of these micro-level experiments. The reason is simple. The experimental and data-collection costs are usually in a market research budget, which is not considered to belong to the same framework as the budgets for advertising, pricing, promotion, and distribution, all of which market research supports. A $200,000 cost for data seems like a lot of money to put into a market research budget. When one looks at the leverage that advertising, promotion, and the sales force get and the improvement of decisions that comes from such data, however, the costs seem inconsequential.

The second problem is management's tendency to interpret results using simple data analysis methods. One has to use the appropriate model and statistical analysis to ensure that the results are indeed real and not statistical artifacts.

How to Avoid the Pitfalls

We have observed a tendency in marketing (as well as in other areas) to use computers to make employees' jobs easier rather than to enable employees to do their jobs better. Managers have a tendency to favor computers to eliminate clerical labor and automate the tedious parts of management jobs. But the real potential of the new technology lies in improving marketing decisions. Since most of the clerical procedures formerly used to analyze marketing data were fairly simple, managers have gravitated toward very simple computer marketing analyses.

The new technology also has great potential for misuse. For example, there has been a growing use of menu-driven computer systems. These systems have lists of reports that managers may choose from. But such systems limit the complexity of an analysis because they look at data two factors at a time. They use cross-tabulation or various plots of marketing instruments such as advertising and sales over time. These systems can be wonderful for hypothesis generation or for developing questions that need detailed answers. Without appropriate checks and interpretation by knowledgeable, sophisticated analysts, however, these reports can cause more harm than good.

It is possible to use the new data bases to estimate the degree to which various marketing factors influence sales, but the standard technology to automate complete market response analysis is just not here yet.

There may be other extraneous factors causing sales response. For example, if you take a cross-sectional look at the advertising and sales for a product, you may conclude that the advertising causes the sales. After all, the graph a computer menu produces may show a rise in advertising associated with a rise in sales.

But what this analysis may really be saying is that large cities are bigger than small cities. Obviously, large cities have larger sales and larger advertising budgets than small cities. If population is statistically factored out of the analysis, a very different picture can emerge. Not only is population a factor that should be included, but promotion, distribution, and pricing—of both the product and the competitors in question—also need to be considered simultaneously.

It is difficult to resist a beautiful graph relating advertising and sales in a striking multicolor format. GIGO, "garbage in, garbage out," was a very true description of the data processing that was popular 10 to 15 years ago. Now a new slogan has become popular and is even more true: "Garbage in, *color* garbage out."

The new generation of managers and young people who are no longer afraid of the computer may be a mixed blessing. The most that any market analysis (no matter how sophisticated) can do is decipher what has happened—that is, what worked and what did not work in the past. No system will necessarily predict aspects of the future that are not similar to aspects of the past. Management cannot use the computer as a substitute for rational, creative thinking. Rather, the computer is best used as a support system for strategy formulation.

An example helps illustrate our point. A large retailer with many stores was seeking to determine the best media through which to advertise a new consumer electronics product. Its advertising agency was recommending magazines, while others in the company were recommending newspapers, radio, and television. The company's managers developed a program whereby two cities would receive one experimental ad campaign for three months.

Data for the product accumulated on electronic cash registers, and the experiment's results were available a week after the experiment was over. The advertising agency simply totaled the sales during the experiment and showed them in comparison with sales before the experiment for each of the treatments. It then concluded that magazines were the best media alternative.

One marketing scientist realized, however, that many factors aside from the media treatment could cause the results that the agency had found. He figured that something about the size of the cities might increase the sales of the product since the magazines happened to be in the largest cities. He then did a statistical analysis with multivariate procedures to isolate the effects of the population as well as the situations in which the experiment had been followed carelessly. He wanted to factor out the statistical effects of jointly having television and radio or television and magazines in some markets for some months.

With statistical precision, he discovered that television advertising is much more profitable than magazine advertising. In fact, using magazines may be no more profitable than using no advertising at all. As a result of this experiment, the company changed its media plan from using magazines heavily to using TV heavily. The company's advertising budget for the new product was $5 million.

How valuable was this experiment? It showed that the company could increase the productivity of its advertising by a factor of two or three. How much was this experiment worth? A lot more than it cost. Even if it had cost $500,000 or $1 million, it would have been worthwhile. Yet how many companies will ever consider spending $500,000 for a media experiment?

ANALYZING CAUSE AND EFFECT

Knowing why your sales have changed in the past can be a very important aid in developing strategy for the future. Market response analysis is a complicated but effective way of analyzing past data. Nevertheless, a company needs a marketing scientist to ensure that conclusions will not be accepted without careful checking and analysis.

For example, when an over-the-counter drug company suffered a decline in its national unit market share for its drug "Abel," company officials attributed the falloff to the competitive efforts of two products. One, product "Baker," was a private-label product sold at half of Abel's price. The second, product "Cain," was produced by another division of Abel's company. The decision support system provided plots of national unit market share over time for all three products (see the three graphs in Exhibit III).

These graphs make clear that products Baker and Cain were taking share from product Abel. Statistical analysis of the numbers on the graphs confirmed that Abel's market share declines correlated with the share increases of Baker and Cain.

A marketing scientist demonstrated to the company's management, however, that this analysis and conclusions were faulty. If indeed Baker or Cain were competitive with Abel, then the competitive effects should be evident at the regional as well as the national level. As a test, the scientist developed several plots to relate the market share changes of product Abel with those of product Baker (see Exhibit IV) and of product Cain (see Exhibit V) by region for a six-month period. Each point in these exhibits represents market share changes for a specific region for two products. These scatter diagrams were also easy to obtain from the decision support system.

As shown in Exhibit IV, except for two observations associated with external events, the share decreases for Abel for a region were associated with the share increases for Baker for the same region. The evidence supported the national competitive effect at the regional level.

A similar plot for Cain, in Exhibit V, shows a very different story. In each region there was a tendency for Abel's share to decrease least where product Cain's share had increased the most. Conversely, the drug's share declined most in regions where Cain was also having its smallest share gains. Another unrelated, noncompetitive phenomenon was causing Abel's share decline. Cain could not have been causing it; Cain was probably helping Abel by combining the two brands' sales force efforts. The marketing scientist's perceptive analysis stopped a potentially damaging interdivisional dispute and reoriented management's strategic thinking about competition.

In some cases the new technology may cause misinterpretation

Exhibit III.   Bimonthly Market Shares
July–August 1979 – July–August 1981

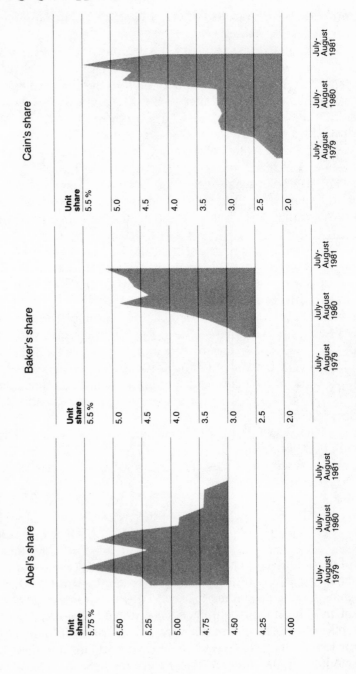

Exhibit IV.   *Regional Market Share Changes, Abel and Baker*
First Half of 1981 in Comparison with Last Half of 1980

Change
**in Abel's
share**
in share
points

0.5	Area 6
0.3	Area 3
0.0	
	Area 5
−0.3	Area 1 / Area 2
	Area 9
−0.5	
−0.8	Area 7
−1.0	Area 8
−1.3	
−1.5	Area 4

−1.0   0.0   1.0   2.0   3.0   4.0

Baker's change in share
in share points

of marketing effectiveness because the data are not integrated with other pertinent information. For example, Exhibit VI is a graph that shows a marketing decision support-system software program of monthly factory shipments for an over-the-counter drug. The spikes in the shipment data are associated with trade promotions, or temporary price reductions to the trade for a limited time. One module of the program produced the dotted line, which is an extrapolation of normal months to establish a baseline of what

Exhibit V. Regional Market Share Changes, Abel and Cain

First Half of 1981 in Comparison with Last Half of 1980

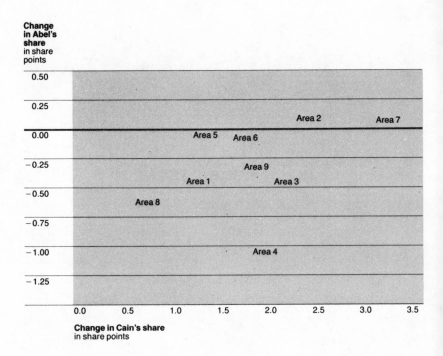

sales might have been had there been no promotion. Obviously, the trade promotions were very effective in stimulating sales.

Data from the same period but examined from another perspective suggest a very different conclusion. Exhibit VII shows retailers' warehouse withdrawals for the same product and a similarly constructed baseline. Warehouse withdrawal data are much closer to consumer sales. This graph shows minimal effects from the trade promotions on sales to consumers. Indeed, the trade intermediaries in this case were simply using the promotional discount to stock

Exhibit VI. *Warehouse Withdrawals of an Over-the-Counter Drug During a Four-Year Period*

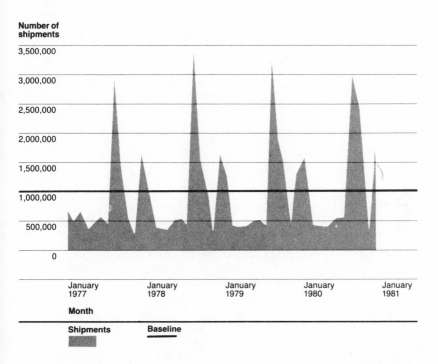

up their warehouses with goods that they would have bought later at regular prices.

Until the warehouse withdrawal data were brought into the analysis, management was confident that the trade promotion program was highly profitable. After the new data were brought in, the managers changed their minds. This example illustrates the need to put all pertinent information in the same decision support system. Leaving even one data source out of consideration can be dangerous.

MINIMIZING THE DANGERS

What can management do to simultaneously reduce these dangers and take advantage of the potential that the new technology

Exhibit VII.   **Regional Market Share Changes, Abel and Cain**
First Half of 1981 in Comparison with Last Half of 1980

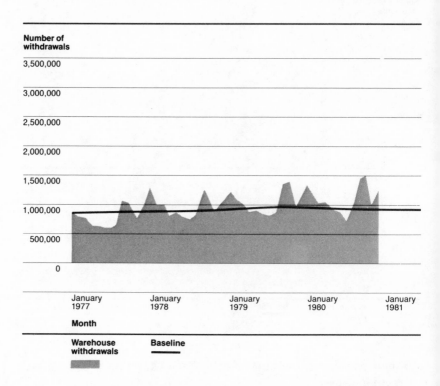

Number of withdrawals

3,500,000	
3,000,000	
2,500,000	
2,000,000	
1,500,000	
1,000,000	
500,000	
0	

January 1977   January 1978   January 1979   January 1980   January 1981

Month

Warehouse withdrawals   Baseline

offers? At present, the computer terminal and television screen are not the best interface between management, which can be somewhat naive, and the new technology. Just because the technology makes using the computer terminal easy does not mean that the results will be perfectly correct or easy to implement. Persons with expertise in marketing science, employed either as full-time staff or as external consultants, can improve decision making when they serve as the liaison between the manager and the new technology.

The liaison people have two very important skills. They understand the business and the strategic problems that management faces. They also understand enough about data analysis, statistical analysis, and modeling to make sure that the appropriate checks and questions have been asked when a recommendation based on computer analysis is made. These people should report directly to top and middle management as part of staff groups. That way, they will control the quality of the analysis being done. We cannot emphasize enough the importance of having someone who understands data analysis review management's decisions on strategy.

Eventually this group of liaison people may be unnecessary. Ongoing artificial intelligence research will enable the computer to do as careful a market response analysis as a very good analyst. Until that happens, the liaison is important.

Taking Advantage of the New Data

To make optimal use of the new information, methods, and technologies, a company must combine the data, models, and tools of analysis. A marketing decision support system can do so. Its software and computers will help the organization translate data into information that is relevant to evaluating marketing decision alternatives.

The marketing decision support-system software must be able to leverage all the latest data, models, and statistical analysis procedures. The software must have the capacity for data-base management, analysis, display, and modeling—all in a user-friendly environment. The data base should organize information in ways that can be easily altered when situations or services change. For example, without doing massive reprogramming, a company must be able to incorporate new products or changes in sales districts into the data base. The software should have the capacity to allow many users to access the same integrated data base. The system needs a wide variety of output capabilities, ranging from simple tables to presentation-quality graphics and reports. To be able to divide and aggregate the data simultaneously into such categories as product, region, salesperson, and time period is very important.

Not only are simple "cuts" at the data necessary but also a wide variety of statistical and modeling capabilities to test and refine hypotheses generated by initial plots and tables of the data. We have seen many marketing decision support systems stop dead because the initial software selection did not anticipate how integrated, powerful, and flexible the software needs would be.[2]

To keep the system as productive as possible, it must have the support of an internal organization of specialized professionals as well as the sanction of top management. The support organization would carry out the following functions.

1. Install, operate, and maintain the computer hardware.
2. Administer the data base by recording which data are and which are not included in the system, updating the data base as new data became available, maintaining the documentation of available data, and ensuring data integrity.
3. Train administrators and users of the system at all levels of expertise and in all kinds of documentation needed.

A typical company with a mature support organization might include six people besides the manager—two persons in computer operations, two in data-base administration, one to develop additional capabilities and support users, and one to train new employees.

Looking Ahead

The future practice of marketing will bear little resemblance to that of the past. Changes in the managerial environment—the data, computers, human resources, and software—dictate a change in managerial practice.

Whereas a good marketing sense has led to many successful marketing careers, the future confronts us with the infusion of new marketing technologies and information sources. Appropriately supported, this new information will lead to a more accurate understanding of the business environment and to more profitable marketing strategies.

New, more powerful racing cars enable expert drivers to get around the Indianapolis Speedway increasingly faster. If these same cars are driven improperly, however, they will get into increasingly severe accidents. The same principle applies to the new data and computer technology. We must "drive" them with caution and the appropriate expertise.

Notes

1. These results were taken from Alan Kuritsky, Emily Bassman, John D.C. Little, and Alvin J. Silk, "The Development, Testing,

and Execution of a New Marketing Strategy at AT&T Long Lines," *Interfaces,* December 1982, p. 22.

2. For a detailed checklist of capabilities required in marketing decision support-system software, see John D.C. Little and Michael N. Cassetari, "Appendix," *Decision Support for Marketing Managers* (New York: American Management Association, 1984).

3. For more details, see Little and Cassetari, *Decision Support for Marketing Managers.*

5
Putting Expert Systems to Work

Dorothy Leonard-Barton and John J. Sviokla

Executives are intrigued by stories of computer programs that can analyze mud during oil drilling or configure complex computer systems. N L Baroid Company's MUDMAN and Digital Equipment Corporation's XCON perform tasks previously thought too complicated or not routine enough for computers. MUDMAN and XCON are not ordinary computer programs though. They are "expert systems"—programs that mimic the thinking of the human experts who would otherwise have to perform the analysis, design, or monitoring. Through a complicated series of "if . . . then" rules— "If there is a disk drive that has not been assigned and there is capacity for at least one disk drive, then assign the disk drive to the current computer configuration"—such programs allow computers to solve difficult, one-of-a-kind problems.[1]

Growing numbers of managers are asking whether expert systems are right for them, and if so, how they can start using them. Those who want to exploit the new technology can learn from the early users of large, commercial expert systems. Their experience shows that expert systems are indeed a valuable tool for capturing and disseminating skill and knowledge, often to create competitive advantage. But prospective users may be encouraged to learn that despite the fascination with applying the new technology to more sensational tasks like space exploration or warfare, some of the greatest opportunities for expert systems lie in small, everyday tasks like credit verification or capital budgeting analysis.

Real Benefits

Expert systems (ESs) have been used successfully for design, diagnosis, and monitoring in a range of industries—from computers to accounting. Probably the most famous business application is XCON (for eXpert CONfigurer). Digital has a wide range of computer components that continually change and can be configured in a vast number of ways. During the early 1970s, human experts—known as technical editors—ensured that each computer system on order had all the necessary components and no extras and made diagrams showing how to assemble the system. The process is known as "configuration."

At Digital the initial configurations sometimes contained omissions or errors that had to be fixed before manufacturing could schedule production. Then 90% of the systems were checked again at Digital's final assembly and test facility in Westminster, Massachusetts, where the pieces of the computer were physically plugged together and run. Once they passed this test, the computers were disassembled and shipped to the customers.

In 1973, faced with the prospect of adding tens of millions of dollars worth of assembly and test facilities to accommodate sales growth, Digital sought an alternative. The result was XCON, an expert system that checks sales orders and designs the layout of each computer order it analyzes. The new system, along with the creation of a data base and an improvement in component quality, allows Digital to ship most components directly to the customer site for final assembly, thereby eliminating the need for additional final assembly facilities.

N L Baroid, a drilling services company, created MUDMAN to analyze the drilling fluids, or "muds," that are pumped down the shaft to facilitate drilling by lubricating, carrying shaving back to the surface, and so on. On deep or difficult wells an engineer on site often has to sample and analyze the mud at least twice a day. The engineer analyzes readings on some 20 parameters including viscosity, specific gravity, and silt content. MUDMAN helps the on-site engineer do the job more consistently. It evaluates the data the engineer enters and, by combining these with historical data for that particular well, identifies trends. It can then recommend adjustments to the mud composition and alert the mud engineer to potential problems.

Muds are a commodity business whose buyers are few and powerful. Major oil companies shop for price and ration purchases among many eager suppliers. But MUDMAN gave Baroid something unique to offer customers. Suddenly the company could differentiate itself from competitors. At one site in the North Sea, MUDMAN correctly diagnosed a mud contamination problem that human experts had misdiagnosed for more than a decade. The oil company customer was so impressed that it bent its policy and invited Baroid to bid on "more than the normal" share of business.

Westinghouse Electric Corporation designed an ES to monitor the steam turbines it sells. When a turbine fails, it sometimes throws pieces of steel, whirling at thousands of revolutions per minute, into protective castings, causing tens of thousands of dollars worth of damage and weeks of downtime. Detection of potential failures is thus extremely useful. Westinghouse's process diagnostic system (PDS) continuously tracks data from monitors on the turbine and makes recommendations for maintenance. PDS is sold as part of Westinghouse's service contract.

American Express Company uses an expert system to help its credit authorization staff sort through data from as many as 13 data bases. The American Express credit card has no set spending limit. That feature is important for competitive reasons, but determining the credit level for each customer poses a stiff administrative challenge. Each time the customer makes a large purchase, the merchant telephones AMEX to authorize the charge. The AMEX employee then has to make a quick judgment call. Authorization requests outside the normal buying pattern require a search of the data bases for more information. Now the Authorizer's Assistant ES performs that search and makes recommendations to the person who makes the authorization decision. The entire process takes only seconds; the merchant is still on the phone.

Coopers & Lybrand has an ES called ExperTAX that helps accountants in reviewing the way their clients accrue taxes and in offering tax planning advice. ExperTAX improves the quality of the tax service because it never forgets a question and it checks each policy against the client's financial statistics. Furthermore, in substituting for the experience junior people lack, it allows them to perform more complete and accurate tax planning.

XCON, MUDMAN, Authorizer's Assistant, and ExperTAX didn't disappoint the companies that funded them. The improvements they delivered were real and measurable. Today roughly 90% of Digital's dollar volume of systems is shipped as components and assembled at the customer site. Digital managers attribute to XCON some $25 million of the savings realized from minimizing the final assembly and test process. They also cite XCON as an important contributor to Digital's long-time strategy of offering customers many options.

Differentiation of a commodity product via MUDMAN won new business for Baroid. AMEX expects its Authorizer's Assistant not only to raise an authorizer's productivity by as much as 20% but also to reduce losses from overextension of credit (the exact financial benefit is kept secret). Authorizer's Assistant supports the company's strategy to differentiate itself by offering individualized credit limits. ExperTAX makes better use of junior people's time.

As these examples show, expert systems can support various competitive strategies by differentiating a product or by lowering costs. Sometimes projects begun with one objective in mind have led to the other. In some instances, new businesses have sprung up. Both Texas Instruments and Digital first developed expert systems for internal use but have since spun off organizations based on the technology that offer new products, such as expert systems "shells," and consulting and training. (An ES shell is a software tool that provides an integrated set of building blocks that can be used to create an ES program.)

Often more interesting—and ultimately more valuable—than the hoped-for gains in productivity and effectiveness are the many unexpected benefits that flow from ESs. One such benefit is the way an ES can help people in the organization understand a problem better. For years IBM had a set of standard prices for provision of after-sales services to install, relocate, or remove computers. These prices were the starting point for negotiations among the customer, the field service representative, and service management. Because each customer had different ducting, wiring, and flooring and because experience of the estimators varied widely, consistent bidding was a problem. IBM field service employees needed a better shared understanding of how to price complex jobs or how far to alter the standard price.

Now IBM uses an ES called CONSULTANT to help field service reps price bids. The rep simply specifies the machine types and the location-specific factors and the system generates a bid. Bids are negotiated only if the field person's price differs from CON-SULTANT's by more than 20%. This procedure has eliminated many administrative problems.

Once expertise is revealed, it can be reviewed, discussed, and communicated in whole new ways. Studies have shown that experts are seldom able to retrace the analytic steps taken to arrive at a particular decision. They may be able to highlight important factors that went into a decision but usually cannot describe the whole process. They are not being intentionally evasive. In the process of becoming expert, individuals distill many observations into intuition and deep understanding but cannot articulate them.

That fact makes it hard to mine the expert's knowledge. But once the information has been drawn from the expert and the software created, the rules, examples, and data provide a mental mirror with which the expert can explore, explain, and elucidate the nature of his or her expertise. The understanding revealed is therefore of value both to the expert and to the members of the organization dependent on the expertise.

Once expertise is outside someone's head, more people can work at refining it, and as it is fine-tuned, problem solving moves from art to science. It can then be more easily captured in other computer languages. Thus, today's ground-breaking ES may be tomorrow's traditional solution. It will be tempting to look back at an ES and say that the task should have been solved with a more traditional programming approach. But to take that position is usually to misunderstand (and underestimate) the process by which expertise is captured. Once the problem is solved, the solution seems obvious.

Another benefit of ES is that once the knowledge has been captured in code, it can be protected and shared. If a human expert is hired away or is too busy to teach younger colleagues, an ES can help by serving as a training tool. Many people can, in effect, become apprentices to a few experts. People who are afraid to ask questions because they are expected to know the answers can consult with an ES in private. And the experienced person can benefit by seeing how another expert approaches the task.

Finally, building an ES is a foot in the door to artificial intelligence. Most systems are custom built, and even the few available turnkey systems often need customization. Knowledge engineers are scarce, and it takes time to develop people with the skills needed to make ESs and AI work. Of course, these facts can be used competitively. By getting in early, an organization can gain experience and develop technical staff, thereby creating a barrier competitors will have a hard time overcoming.

Finding the Leverage Points

It's one thing to study the successes of other companies and another to produce a success of one's own. So how does a manager court the new technology?

The first step is to identify the opportunities. Look for design, diagnosis, or monitoring procedures that are not being performed as well as they could be. Ask, *Is there a task in my organization that would be improved if . . .*

. . . we had more time? AMEX employees understood well the process of credit authorization. If each authorizer had half an hour to process a request, an expert system would hardly be necessary. But when a creditor telephones for a credit check, time is measured in seconds, not hours. AMEX's Authorizer's Assistant can use the rules and data much faster than a human expert.

Organizations are replete with tasks for which doing things faster means doing them better. Basic transaction systems for credit, purchasing, and so on are promising areas to explore.

. . . the best expert always did the job? Companies don't always have enough of the expertise they need. At Honeywell, for example, the skill of field service technicians varies, usually with the technician's experience. By using an ES called Mentor to help diagnose problems with commercial air conditioning systems, Honeywell ensures that the quality of service calls is uniformly high.

Digital couldn't afford to have its design engineers configuring computer systems, even though they understood the process best. XCON allows the company to apply expert knowledge to a task that is routine but important.

. . . we had consistent decisions? When a drilling rig is having trouble with a well, the people involved must stay on the job sometimes for days at a time. Just when the mud engineer's judgment must be keenest, he may be most fatigued. MUDMAN's analyses are consistently careful, regardless of the work conditions.

The notion of a thinking machine is seductive. ES builders are often drawn to the flashy applications. But observation of dozens of systems in development and use indicates that the more mundane tasks are among the most fruitful areas for new applications. Business and government have many jobs that are important but routine or even boring. Tasks such as contracting, negotiating, and auditing pervade business and are promising opportunities. Likely candidates are those jobs that currently make use of complex questionnaires. Meeting the requirements of government agencies like the Environmental Protection Agency or the Occupational Safety and Health Administration could be simplified by encoding the regulations in an expert system and making it available to companies who need to comply.

The improvements in quality, timeliness, or consistency may seem small, but they can have a great impact on the overall business. Texas Instruments uses its Capital Investment Expert System to help employees who are making capital budgeting requests. The ES provides a complete and consistent set of questions covering all aspects of any proposal. The system guides the user through the questions relevant to the particular project. Higher executives at TI are thereby assured of comparable analyses, so they can make more informed capital allocation decisions. The system also helps individual managers analyze their situations more completely.

People sometimes talk of a "standard" ES application, but that is often an oxymoron. If a company needs experts to solve a particular problem, it usually needs a customized approach. Consequently, implementation of an ES is often as much a process of transferring a point of view or set of beliefs as it is providing a solution to a problem.

Once you've identified the ES opportunities, you must assess the feasibility of applying the new technology to those tasks. Look, for instance, at the size of the problem. One that can be solved in a few minutes to a few hours is a reasonable candidate. Issues that take days to resolve are probably too ambitious.

And think about whether the problem can be described in words. Could it be solved over the phone? If the expert needs to see or touch the data, the task may not be well suited to an ES. In one case, after six months of work on a prototype ES designed to diagnose problems in soldering of computer components, the project developers reached a dead end. They had assumed operators could detect defects which could then be diagnosed by the software. However, discerning the subtle irregularities that were visible to an expert's eye proved beyond the operators' capabilities, and the developers could not write software to perform that expert task. Therefore, the project was refocused to address problems readily identifiable, even by novices.

In creating ExperTAX, Coopers & Lybrand used a pragmatic technique to simulate the limitations of the computer screen. They sat three experts on one side of a table, a novice with all the data on the other, and put a curtain down the middle. The tax experts were charged with performing tax accrual and tax planning for the "client." They could ask any questions they wished, but they could not get up and look at the data. They were therefore forced to specify the data they needed and explain why. Coopers videotaped the process and used it as the basis for the ES. A third test of feasibility is whether you can identify the abilities that differentiate an expert from a novice. Making the distinction is necessary because you must know what experts should be involved in building a system and you must have a clear idea of what standard to use when measuring its performance.

Meeting the Implementation Challenge

If the opportunity is ripe and applying an ES is feasible, it's time to start the development process. In many ways, development and implementation of an ES are the same as for any new technology. All new technologies involve technical risk, necessitate some organizational adjustments, and require skillful handling of perceptions so that prospective users don't develop unreasonable expectations. And of course, commitment by management is essential.

With ESs, though, the technical and organizational challenges are heightened, in part because of the way these systems are built. Most businesspeople are accustomed to seeing carefully laid-out specifications before developers actually start on the software development project. ESs, however, are developed via rapid prototyping—that is, the quick production of a preliminary version whose use provides feedback for correcting the design. The problems the developers encounter are sometimes so great that they have to redesign the system from scratch. Some managers find this horribly wasteful. They don't realize that the most important part of the development process is not the coding itself but the progressive discovery of knowledge.

As with decision support systems, prototyping ESs involves choosing the relevant data, presentation mechanisms, and analytical models. But ESs also generate evaluations and recommendations based on the data and models. The experts must evaluate each version of the system and compare the reasoning that is being embedded in the system with their own thinking. Managers and experts must be involved throughout the process to make sure that the project is on the right track.

The exploratory nature of the development process makes it hard to predict how useful the project will be. Managers may find that uncertainty frustrating. They cannot eliminate the uncertainty, but the more they understand ESs, the better their chances of creating a valuable system.

SCALE

An issue that arises in the development stage is whether to start on a large scale, a small scale, or a combination of the two. One way to start small is by making PC-based shells widely available to end users. The idea is that, as people become comfortable with the technology, they will discover useful applications on their own. Du Pont, for instance, gives employees small, PC-based ES shells and encourages them to build systems tailored to their specific needs. Such systems are expected to be small, have a short development time (months, at most), and provide a quick payback. The money Du Pont might otherwise have spent on consultants it spends on training people in the use of the shells.

Companies including IBM and Texas Instruments have a combination of large-scale and small-scale projects. The key to this approach is to establish an infrastructure of support and assign an individual (or group) with the responsibility for monitoring ideas and spreading successful projects throughout the organization.

Other organizations, such as Digital, Boeing, and Arthur Andersen, have undertaken large-scale projects. These projects require a team of people with the right mix of talent and take from six months to at least two years to create and implement. PlanPower, a personal financial planning ES developed by Applied Expert Systems, took approximately two years from design to delivery. The same is true for Palladian's Financial Advisor—a capital budgeting expert system—and for MUDMAN.

Needless to say, it will take these companies less time to deliver complementary products and new ESs because of the learning that has already taken place. Organizations that build one system learn in the process how to do it faster and better the next time. Still, improvements in the ES development process are slow in coming, and development of a large-scale ES remains a lengthy proposition.

Of course, this long incubation period can constitute a competitive advantage.

TALENT

The development team for large-scale projects should have three types of talent: domain, technical, and managerial. The domain expertise, or knowledge of how to perform the task, is usually provided by the expert who has been doing the job. In the case of ExperTAX, for example, tax and audit experts furnished the domain expertise.

The technical skill—that is, knowledge of the hardware and software tools available and used in the project—can come from a number of places: universities, consulting companies, computer vendors, in-house MIS staff, or salaried ES experts. Drawing talent from any of these sources has its advantages and drawbacks. Outside experts are expected to have a deep understanding of ES tools and methodology so they can develop a working system quickly, and they bring a fresh perspective. But they are expensive, and learning the client's business takes time. On the other hand, people inside the company, however knowledgeable they are about the business, usually lack experience with ESs. And hiring a full-time staff that knows ESs is for most companies prohibitively expensive. For pragmatic reasons, most companies turn to experts outside the company who are practiced at eliciting and encoding an expert's rules of thumb.

Some companies contract with university researchers to create prototypes that are developed in-house; MUDMAN and XCON both began with prototypes developed at Carnegie-Mellon University. Others rely heavily on consultants. General Motors purchased an equity stake in Teknowledge, Inc., an ES consulting firm it had been using. Texas Instruments is moving aggressively on all fronts. It provides in-house training and uses consultants.

The need for domain and technical talent is so obvious that these two are never overlooked. They do, however, sometimes exert too much or too little influence. When technical experts alone determine the performance and application characteristics, the applications often fail to meet a real business need. The projects that succeed are usually driven by a domain expert or business manager. That person, being the best judge of the trade-offs that often must be made during development, should have the last word on the content and process of the actual ES.

Digital's experience attests to that fact. The technical editors at Digital couldn't use the first version of XCON. While it was technically accurate, it did not fit the way business was customarily conducted. Manufacturing often partially assembled a system while awaiting a salesperson's approval of the other parts. XCON would totally reject such a design. Only when XCON was revised to make two checks—one for review and approval by sales and one for manufacturing—did it perform adequately.

Because ES technology appears different from other computer projects, senior management is often unsure whether the management information systems department should handle it. The answer depends. If the MIS department is insular or preoccupied with the maintenance and upgrading of existing systems, it is unclear what role it should play. Most ESs currently in wide use in companies originated in a functional area, not the MIS department. If, however, the MIS department has a history of supporting and implementing user-initiated systems and can attract the necessary talent, then giving MIS a major role in the ES development project is probably a good idea.

The third type of talent, managerial, is the one most often neglected or dealt with ad hoc. Managing any software development project requires a rare combination of technical ability and interpersonal skills, but because ESs explore complex and ill-defined domains, they pose a particularly tough managerial challenge. The project overseer must be able to tolerate the high degree of ambiguity inherent in developing ESs.

USAGE

Less clear than the makeup of the development team is the question of who will be the user. The system might help experts work faster, apprentices work more consistently, or novices get started at the job. Some ESs are used regularly to get the job done and others are used sporadically, more like a training tool.

Expert systems can be used as an extension of an expert to take over routine tasks and free that person for more demanding problem solving, or they can be handed down to a less-experienced individual. Hand-me-down technologies can create a whole new class of technical experts. This has occurred in many cases in which the roles of individuals who used the ES have changed greatly. Through use of PlanPower, for example, a clerk began to acquire the expertise of a financial planner.

Each pattern of use implies different system designs and different benefits. An ES used by novices differs from one used by the experts themselves. And the organizational impact—the creation of new job categories, the necessity for training programs, or the alteration of career paths—also varies.

Targeting a particular task doesn't always tell you who the system users will be, because actual usage often diverges from the plan. Companies that study the usage patterns stand to learn a great deal about the way ESs alter operations. One way to enhance the learning that occurs is through organizational prototyping— that is, by conducting experiments that involve either deliberate creation and evaluation of groups of people who use the system differently or comparison of differences in usage patterns that arise naturally. The insight gained can translate into productivity gains, tailoring of job roles, and a better sense of users' needs for future systems.

Digital's XSEL (eXpert SELling assistant) was designed to interact with XCON. It was originally intended to be used by salespeople to check the configuration at the time they created a new order for a computer system. Among the earliest users in Europe, three different patterns of usage emerged. In some offices, salespeople used XSEL as intended. In other offices, configurations were checked manually by a technical assistant, who did not use XSEL. In yet other offices, the technical assistants used XSEL. This third pattern is the one that has persisted in Europe, and Digital has adjusted to it. XSEL developers no longer assume that all system users will be sales reps, especially in Europe.

MEASUREMENT

Some managers use the total number of users or amount of usage as measures of success. Yet those may not be the best indicators of the system's value. For example, some ESs are used like a training tool: novices use the ES extensively for a few months until they've learned all it has to offer, after which usage drops off until a new batch of beginners appears on the scene. Others are used by a few people or infrequently but at critical decision points. So the manager of an ES project should treat the measurement issue pragmatically. The organizational prototyping mentioned earlier can help to highlight the best measures of success.

Manage Expectations

As exciting and promising as ESs are, overenthusiasm can sometimes lead to unfounded assumptions and unrealistic expectations.[2] A typical claim is that expert systems help companies "clone experts." That claim is overblown. Problem solving is only a small part of what an expert does in a company. The best ESs to date capture only a portion of the expert's knowledge. Moreover, even the most advanced expert systems, such as XCON, do not replace experts but rather augment their capabilities or allow less-experienced individuals to perform better. Generally speaking, humans are supported by—not replaced by—expert systems. Moreover, expert systems are regularly, if not continually, monitored and updated by humans.

ESs are not 100% correct 100% of the time. People tend to expect much higher and more consistent performance from a computer program than they would ever expect from a human expert, but such lofty expectations court disaster. One can expect consistency from an ES, but ESs mimic the frailties as well as the strengths of human judgment. Besides, assessing whether an answer is "correct" is often a matter of opinion. This is true in credit authorization as well as in computer configuration. Many configurations will work, but choosing the best one is a matter of judgment.

Hypesters often make mistakes about the utility of ESs because they implicitly compare ESs to mechanical automation. Steam power removed horsepower and manpower. Computers removed clerical staff in industries like insurance. Continuing this logic leads one to think of ESs as the automation of experts. But this line of reasoning has two flaws. First, the effects of earlier types of automation were not that direct. Second, an ES is often more of a corporate technology asset than an investment in labor replacement.

Research has shown that it is hard for people to consciously process more than nine pieces of data simultaneously; any problem with more than nine parameters boggles the mind. Yet we have trouble assessing the degree of that complexity because 20 parameters are as difficult for us to comprehend as 100. In either case, it is well beyond our ability to retrieve them readily. This inability to gauge the depth of complexity tends to inflate our expectations of expert systems.

An early version of a system can appear to be more impressive than its true capabilities warrant, leading people to underestimate the amount of work left to be done before the system is ready for use. In some cases, managers' inflated expectations from early demonstrations of the prototypes caused them to jump to the erroneous conclusion that the projects were behind schedule. Some managers even went so far as to deny resources allocated to the project because progress was so much slower than anticipated.

These caveats notwithstanding, expert systems have demonstrated their value to the business community, and managers should assume responsibility for using ES technology thoughtfully. Use of these systems is allowing organizations to leverage existing expertise to improve the timeliness and performance of many routine but critical business decisions. Moreover, the learning garnered in the process of questioning experts and structuring their knowledge provides valuable insight that often leads to efficiencies in task execution. Implementing these tools drives organizations into new managerial territory. Executives have lots of experience dealing with the transfer of expertise from one human to another. They have much less experience managing expertise when machines help record and animate human efforts to capture and transfer knowledge.

We do not yet know the full set of potential benefits and limitations of man-machine systems, but we are beginning to learn. As we have seen, expert systems have already allowed novices to perform expertlike tasks. In some cases, they have helped organizations understand vital processes and procedures. The next wave of ESs may be even more powerful and valuable. Realization of the potential of this evolving combination of human and machine knowledge hinges as much on management as on the technology itself.

Notes

1. The example is a modified rule from Digital's XCON expert system.
2. For discussion of realistic expectations, see, for example, Beau Sheil's "Thinking about Artifical Intelligence," *Harvard Business Review,* July-August 1987, p. 91.

About the Contributors

Brandt R. Allen is James C. Wheat, Jr., Professor of Business Administration at University of Virginia's Colgate Darden Graduate School of Business Administration.

Lynda M. Applegate is assistant professor, Harvard Business School, where she teaches courses on management information systems and managerial economics.

Robert I. Benjamin, recently retired from Xerox Corporation's information management staff, is a visiting scientist at the Center for Information Systems Research at Massachusetts Institute of Technology's Sloan School of Management.

William J. Bruns, Jr., is professor of business administration, Harvard Business School. He is the author of several books, including, with Robert S. Kaplan, *Accounting and Management: Field Study Perspectives* (Harvard Business School Press, 1987), as well as numerous articles.

James I. Cash, Jr., is James E. Robison Professor of Business Administration, Harvard Business School. He is co-author with F. Warren McFarlan and James L. McKenney of *Corporate Information Systems Management: The Issues Facing Senior Executives* (Dow Jones-Irwin, 1988) and has completed a video program for the Harvard Business School Publishing Division, *Competing through Information Technology.*

Eric K. Clemons is associate professor of decision sciences at the Wharton School and of Computer and Information Science at the Moore School of Electrical Engineering, both at the University of Pennsylvania. He is project director for the Reginald H. Jones Center's Sponsored Research Project in Information Systems, Telecommunications, and Business Strategy and is associate editor of *Management Information Systems Quarterly.*

J. Daniel Couger is Distinguished Professor of Computer and Management Science at University of Colorado, Colorado Springs. He was named U.S. Computer-Science Man of the Year in 1977 and has been a consultant to more than 30 major corporations.

Thomas H. Davenport was, at the time his article was published in the *Harvard Business Review,* senior research associate at the Harvard Business School. He was formerly with Index Group, a consulting and research firm in Cambridge, Massachusetts, where he was director of research.

John J. Donovan is chairman and chief executive officer of the Cambridge Technology Group in Cambridge, Massachusetts, which builds major strategic applications for a variety of organizations. He is also adjunct professor of management science at Massachusetts Institute of Technology's Sloan School of Management and the author of *Systems Programming* (McGraw-Hill, 1972).

Peter F. Drucker is Marie Rankin Clarke Professor of Social Science and Management, Claremont Graduate School. Widely known for his work on modern organizations and management practice, he is the author of numerous articles and books.

Michael Hammer is president of Hammer and Company, a consulting and research firm in Cambridge, Massachusetts. He is the research director for the Partnership for Research in Information Systems Management (PRISM).

Max D. Hopper is senior vice president for information systems at American Airlines, a subsidiary of AMR Corporation, and vice chairman of AMR Information Services. He joined American in 1972 as director of SABRE, the airline's computerized reservation system.

Russell Johnston is associate professor of management at Boston University.

Benn R. Konsynski is visiting professor at the Harvard Business School. He was formerly a professor at the University of Arizona where he was co-founder of the university's decision support laboratory.

Paul R. Lawrence is Wallace Brett Donham Professor of Organizational Behavior, Harvard Business School. He is the author of numerous articles and books, including, with Davis Dyer, *Renewing American Industry* (Free Press, 1983), and with Charalambos Vlachoutsicos, *Behind the Factory Walls* (Harvard Business School Press, 1990).

Dorothy Leonard-Barton is associate professor of business administration at the Harvard Business School. The author of numerous articles on technological capabilities, she has served as an adviser to the National Academy of Sciences and on the editorial boards of *Organizational Science* and *Journal of High Technology Management and Market Research*.

Leonard M. Lodish is professor of marketing at the University of Pennsylvania's Wharton School. He is the author of *The Advertising Promotion Challenge: Vaguely Right or Precisely Wrong* (Oxford University Press, 1986).

Thomas W. Malone is Patrick J. McGovern Professor of Information Systems at Massachusetts Institute of Technology's Sloan School of Management and is a member of the MIT Artificial Intelligence Lab.

F. Warren McFarlan is Ross Graham Walker Professor of Business Administration and director of research, Harvard Business School. He is co-author, with James I. Cash, Jr., and James L. McKenney, of *Corporate Information Systems Management: The Issues Facing Senior Executives* (Dow Jones-Irwin, 1988). With James I. Cash, he is featured in a video program, *Competing through Information Technology*, which examines how information technology alters competitive conditions in industry.

William G. McGowan is a founder of MCI Communications Corporation, a major supplier of telecommunications services, and has been its chairman since 1968. He has received many awards and honors, including being named executive of the decade by the Communications Network organization and receiving the Industry Achievement Award from the International Communications Association. He is only the second individual to have received the latter award. McGowan received his M.B.A. from Harvard Business School.

Tauno Metsisto is vice president of Index Group, a consulting and research firm in Cambridge, Massachusetts, where he is responsible for the firm's technology architecture practice.

Victor E. Millar retired in 1986 from Arthur Anderson & Co., where he was managing partner for practice and worked extensively with executives to increase their understanding of information in the management function.

D. Quinn Mills is Albert J. Weatherhead, Jr., Professor of Business Administration, Harvard Business School. He is the author of several books, including *The IBM Lesson: The Profitable Art of Full Employment* (Times Books, 1988).

Rowland T. Moriarty is associate professor of business administration, Harvard Business School. Formerly, he held sales management and marketing positions at Xerox and IBM.

Michael E. Porter is professor of business administration at the Harvard Business School. An authority on competitive strategy, he is the author of nine books and over thirty articles. His latest book, *The Competitive Advantage of Nations* (Free Press), was published in 1990. He is featured in a video program, *Michael Porter on Competitive Strategy*, offered by the Harvard Business School Publishing Division.

David J. Reibstein is professor of marketing at the Wharton School, University of Pennsylvania, where he also serves as vice-dean and director of the Graduate Division. He is the author of *Marketing Concepts: Strategies & Decisions* (Prentice-Hall, 1985).

John J. Sviokla is assistant professor of business administration, Harvard Business School, where he teaches courses on knowledge-based systems and research topics in information systems.

Gordon S. Swartz is research associate at the Harvard Business School and was formerly research director at the Competitive Assessment Center, a computer industry research company.

JoAnne Yates is senior lecturer and management communications coordinator at Massachusetts Institute of Technology's Sloan School of Management.

INDEX

pricing, 76
structure, 191–192
substitute, 101
transformation, through information
technology, 60, 68–69, 70–71
See also Marketing and distribution;
Marketing and sales productivity
(MSP) systems; Sales
Profit-center approach to information
services, 167–168, 171, 172, 173–181
Programming and programs, 141, 142, 146
big brother approach to, 145–146, 147,
149
budgets, 147
end-user, 155–165, 181
English-like development languages,
155, 156
expert systems and, 255
helping hand (indirect control) approach to, 146–149
watchdog approach to, 149–150
See also Language packages
Proprietary computer systems, 113, 114
Prototyping, 163, 262, 263

Remote devices, 84
Research and development, 94
competitive advantages of, 92
computer systems, 40, 134
information storage, 88
marketing, 231–248
specialized, 6
technology, 35–36
vertical integration and, 27
Retail Operations Intelligence system, 119
RISC (reduced instruction set computing)
architectures, 115
Rockefeller, John D., Sr., 14
Rolm, 76
Ryder System, 52, 54

SABRE reservation system, 51, 103, 108,
113, 123
AMR and, 116, 124
competition and, 120–123
performance capabilities, 117
software, 119
Travel Information Network, 121
Sales
after-sales service, 194–195
barriers to entry and, 85
budgets, 92
competitive advantage of computers in,
83
costs, 213, 214

electronic/computerized, 49–50, 52–53,
54–55, 148
information technology and, 202–203,
214
just-in-time, 50, 64, 89, 95, 103, 189
management, 216
productivity and, 213, 219–220
single-source, 49, 50, 51, 53, 122, 137
telecommunications and, 192–194
value adding and, 85
See also Product(s)
Schlumberger, 68
Sears, Roebuck, 52, 77, 104
SelectQuote Insurance Services, 54
Siemens, Georg, 13–14
Siemens, Werner, 14
Sloan, Alfred P., 14
Source, The, 108
Specialists and specialization of operations, 5, 6, 10, 11, 14
expert systems and, 255, 260–262,
263, 264
management and, 34
marketing, 246–247, 248
rotation of, 11–12
telecommunications, 196–197
See also Expert systems (ESs)
Split-cable technology, 231, 232–233,
235, 236, 238
Spreadsheet technology, 148, 157, 162,
201, 206
State Farm Insurance, 54
Strategic business units, 90–91
Sulzer Brothers, 66, 75
Switching costs, 86, 107, 114, 186, 188,
191, 197, 198. *See also* Competition

Tandy, 116
Task force teams, 6, 11–12
adhocracies, 41
end-user, 159, 162–163
information technology, 132, 134–136,
138–139
management rotation in, 46
multidisciplinary, 37
programming, 149
project-oriented, 41, 43
telecommunications, 196–197
Technology risk, 135
Teknowledge, Inc., 260
Telaction shopping system, 52
TELCOT system, 55
Telecommunications, 34, 76, 77, 138
advantages and risks, 185, 197–199,
206
applications, 186–187, 197–199